DOCUMENTS OF MODERN HISTORY

General Editor:

A.G. Dickens

Already published in this series
The Renaissance Sense of the Past
Peter Burke

Martin Luther
E. G. Rupp and B. Drewery

The Reformation in England to the Accession of Elizabeth I
A. G. Dickens and Dorothy Carr

Erasmus
R. L. DeMolen

Elizabethan People: State and Society
Joel L. Hurstfield and Alan G. R. Smith

English Colonization of North America
Louis B. Wright and Elaine W. Fowler

Sweden as a Great Power 1611 – 1697
Michael Roberts

The Divided Society: Party Conflict in England 1694 – 1716
Geoffrey Holmes and W. A. Speck

The Age of Peel
Norman Gash

The Great Powers and the Near East 1774 – 1923
M. S. Anderson

Government and Society in France 1814 – 1848
Irene Collins

Victorian Nonconformity
J. H. Y. Briggs and I. Sellers

Bismarck and Europe
W. N. Medlicott and Dorothy Coveney

The Growth of the British Empire 1880 – 1932
I. M. Cumpston

From Isolation to Containment. American Foreign Policy 1921 – 1952
Richard D. Challener

The Diplomacy of World Power: The United States 1889 – 1920
Arthur S. Link and William M. Leary Jr

Education in Tudor and Stuart England
David Cressy

Post-War Integration in Europe
Richard Vaughan

Huldrych Zwingli
G. R. Potter

The Development of the British Welfare State 1880 – 1975
J. R. Hay

Germany in the Thirty Years War
Gerhard Benecke

The Conflict of Nationality in Modern Ireland
A. C. Hepburn

The Middle East, 1914 – 1979
T. G. Fraser

The Lost Peace: International Relations in Europe, 1918 – 1939
Anthony Adamthwaite

The Lost Peace
International
Relations in
Europe, 1918 – 1939

Anthony Adamthwaite

EDWARD ARNOLD

First published 1980 by
Edward Arnold (Publishers) Ltd
41 Bedford Square, London WC1B 3DQ

British Library Cataloguing in Publication Data

The lost peace – (Documents of modern history).
  1. Europe – Foreign relations – Sources
  I. Adamthwaite, Anthony   II. Series
    327.4   D 727

Printed and bound in Great Britain at
The Camelot Press Ltd, Southampton

Contents

Abbreviations   xi
Acknowledgements   xiii
Preface   xv
Map 1: European Frontiers after the First World War
Map 2: Europe, 1938 – 39
Map 3: The Far East c. 1939

Introduction   1

I   Peace-making, 1918 – 23   14

  1 The United States threatens to withdraw from the war,
     30 October 1918   18
  2 The German Cabinet considers Allied peace terms, 21
     March 1919   20
  3 Conversation between Wilson, Clemenceau, Lloyd
     George, Orlando 27 March 1919   24
  4 President Poincaré argues for indefinite occupation of
     the Rhineland as security for payment of German
     reparations, 28 April 1919   30
  5 Smuts encourages Keynes to denounce the Treaty of
     Versailles, 10 June 1919   32
  6 The German army looks to the resurrection of Germany,
     28 June 1919   34
  7 The United States and the League of Nations, 25
     November 1919   35
  8 The British Cabinet sums up its policy on Russia, 29
     January 1920   38
  9 Excerpt from the Theses on the National and Colonial
     Question adopted at the Second Congress of the
     Communist International, 1920   39
10 Britain at the Washington Conference, 11 November
     1921   41

11 Japan at the Washington Conference, 27 December 1921   42

12 Lloyd George and Briand discuss an Anglo-French alliance, 21 December 1921   44

13 Reparations and War Debts. Cabinet minutes 22 December 1921   46

14 Cecil's proposals for a Draft Treaty of Mutual Assistance, with comments by the Foreign Office, 1 July 1922   50

15 Seeckt calls for the partition of Poland between Germany and the Soviet Union, 11 September 1922   54

16 Baldwin and Poincaré on Anglo-French differences, 19 September 1923   54

17 Canadian views on British empire and British foreign policy, 3 October 1923   58

18 Britain considers financial pressure on France, 14 November 1923   63

II   Détente, 1924 – 8   65

19 MacDonald and Herriot conclude a 'moral pact of continuous cooperation', 21 June 1924   67

20 Germany evades the disarmament clauses of Versailles, 20 February 1925   68

21 Britain as honest broker, 19 March 1925   70

22 Stresemann's foreign policy goals, 7 September 1925   72

23 *Mein Kampf*, 1925   73

24 France and Locarno, 12 February 1926   76

25 Germany's aims, 6 March 1926   79

26 Foch opposes early withdrawal from the Rhineland, 8 March 1926   79

27 Stresemann and Briand discuss Franco-German rapprochement at Thoiry, 17 September 1926   82

28 Disarmament: A British view, 31 January 1928   87

29 Monetary reconstruction in Europe: Anglo-French rivalry, 27 – 28 April 1928   93

30 Anglo-American relations assessed, 12 November 1928   97

III   Disintegration, 1929 – 33   105

31 Naval disarmament: France versus the Anglo-Saxon powers, 13 January 1930   109

32 French plans for Franco-German economic cooperation, 11 February 1930 — 113

33 Britain assesses Briand's proposal for a European federal union, 30 May 1930 — 116

34 President Hoover's proposal for a Moratorium on War Debts and Reparations, 20 June 1931 — 120

35 Sir John Simon on the Manchurian crisis, 25 November 1931 — 122

36 Britain's dilemma in the Far East, 1 February 1932 — 124

37 France's scheme for a Danubian economic entente rejected, 11 May 1932 — 126

38 Hitler's letter to Colonel von Reichenau, 4 December 1932 — 130

39 General Weygand reviews French defence policy, 16 January 1933 — 136

40 Hitler's first speech to the generals, 3 February 1933 — 139

41 Japan withdraws from the League of Nations, 27 March 1933 — 140

42 Debts, depression and disarmament, 7 April 1933 — 141

43 Britain, France and the United States must call Germany's bluff, 16 May 1933 — 143

44 Roosevelt urged to broadcast to Germany, 17 October 1933 — 149

45 Open versus secret diplomacy, October – November 1933 — 150

46 Franco-Soviet-Czech discussions at Geneva, 25 November 1933 — 154

IV Challenge and Response, 1934 – 36 — 158

47 The Soviet ambassador in Paris on France's delay in negotiating an alliance, 25 January 1934 — 161

48 Neville Chamberlain suggests an Anglo-Japanese pact, 1 September 1934 — 161

49 Roosevelt opposed to an Anglo-Japanese pact, 9 November 1934 — 163

50 Mussolini on Abyssinia, 30 December 1934 — 164

51 Clifford Allen meets Hitler, January 1935 — 166

52 Hoare-Laval talks on Abyssinia, 7 December 1935 — 167

53 Hitler considers the reoccupation of the Rhineland, 14 February 1936 — 172

54 France's Popular Front government divided on Spain, 25
    July 1936   175
55 Britain stresses the urgency of a non-intervention
    agreement, 7 August 1936   176
56 Japan's aims, 7 August 1936   177
57 Hitler on the Four Year Plan, August 1936   180

V Undeclared War, 1937 – 39   184

58 Italy will not save Austria, 6 November 1937   187
59 The Hossbach Memorandum, 10 November 1937   188
60 The United States must take firm action against Japan,
    14 November 1937   193
61 General Jodl's amendment to 'Operation Green', 7
    December 1937   195
62 The British Cabinet reviews its foreign and defence
    policies, 8 December 1937   197
63 The aims of the Japanese army, 3 July 1938   200
64 Roosevelt suggests a conference on Czechoslovakia, 27
    September 1938   205
65 Italy and the Munich crisis, 27 – 30 September 1938   206
66 Japan instructs its ambassadors in Germany and Italy on
    the conclusion of a tripartite pact, 25 January 1939   211
67 Beck defines Poland's position, 24 March 1939   214
68 British and French public opinion polls, 1938 – 9   215
69 A meeting of the military missions of Britain, France
    and the Soviet Union, 14 August 1939   219
Chronology   221

Further Reading   227

Biographical Sketches   232

Anne-Marie, Katherine, Christian and Jonathan 'Like as the arrows in the hand of the giant: even so are the young children.
Happy is the man that hath his quiver full of them: they shall not be ashamed when they speak with their enemies in the gate.' Psalms, cxxvii

Abbreviations

DBFP	*Documents on British Foreign Policy, 1919 – 1939* (continuing), (London, HMSO, 1946 –)
DDF	*Documents diplomatiques francais, 1932 – 1939* (continuing), (Paris, 1963)
DGFP	Documents on German Foreign Policy, 1918 – 1945 (London, HMSO, 1949)
FRUS	*Foreign Relations of the United States* (continuing) (Washington, USGPO, 1933 –)

Acknowledgements

Grateful acknowledgement is made to the following sources of material used in this book.

The Controller of HM Stationery Office for permission to reproduce Crown Copyright records; the Directeur des Archives Diplomatiques for permission to quote from French diplomatic documents; the Directeur des Archives Nationales for extracts from the Painlevé Papers; the Directeur du Services des Archives de l'Assemblée Nationale for excerpts from the minutes of the Chamber of Deputies foreign affairs committee; the University of Birmingham for material from the Austen Chamberlain Papers; Lord Hankey for permission to quote from the papers of the first Lord Hankey; Professor Ann K.S. Lambton for material from the papers of Viscount Cecil of Chelwood; Mr J.C. Smuts for material from the Smuts Papers; Dr Esmonde M. Robertson for the translations of Hitler's letter to von Reichenau and Mussolini's directive on Abyssinia; Mr Keith Payten for translations of Soviet diplomatic documents; George Allen and Unwin Ltd, for permission to reproduce material from my *Making of the Second World War* (1977); Jonathan Cape Ltd and A.D. Peters and Co. Ltd., for *Documents on Nazism, 1919 – 1945*, eds. Jeremy Noakes and Geoffrey Pridham (1974); Jonathan Cape Ltd for an extract from David Marquand, *Ramsay MacDonald* (1977); Columbia University Press for extracts from Waclaw Jedrzejewicz (ed), *Diplomat in Paris, 1933 – 1939: Papers and Memoirs of Jozef Lipski* (1968) and James William Morley (ed), *Deterrent Diplomacy: Japan, Germany and the USSR*, 1935 – 1940 (1976); Cambridge University Press for an extract from R.S. Sayers, *The Bank of England, 1891 – 1944*, vol.3 (1976); Bodley Head Ltd and Little, Brown & Co for an extract from Max Freedman (Ed), *Roosevelt and Frankfurter: Their Correspondence 1928 – 1945* (1967); Eyre Methuen and Co. Ltd for an extract from J.H. Morgan, *Assize of Arms*, vol.I (1945); Franco Angeli Editores for an extract from G. Rochat, *Militari e politici nella preparazione della campagna d'Etiopia: Studio e documenti*, 1932 – 1936 (1971); Harvard University Press for extracts from Edgar B. Nixon (ed), *Franklin D. Roosevelt and Foreign Affairs*, vol.I (1969); Heinemann Ltd for the extract from Martin Gilbert, *Winston S. Churchill*, IV, Companion volume, part 3 (1977); Longman Ltd for the extract from Martin Gilbert (ed), *Plough My Own Furrow: The Life of Clifford Allen* (1965); and J.C.G. Röhl, *From Bismarck to Hitler* (1970); Hutchinson Publishing Group Ltd and Houghton Mifflin for Adolf Hitler, *Mein Kampf*, trans. Ralph Mannheim (1969); Librairie Droz for Paul Mantoux, *Paris Peace Conference 1919: Proceedings of the Council of Four* (1964); Macmillan London and Basingstoke for *Gustav Stresemann, His Diaries, Letters and Papers*, ed. and trans. Eric Sutton, vol.2 (1937) and *Economic History of Europe: The Twentieth Century*, ed. Shephard B. Clough (1969); Oliver and Boyd Ltd for *The League of Nations*, ed. Ruth B. Henig (1973); Oxford University Press for the extract from *The Communist International 1919—1943: Documents*, I, selected and edited by Jane Degras (1956) and F.L. Carsten, *The Reichswehr and Politics 1918 – 1933* (1966); Princeton University Press for Raymond B. Fosdick, *Letters on the League of Nations* (1966); Random House for *Gallup International Public Opinion Polls*, ed. George H. Gallup (1977) vol.2, *France, 1939, 1944 – 75*; Routledge and Kegan Paul Ltd for extracts from C.J. Lowe and M.L. Dockrill, *The Mirage of Power*, 3, *The Documents* (1972), C.J. Lowe and F. Marzari, *Italian Foreign Policy, 1870 – 1940* (1975), Ian Nish, *Japanese Foreign Policy, 1869 – 1942* (1977); Stanford University Press for *The Political Institutions of the German Revolution 1918 – 1919*, eds. Charles B. Burdick and Ralph H. Lutz (1966).

Preface

Until relatively recently scholarly attention was focused on the origins of the Second World War. Post – 1918 international relations were seen entirely in the context of the historiography of war origins. The fact that in the 1940s and 1950s governments gave priority to the publication of material on the late 1930s confirmed this distortion. Consequently, students anxious to make a start on the study of sources for interwar diplomacy are not well served. There are several selections of documents on the origins of the Second World War but nothing on the problems of peace-making. This selection of documents has a double purpose: to illustrate the attempts to create a lasting peace after the First World War and to illuminate the frustration of those attempts and the subsequent collapse of the peace settlement. It is misleading to describe international affairs after 1918 as one long slide to inevitable catastrophe. Different policies might have averted disaster at several turning points. Post-Versailles Europe was not doomed from the beginning. *Dis aliter visum*.

Space makes it impossible to illustrate all aspects of interwar European diplomacy and this has led to many omissions, of which I am fully conscious. I have thought it better to select substantial passages rather than to make the book an anthology of snippets. The focus is on international relations in Europe because Europe was still the centre of the international system but I have tried to show the increasing influence of the United States of America and Japan. The aim of the selection is not to chronicle the *res gestae* of foreign policy but to give students some idea of its formulation. Accordingly, official dispatches have been largely omitted in favour of the diaries and private correspondence of ministers and officials and the records of policy-making discussions. The selection draws on the main published collections and includes some hitherto unpublished French material as well as German and Soviet documents translated for the first time. I am grateful to Mrs Molly Marriott for her careful typing of part of the manuscript.

1   European Frontiers after the First World War

2 Europe, 1938–1939

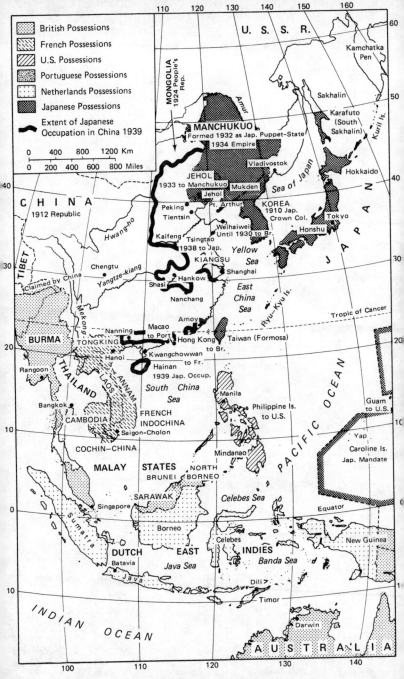

3 The Far East 1939

Introduction

On his arrival in Europe in December 1918 President Woodrow Wilson of the United States was greeted as a saviour who would inaugurate an era of permanent and universal peace. A French workman pointed to the president's ship and said: 'That man is going to make it all right'. No peace settlement could have fulfilled the millenial hopes of a new heaven and a new earth. It was the destruction of these Utopian hopes that provoked the denunciations of the settlement.

The balance of power which had broken down in 1914 was completely shattered in 1918. The war showed that Germany, with only modest help from Austria-Hungary, could defy a coalition of four leading European powers — Britain, France, Russia and Italy. Only the intervention of the United States in 1917 saved the Entente powers from defeat or deadlock in the west and only a continuing American presence could have stabilized Europe.

Though vanquished in the west, Germany was victorious in the east. By the armistice of 11 November 1918 the allies acknowledged the survival of Germany as a great power. Germany had to make peace but the allies tied their own hands because the armistice was concluded with representatives of the new Weimar Republic, and the preservation of the moderate Socialist government against Bolshevism became a principal allied interest. Only a stable government could be relied upon to honour the armistice conditions. But Germany remained a great power and would sooner or later contest the verdict of 1918.

The peace settlement confirmed the existing instability because it lacked moral force. Almost to a man Germans denounced the *Diktat* of Versailles. One reason for German resentment was the fact that they had been encouraged to expect a treaty inspired by President Wilson's Fourteen Points (2). In fact the principle of self-determination seemed to work against Germany, for example in the creation of the Polish Corridor. The peace treaty with Austria prohibited an *Anschluss* with Germany. The War Guilt clause was also resented. Yet the heart of the matter was *amour propre*. Germany would not accept her defeat and would almost certainly have resented any peace treaty however mild.

What augured ill for the future was the territorial settlement in central and eastern Europe. The collapse of Austria-Hungary left a vacuum. The confirmation of national self-determination created new tensions. Ethnic minorities were included in the successor states in order to give them political and economic viability—Sudeten Germans and Poles under Czechoslovak rule, Germans under Polish rule. The new states of Czechoslovakia and Poland were at daggers drawn. In 1919–20 Poland had to fight for her existence against Bolshevik Russia. The Little Entente states of Czechoslovakia, Romania and Yugoslavia were menaced by Hungary, embittered by territory lost at the peace conference.

Much more can be said for the peace settlement than was conceded at the time. Versailles was a brave attempt to deal with intractable, perhaps insoluble, problems. Peace-making went on for five years after the armistice of 1918, but after 1945 the process went on in Europe for nine years, with Japan for eleven years, and no peace treaty has been concluded with Germany. The Paris peace conference has been compared unfavourably with the Congress of Vienna. The comparison is not a fair one. The collapse of four empires in Europe and the Near East confronted the Paris statesmen with problems on a scale which no previous peace congress had encountered. The pressures were enormous. The conference met against a background of revolution, famine and economic chaos which had not been experienced since 1848 (3). The Vienna statesmen safely ignored the incipient nationalism of their world, allied leaders in 1919 were presented with a *fait accompli*—self-determination in central and eastern Europe was a reality. The Europe of 1815 was a self-contained system; in 1919 the old balance of power had gone for ever. Russia, a central link in the old balance, was torn by civil war and absent from the conference. The United States disavowed Wilson's work and withdrew from political commitments in Europe.

The decline of Europe added to the instability of the international system. Before 1914 political, demographic and economic forces were eroding Europe's primacy but the First World War accelerated the process. Japan, hitherto a Far Eastern power only, was now admitted to the ranks of the leading great powers (11). Until 1914 Britain, France and Germany were the main investors of capital, after 1918 all three became major debitors of the United States. During the war the established overseas markets and colonial territories of the European powers were deeply penetrated by American investment. The war speeded the winds of nationalist revolt against European colonial rule. France faced challenges in her North African territories, in Mandated Syria and in Indo-China. Britain's main anxieties were Egypt, India and Palestine. This running fight against nationalism was a constant drain on the energies and resources of the two leading European powers. The expenditure of so much effort produced a determination to hang on to empire at almost any cost. The consequences were caution and compromise in Europe.

The moral consensus underpinning the pre – 1914 balance of power was destroyed and nothing replaced it. Five years of conferences and treaties between 1919 and 1923 left Europe disillusioned and dissatisfied. The problem of Germany was unsolved. Two main alternatives were open in 1919: power politics and traditional alliances; or one of the two new forms of internationalism. Neither of the alternatives was effectively pursued and European postwar diplomacy was an uneasy compromise between old-fashioned power politics and the internationalism enshrined in the Covenant of the newly established League of Nations.

With Germany disarmed and Britain rapidly disarming, France was the leading military power but the effects of the war and the inadequacies of the treaties sapped her strength. Bled white by the carnage, overwhelmed by the cost of paying for the war and restoring the occupied territory, France lacked the will to assert her predominance. Versailles was in many respects a defeat for France. Marshal Foch, allied generalissimo, had urged his government to insist on possession of the left bank of the Rhine. President Poincaré counselled Clemenceau to ask for the indefinite occupation of the Rhineland as security for the payment of German reparations (4). In return for the offer of an Anglo-American Treaty of Guarantee France abandoned her demand for territorial safeguards. But the Treaty of Guarantee fell through in November 1919 when the United States Senate refused to ratify the Treaty of Versailles. Although British and American forces could not have landed in time to prevent a German invasion, the guarantee would have buttressed French morale. The creation of an independent Poland destroyed much of the usefulness of a Franco-Russian alliance since Germany now had no common frontier with Russia and Russia was unable to put direct pressure on Germany.

Moreover the establishment of Poland out of German and Russian territory gave both powers a common interest, a possible prize. France lacked powerful allies — Russia was eclipsed, Britain refused to renew the wartime military alliance, the United States shunned political involvement, Italy was dissatisfied by the settlement, Japan was too remote to contribute to European security. France's eastern allies — Poland, Czechoslovakia, Romania and Yugoslavia — were weak and divided.

The limits of French power were demonstrated in 1923 when France, assisted by Belgium, occupied the Ruhr to enforce payment of German reparations (16). Anglo-American disapproval and financial crisis compelled France to accept the recommendations of the Dawes Committee, an international committee of experts. The Dawes Plan of 1924 marked a substantial revision of the reparations chapters of Versailles. France's military occupation of the Ruhr weakened the Weimar Republic. The memory of 1923 — hyperinflation, middle-class impoverishment, the humiliation of French colonial troops stationed on German soil — inflamed German nationalism.

Nonetheless the mixture of traditional power politics and internationalism might have kept the peace if Britain and France had worked in harmony. However the *mésentente cordiale* which prevailed for much of the five years of peace-making greatly aided Germany's revival (12, 23). Germany exploited Anglo-French differences and France's efforts to resurrect the wartime military alliance were rebuffed (12). In the Ruhr crisis of 1923 Britain even considered employing financial pressure to bring about a change in French policy (18).

Britain's refusal to join forces with France was motivated by war-weariness, dislike of the peace treaties and a sense of diminishing strength. The war eroded British power and left a sense of insecurity. Sea power was no longer sufficient and Britain's dethronement as the supreme naval power was formalized by the Washington Naval Treaty of 1922. Under American pressure Britain abandoned in 1921 the Anglo-Japanese alliance of 1902 (10). Economic changes contributed to Britain's loss of power. By 1914 Britain's industries lagged behind those of Germany and the United States. Postwar unemployment seemed to confirm the argument of J.M. Keynes in *Economic Consequences of the Peace* (1919) that Europe's economic health was dependent on Germany's recovery. Although the British empire was enlarged in 1919, it was beset with tensions. Attempts to achieve a federated imperial structure had failed and participation in the war imbued the Dominions with a taste for full independence (**17**). By the Balfour resolutions of the Imperial Conference of 1926 and the Statute of Westminster of 1931 Australia, Canada, New Zealand and South Africa were authorized to conduct their own internal and external affairs.

The upshot of Britain's political and economic preoccupations was that she assumed a mediatory role, promoting a European détente but avoiding hard and fast commitments. Arguing that neither Britain nor France was strong enough to control the Continent, the Foreign Office, seconded by the Treasury, worked for Germany's political and economic recovery. Only German acceptance of the status quo, it was argued, could in the long run safeguard the peace.

Neither of the rival forms of internationalism, the League of Nations and the Third International, succeeded in supplanting traditional power politics. The Third (Communist) International, the Comintern, was created by Lenin in March 1919 in order to exploit what was seen as a world crisis of capitalism. With Soviet republics established in Munich and Budapest in the spring of 1919 and industrial unrest in Britain and France world revolution seemed in sight. By the end of the year the revolutions in central and eastern Europe had been crushed and capitalism was on the mend. The Third International's definition of aims and principles in the Twenty-One Points of July 1920 did not secure the general support of European socialists. Doctrinal divisions destroyed the solidarity of the pre – 1914 international labour movement. The policies of the Third International and the Soviet Union envenomed the international and domestic politics of the interwar years. Bolshevik leaders spoke with two voices. On the one hand they sought good relations with capitalist states and these states responded with diplomatic recognition and commercial treaties. On the other hand this policy was nullified by the Comintern's propaganda in Britain and France and in their colonial possessions (**9**).

Similarly the League of Nations failed to win a commanding influence in world politics. From its creation it had serious short-comings. Germany was excluded and Russia absent. By making the Covenant of the League a part of the Versailles treaty allied statesmen committed a strategic error. Germans saw it as a victors' club to enforce the territorial settlement. More serious was the hostility and indifference of American opinion following the Senate's refusal to ratify the peace treaty (**7**). The Covenant had its flaws. The League had a permanent secretariat in Geneva but no peace-keeping force.

Members were required to cooperate in the collective attempt to keep the peace but policy decisions by the League Council and Assembly needed the unanimous consent of all states represented. Proposals to strengthen the Covenant were shipwrecked on the rock of national sovereignty (14). The League was successful in settling a number of disputes—Danzig, the Aaland Islands, Upper Silesia—and its agencies performed valuable welfare work. Yet it made no progress on disarmament. And on two crucial issues in 1923—Italian seizure of Corfu and French occupation of the Ruhr—the League was bypassed.

Arguably the greatest cause of Europe's instability was the withdrawal of the United States. Not that the retreat was total. Throughout the 1920s the United States pursued a coherent economic diplomacy towards Europe, aimed at rebuilding a war-torn economy and thereby protecting key markets as well as blocking Bolshevism. An Anglo-American financial entente was crucial in the resolution of the reparations issue in 1923 – 24. Unfortunately by the end of the decade Anglo-American rivalry had resurfaced (30). The fallacy of American policy was the assumption that limited economic involvement in Europe was sufficient. American avoidance of political entanglements vastly increased the uncertainties with which European policy makers had to reckon.

Some security was better than none and France accepted the international guarantees offered in the Locarno agreements of October 1925. Germany, France and Belgium agreed to recognize their existing frontiers as permanent, including the demilitarized Rhineland zone; Britain and Italy guaranteed this arrangement and the treaty provided for the settlement of all disputes through the League of Nations. The treaty was a mixed blessing for France (24). Though Germany freely recognized the territorial settlement in western Europe she did not abandon her opposition to the settlement in the east. Thus Locarno confirmed the quandary of French policy. France was guaranteed but not her eastern allies.

Locarno fostered an illusion of détente, an illusion nourished as much by the economic prosperity of the mid – 1920s as by the treaty itself. Germany's admission to the League in 1926 encouraged hopes of amity. The conversation between the French and German foreign ministers at Thoiry in September 1926 seemed at the time to contain the seeds of great things, but bore no fruit (27). By 1929 the Locarno spirit had evaporated. It had meant different things to different statesmen. For the German foreign minister, Gustav Stresemann, Locarno was the first step towards treaty revision, for his French colleague,

Aristide Briand, it was the first step on the road to compliance; for the British foreign secretary, Austen Chamberlain, it was an assertion of British detachment. By guaranteeing the Franco-German frontier Britain implicitly repudiated responsibility for any other European frontier.

France's leaders remained deeply suspicious of German intentions. Germany in collusion with the Soviet Union evaded the Versailles disarmament clauses. The Treaty of Rapallo in 1922 normalized German-Soviet relations. The goal of Weimar leaders was the over-turning of Versailles (22, 25). What is not clear is how far Stresemann envisaged the use of force to achieve this aim. He could hardly have expected France to abdicate without a struggle. Reichswehr leaders advocated a German-Soviet alliance with the aim of partitioning Poland (15).

The world economic crisis of 1929 – 33, by causing deep social fissures within states and by disrupting the international economy, contributed to the collapse of the territorial settlement. Economic breakdown led to political upheaval which in turn destroyed the international status quo. Germany was the most striking example of this interaction. Without the depression Hitler would not have gained power. Mass unemployment reinforced all the long-standing resent-ments against Versailles and Weimar democracy.

The economic blizzard provided compelling reasons for con-ciliating the fascist dictators. War, it was feared, would destroy the prospects of economic recovery. Rearmament was delayed because massive spending on arms was seen as the short road to ruin. By the mid 1930s Britain and the United States were on the way to recovery but apprehensions of a relapse were revived by the Roosevelt recession which engulfed the United States in 1937. European bourses registered the recession in the winter of 1937 – 8. The slump spurred forward the search for agreement with Germany and Italy in 1938.

With depression came class conflict. Though the worst of the storm was over by the end of 1933 the propertied classes lived in fear of imminent social disaster. Unemployment and low wages fuelled the conflict between left and right. Economic misery divided society in Britain and France and prevented national unity when it was most needed. The prevailing uncertainty, anxiety and pessimism furnished a powerful argument for seeking some accommodation with the dictators. A European war seemed certain to end in the victory of Bolshevism.

Domestic preoccupations determined the reactions of the powers in the Far Eastern crisis of 1931 – 33. In September 1931 Japanese forces seized key points in Manchuria from Chinese garrisons. In May 1933 Japanese armies swept southwards menacing Peking and the North China plain. At this point the Japanese stopped and concluded a truce with the Chinese. The truce lasted until July 1937 when a full-scale Sino-Japanese war began.

In the light of the Second World War the Manchurian affair was widely believed to have been the beginning of the slide to disaster. For a long time a conspiracy theory held sway, according to which British ministers and City interests, indifferent to the League and jealous of American economic and naval power, cynically disregarded Chinese interests and favoured Japan. Hitler and Mussolini were thus encouraged to try their luck in Europe and Africa. The United States, it is said, was ready to resist aggression but her initiatives were spurned.

There is no evidence to support the conspiracy theory. The myth that the Far Eastern crisis was the detonator of later crises has been effectively demolished. Inevitably the Manchurian affair was linked to later events but it did not 'cause' them. Neither Mussolini's invasion of Abyssinia in 1935 nor Hitler's march into the Rhineland in 1936 can be related to Manchuria. That the League and collective security suffered serious injury is undeniable. Chinese appeals to the League were answered by the dispatch of a commission of enquiry, the Lytton Commission. Meanwhile the Japanese conquest proceeded unhindered. The League voted against recognition of the Japanese puppet state of Manchukuo. The sanctions imposed were derisory – refusal to recognize Manchukuo passports, currency and postage. Japan replied by leaving the League in March 1933 (41).

The first great test for the European security system came in 1932 – 34. Germany's demand for equality of rights in the Geneva disarmament talks challenged France's leadership. Germany walked out of the disarmament conference in October 1933 and France rejected further disarmament negotiations in a note of 17 April 1934. The logical result was rearmament. Nothing happened. French rearmament did not begin until the autumn of 1936. By 1934 France had lost the initiative in Europe and Britain became the senior partner in the entente.

Instead of rearming France fell back on diplomatic expedients – complicated and protracted negotiations for an eastern Locarno linking Germany, France, the Soviet Union and France's eastern allies, bilateral talks for a Franco-Soviet pact (46), a rapprochement with Italy. The eastern Locarno negotiations proved abortive. A Franco-Soviet pact was signed in May 1935 but it meant little since France refused Stalin's offer of staff talks. The Franco-Italian rapprochement resulted in the Rome Agreements of January 1935 but the alliance did not survive the Italo-Abyssinian war of 1935 – 36.

Hitler's coming to power in January 1933 focused and fuelled German discontents. The driving force of Hitler's foreign policy sprang partly from traditional power politics, partly from the ideology of national socialism. Though nazism drew on pre – 1914 pan Germanism, its peculiar force lay in the fusion of familiar clichés into an official doctrine, mobilizing party and nation. Nazism, as Hitler insisted, was a 'doctrine of conflict'. The movement had to be kept on the move, like a bicycle that topples over if it is not kept in motion. In foreign policy Hitler was both planner and opportunist. In Alan Bullock's words he displayed 'consistency of aim with complete opportunism in method and tactics'.[1] There is ample evidence illustrating the consistency of purpose which informed Hitler's thinking before and after 1933 (**23, 38, 40**).

The European security system, already shaken by Germany's departure from the League of Nations and denunciation of the Versailles disarmament clauses, underwent a decisive test in the Abyssinian crisis of 1935 – 36. The crisis was *the* major step toward war. The consequences of Mussolini's invasion of Abyssinia in October 1935 were far reaching: the recently constructed Stresa front of Britain, France and Italy was shattered, as was the Franco-Italian alliance of January 1935; the League received its *coup de grâce*, Britain and France were estranged. Under cover of the crisis Hitler proceeded with the remilitarization of Germany's western Rhineland frontier a year earlier than he had thought possible. Italy's isolation led directly to the emergence of the Rome-Berlin Axis in October 1936, which in turn brought about the abandonment of Italy's interest in preserving Austrian independence. The way was cleared for Germany's annexation of Austria in March 1938.

When Italian troops invaded Abyssinia on 3 October 1935 the League of Nations imposed economic sanctions but not an oil embargo. British and French ministers were tireless in their efforts to buy off Mussolini (**52**). The fruit of their labours was the Hoare-Laval

---

1 'Hitler and the origins of the Second World War', in Esmonde M. Robertson (ed.), *The Origins of the Second World War: Historical Interpretations* (London, 1971), p. 193.

pact of 8 December 1935 by which two thirds of Abyssinia would have
been ceded to Italy. A press leak of the plan brought swift condemnation from British opinion. Sir Samuel Hoare, foreign secretary, was
compelled to resign. Five months later the Italian conquest was
completed.

While Britain and France were distracted by the Italo-Abyssinian
war Hitler struck his first blow against the territorial order. On 7
March 1936 alleging a contradiction between the Franco-Soviet pact
and the Treaty of Locarno he sent a force of 22,000 into the
demilitarized Rhineland, violating the Versailles and Locarno
treaties. His gamble that Britain and Italy, guarantors of Locarno,
would remain passive and that France would not dare to act alone
proved correct.

The Rhineland reoccupation was the beginning of the end for
France's eastern allies. The strategic situation was never again as
favourable to France. By closing the gap in Germany's western
frontier Hitler could block a French offensive in aid of Poland or
Czechoslovakia. German rearmament received a new impetus in the
four year plan of August 1936 (**57**).

The Spanish Civil War which began on 18 July 1936 and lasted
nearly three years created a climate of war. On 20 July the Spanish
Popular Front government asked France for arms and at the same
time General Franco, leader of the military insurrection, requested
help from Germany and Italy. Within weeks Germany, Italy and the
Soviet Union were supplying men and arms. Only speedy and
substantial French aid could have saved the sister Spanish Republic.
On 2 August the French Popular Front government which had
promised help on 20 July changed its mind and proposed a Non-
Intervention Agreement. Although Germany, Italy, the Soviet Union
and Britain signed the agreement it proved a complete farce. Britain
alone respected it while France allowed a trickle of military supplies to
reach the Republic. The European left claimed that the French
government had been bullied by Britain into non-intervention. Some
British pressure was applied but the decisive considerations for French
ministers were the danger of a general war and the risk of civil war in
France (**54**).

From the autumn of 1937 the immediate origins of the Second
World War can be discerned. Hitler set Germany on a course of
territorial expansion in central Europe (**59**). The new tempo was a
natural extension of previous successes. How far economic pressures
were pushing Hitler towards war is hard to say. Germany was troubled

by economic difficulties in 1937 – 39 and some observers believed that the economy was in a serious plight but there is no evidence that economic difficulties decisively influenced Hitler's decision making.

German rearmament sheds some light on Hitler's intentions. Germany was rearming in breadth but not in depth. Hitler was not preparing for war with the great powers. In 1939 Germany had an army of 51 divisions but only six weeks' supply of munitions. Hitler adopted a *Blitzkrieg* strategy—a series of short wars, against Czechoslovakia in 1938, Poland in 1939, the Soviet Union in 1941. The war that the western democracies expected and prepared for— a war of attrition similar to 1914 – 18 – was the war Hitler wanted to avoid.

As Hitler accelerated his programme of expansion the British prime minister, Neville Chamberlain, initiated new approaches to Germany and Italy. Anglo-Italian talks started in mid-February 1938 and on 3 March a British plan for a general settlement was handed to Hitler. Hitler showed no interest. Austria absorbed his attention. As an Austrian, Hitler stated his goal of *Anschluss* on the first page of *Mein Kampf* (**23**). Exploiting the opportunity provided by the decision of Austria's chancellor, Schuschnigg, to hold a plebiscite, Hitler improvised invasion plans and German troops occupied Austria on 12 March. Next day Hitler proclaimed the annexation of Austria.

After the *Anschluss*, Czechoslovakia's days were numbered. With a strong army and alliances with France and the Soviet Union Czechoslovakia was a barrier to German control of central Europe. Hitler found a convenient stalking horse in the grievances of the three and a half million Sudeten German minority. Britain and France without consulting each other finalized their policies towards Czechoslovakia. France decided that she could not help her ally directly. Britain decided that Czechoslovakia was indefensible and that no guarantee should be given to France in respect of her ally. Both governments agreed that Czechoslovakia should be urged to make substantial concessions to the Sudeten German minority.

Although the motives which had always assured Germany some sympathy still mattered—horror of war, condemnation of the peace treaties, detestation of Bolshevism, by 1937 – 38 British and French policy-making was increasingly dominated by strategic and military considerations. Italy and Japan were now counted with Germany as potential enemies. Britain could not confront Germany, Italy and Japan simultaneously (**62**). French governments could think of no alternative to conciliation. Efforts to resuscitate the eastern pacts in

1936 – 37 had failed. Preliminary Franco-Soviet staff talks proved abortive. Belgium's decision in the autumn of 1936 to abandon a 1920 military agreement with France and return to her pre – 1914 policy of full neutrality threw French plans into disarray. The Maginot Line stopped at the Franco-Belgian frontier and it had been assumed that in the event of war French troops would at once advance into Belgium.

On 30 May 1938 Hitler secretly decided to smash Czechoslovakia in the near future. Military preparations were to be completed by 1 October 1938. In the last week of September German storm troops were massed on Czechoslovakia's borders. As trenches were dug in Hyde Park appeals for a conference reached Hitler from Mussolini, Chamberlain and President Roosevelt of the United States (**64**). Since his public demands were virtually assured Hitler issued invitations to a conference in Munich on 29 September (**65**). The Agreement signed provided for German occupation of the Sudetenland in ten days from 1 October. The operation was to be supervised by an international commission of Britain, France, Germany, Italy and Czechoslovakia. A Four Power guarantee of the dismembered state would replace the Franco-Czechoslovak treaty once Polish and Hungarian claims on Czechoslovakia were settled. Militarily there was a case for resisting Germany in September 1938. France had a last chance of fighting Germany on better or at least even terms. Apologists of Munich have always stressed the divisions of opinion and the public support for the Agreement (**68**). However it is arguable that given other men in power in Britain and France determined to resist Germany from the outset of the crisis the climate of opinion might have been different.

In January 1939 secret reports reached London that Hitler was planning an invasion of the Low Countries and an air attack on Britain. On 1 February 1939 the British Cabinet reversed its policy of the past twelve months and decided that a German attack on the Netherlands and Switzerland would constitute a *casus belli* because it would afford clear evidence of a bid to dominate Europe by force. Two conclusions followed: a return to a continental field force and full Anglo-French staff talks. In short an Anglo-French military alliance.

There is no evidence that Hitler was planning a descent on the Low Countries and Britain. His immediate objectives in the winter of 1938 – 39 were an agreement with Poland on Danzig and the Polish Corridor, a military alliance with Italy and Japan, and the liquidation of rump Czechoslovakia. Japan evaded Germany's efforts to commit her to action against Britain, France and the United States (**66**). The first issue to be settled was Czechoslovakia. On 15 March 1939

Germany occupied Prague and announced the annexation of Bohemia and Moravia. The same day Hungary occupied the Carpatho-Ukraine. Slovakia survived as a vassal state.

Hitler's Prague coup is usually said to have precipitated a diplomatic revolution: Anglo-French guarantees were given to Poland on 31 March, Greece and Romania on 13 April, Turkey on 12 May. However two important qualifications must be mentioned. Firstly, the diplomatic revolution was not a revolution in the full sense of the word. Appeasement, although discredited, continued. The aim was still détente but henceforth with more of the stick than the carrot. Secondly, the alarms and excursions that followed Prague were of crucial importance in confirming the new course of Anglo-French policy. On 23 March Hitler occupied Memel and on 7 April Mussolini invaded Albania. The atmosphere was one of imminent European war.

Yet war was delayed for six months. In March Hitler hoped to win Danzig by peaceful means but the seizure of Memel convinced Poland that a German coup was imminent. Colonel Josef Beck, Polish foreign minister, ordered partial mobilization and was unyielding on Danzig and the Corridor (67). The resulting breakdown in German-Polish negotiations brought a fundamental change in Hitler's policy. On 3 April he ordered plans to be prepared for an invasion of Poland by 1 September 1939. In a speech of 28 April he denounced the German-Polish non-aggression pact of 1934. But Hitler was cautious. Poland, he told his generals on 23 May, would be attacked 'at the first suitable opportunity' but 'it must not come to a simultaneous showdown with the west'. The task of German diplomacy was to isolate Poland.

Why, then, did Hitler invade Poland on 1 September and activate the Anglo-French guarantee? Hitler confidently risked a European war because on 23 August Germany and the Soviet Union signed a non-aggression pact, with a secret protocol providing for the partition of Poland and delimiting German and Soviet spheres of influence in eastern Europe. The pact rendered the Second World War inevitable. Thanks to the Soviet Union's benevolent neutrality Hitler was freed from the danger of a war on two fronts. He could attack Poland in safety and then deal with the western powers.

I

Peace-making, 1918 – 23

In assessing the peace-making that followed the First World War several considerations have to be kept in mind. First of all, the German collapse came sooner than expected and caught the allies unprepared. On 5 October 1918 Germany requested an armistice on the basis of President Wilson's Fourteen Points. But the allies had not accepted them and Wilson secured the forced agreement of the allies to these points by the implied threat of an American withdrawal from the war (1).

The allies were unprepared in another respect. Although the content of a peace settlement had been researched, little thought had been given to programmes, procedure and organization. Consequently, when the peace conference opened on 18 January 1919 much of its early work was haphazard, improvised and confused. This structural insufficiency wasted time and allowed conflicting interests free rein. Thirty-two nations were represented but decision making was in the hands of the Council of Ten—two plenipotentiaries each from Britain, France, Italy, Japan and the United States. The Council of Ten proved unwieldy and was replaced on 24 March by the Council of Four of Wilson, Lloyd George, Clemenceau and Orlando. The notes of the French interpreter, Paul Mantoux, were the only record of its deliberations until sir Maurice Hankey became secretary general on 19 April and initiated formal minutes (3).

Much more important than these structural defects were three other constraints—the pressure of opinion for an early peace, the climate of continuing war and revolution, and the conflicting outlooks of the statesmen. The peace conference could not insulate itself from the confused clamour without. The wartime conscript armies demanded demobilization as soon as the armistices were signed. When the ship carrying the British delegation crossed from Dover to Calais on 11 January 1919 it was passed by a string of ships sailing head to tail from Calais to Dover. Each of these was crammed with British soldiers wild with joy at returning home. Once demobilized men were determined not to have to fight again. In short the allied victory was a rapidly wasting asset. Pervading the Paris proceedings was the fear of Bolshevism — social and political collapse on the home fronts. Allied intervention in Russia reached its peak in the spring of 1919 and the idea of making war on the Bolsheviks was not finally abandoned until January 1920 (8). The new Polish state had a double purpose — to prevent German penetration of Russia and to act as a *cordon sanitaire* against the Bolshevik scourge. The conflicting outlooks of the leaders are illustrated in Mantoux's notes of the meetings of the Council of Four (3). Wilson's idealism clashed with Clemenceau's attachment to traditional power politics.

The Treaty of Versailles was the beginning of peace-making, not the end. All too often the peace settlement is equated with Versailles. In fact the process of peace-making lasted five years. In the Near East fighting continued between Greece and Turkey. In the Chanak crisis of September 1922 Britain was on the verge of war with Turkey. The final peace settlement in the Near East was the Treaty of Lausanne in July 1923. In eastern Europe a Russo-Polish war with considerable French participation was not concluded until the Treaty of Riga in March 1921. The Washington Conference of 1921 – 22 dealt with the Far East in two treaties — a Nine Power Treaty guaranteeing the independence of China and the 'open door' and a Four Power Treaty on the Pacific islands.

Of the five treaties which formed the Peace of Paris the Treaty of Versailles signed with Germany on 28 June 1919 was the most important. Germany lost Alsace and Lorraine to France, Eupen and Malmédy to Belgium, Posen and West Prussia to Poland, the ports of Memel and Danzig to the allies (Danzig was made a free state under League of Nations administration). Plebiscites were to decide the future of Upper Silesia, Schleswig and the Saar. The Saar was placed for fifteen years under international administration. Germany lost all her colonies and was disarmed, her army limited to 100,000 men and the east bank of the Rhine was demilitarized to a depth of 50 miles. The land west of the Rhine was placed under allied administration for fifteen years. Of the economic clauses the most contentious was article 231, the so-called War Guilt clause covering the payment of reparations. Germany had to accept 'responsibility. . .for causing all the loss and damage. . .as a consequence of the war imposed. . .by the aggression of Germany and her allies'.

As the allied peace terms became known in February and March

1919, the German government decided to make counter-proposals on individual issues (2). The most important change made to the treaty in response to German objections was the decision to organize a plebiscite in Upper Silesia, as a result of which a considerable area that had been awarded to Poland remained German. Nonetheless German opinion condemned the final treaty terms as unjust, especially the War Guilt clause. On the very day that German delegates signed the treaty General Stülpnagel, chief of the operations section of the High Command, looked ahead to a war with Poland and perhaps with France 'in the foreseeable future' (6). More dangerous however than German generals were allied critics of the treaty. Well before the treaty was signed General Smuts, South African commissioner at the conference, urged J.M. Keynes of the British delegation, to appeal to the 'plain man' (5). Keynes's argument in *Economic Consequences of the Peace* (1919) that reparations were unjust and unworkable profoundly influenced British attitudes towards the treaty.

After Versailles came the treaties of the Parisian suburbs. On 10 September 1919 Austria accepted a treaty signed at St Germain. The non-German parts of prewar Austria were distributed to claimant powers and a population of 28 millions was reduced to less than 8. Over 3 million Austrian Germans in the Sudetenland were placed under the new Czechoslovakia. A veto was placed on an *Anschluss* with Germany. By the treaty of Neuilly on 27 November 1919 Bulgaria was made to cede western Thrace to Greece and to pay reparations. Hungary by the treaty of Trianon signed on 4 June 1920 was deprived of 13 million people of its prewar population of 21 million and surrendered substantial territory to Romania. Both Austria and Hungary had to pay reparations and had their armies reduced in size. By the treaty of Sèvres signed by the allies and the defeated Turkish Sultanate on 10 August 1920 the Greeks were left in possession of Smyrna in Asia Minor. The advent of the Turkish nationalist leader Mustafa Kemal overturned the settlement. He attacked the Greek colonies at Smyrna and won French and Italian support. Britain alone championed the Greeks. The Treaty of Lausanne in July 1923 recognized the Greek defeat in Symrna and the Turkish mainland reverted to the Turks.

By the end of 1923 fighting in Europe and the Near East had ceased but there was little to show for so many treaties and conferences. Relations between France and her allies were strained almost to breaking point by the French occupation of the Ruhr (16). On naval disarmament some small progress was made. The Washington Naval

Treaty of 1922 established capital ship ratios between the powers of 5 (Britain and the United States): 3 (Japan): 1.67 (France and Italy). Although Japan had hoped for better terms, her achievement was considerable (11). She stepped into Germany's shoes as a leading naval power. In effect Britain and the United States handed over to Japan strategic command of the western Pacific. The implications of the Washington treaty became clear in the Far Eastern crisis of 1931 – 33.

Why was so little achieved after five years? Largely because postwar problems were complex, intractable and perhaps insoluble. The illusion of the statesmen was that given time, patience and goodwill the main issues would be resolved. The interdependent, interlocking nature of political, economic and financial questions was a new feature of the postwar world and statesmen were slow to accept permanent instability. The highly unified pre – 1914 international economy had gone and the economies and currencies of the 1920s were weakened by war and revolution. The long duration of the peace-making process divided the allies, dissipated energies and undermined the credibility of the whole settlement.

Nothing illustrates better the interrelatedness of postwar issues than the tangle of reparations (13). The Treaty of Versailles authorized the Reparations Commission to secure 22,000 million gold marks before 1 May 1921 and then to fix the total amount Germany would have to pay. Disputes on this liability led to an allied ultimatum in March 1921 and to an occupation of Düsseldorf and two other German towns. The reparations bill was worked out at 132,000 million gold marks. A payment plan was agreed at the Second London Conference in May 1921 and Germany paid a total of 3,000 million gold marks before stopping payments. Since Germany was in default France and Belgium occupied the Ruhr in January 1923. Of the 132,000 million gold marks fixed by the Reparations Commission in 1921 Germany had paid little more than a tenth by 1932 when reparations were virtually cancelled at the Lausanne Conference. And what Germany paid was more than covered by foreign loans.

There was no speedy and satisfactory settlement of reparations because they were part and parcel of larger political and economic questions. Britain and France assessed reparations in the context of their war debts to the United States. Reparations would enable them to service their debt of 11,000 million dollars. Financially France needed reparations to pay for the reconstruction of the departments laid waste by Germany. Politically French opinion saw German payments as the fruits of victory. In September 1923 Poincaré told

Baldwin that France felt cheated because at every allied meeting since Versailles her share of reparations had dwindled (16). For Germany however reparations were a symbol of humiliation and defeat and it was in Germany's interest to keep payments small and extended over as a long period as possible (2). What mattered for Britain was the connection between reparations, domestic unemployment and European economic recovery. French insistence on large payments, it was feared, would throw Germany into chaos and Bolshevism and prevent Europe's recovery (13).

Both Britain and France campaigned for the cancellation of inter-allied debts. American cancellation of British and French war debts, it was argued, would enable Britain to cancel the debts of her European allies. A smaller reparations bill could then be fixed with the bulk of payments going to France (13). Although the United States refused either to cancel war debts or to recognize a connection between debts and reparations, in 1923 the French were given a hint that their withdrawal from the Ruhr might lead to a generous settlement of their war debt. Allied statesmen tried to bring the Soviet Union into the reparations equation in order to recover some of the Tsarist debts repudiated by the Bolshevik government in 1917. One scheme was that Germany should organize Soviet economic reconstruction and plough back the profits into reparations enabling Britain and France to recoup their lost investments (13).

1 The United States threatens to withdraw from the war

Colonel House, special representative of the president, to secretary of state Lansing, Paris, 30 October 1918

For the President:
Lloyd George, Balfour, and Reading [respectively prime minister, foreign secretary and Lord Chief Justice] lunched with me today and George stated that it was his opinion that if the Allies submitted to Germany's terms of armistice without more [discussion?], Germany would assume that the Allies had accepted President Wilson's fourteen points and other speeches without qualification. So far as Great Britain was concerned, George stated, point 2 of speech of 8 January 1918, respecting freedom of the seas, could not be accepted without qualification. He admitted that if point 2 was made part of point 14 concerning League of Nations, and assuming League of Nations was

such a one as Great Britain could subscribe to, it might be possible for
Great Britain to accept point 2. He said that he did not wish to discuss
freedom of the seas with Germany and [if] freedom of the seas was a
condition of peace Great Britain could not agree to it. Before our
discussion ended it seemed as though we were near an agreement concerning this matter along the lines of interpretation of point 2
heretofore cabled you in Cable No. 5 to the Department.

We then went to conference at Quai d'Orsay attended by Clemenceau, Pichon [respectively prime minister and foreign minister]
Balfour, Sonnino [Italian foreign minister] and myself. Conference
opened with discussion of fourteen points enumerated in President's
address of 8 January last. Clemenceau and others balked at number
[point] 1 until I read them interpretation thereof as cabled to you in
telegram No. 5. They then all accepted number [point] 1. After
number [point] 2 had been read, George made a short speech worded
so as to excite Clemenceau. He reversed his position taken a short time
before with me privately and said respecting point 2: 'We cannot
accept this under any circumstances; it takes away from us the power
of blockade. My view is this, I want to see character of a League of
Nations first before I accept this proposition. I do not wish to discuss it
with Germany. I will not make it a condition of peace with Germany.' I
stated that if these views were persisted in the logical consequences
would be for the President to say to Germany: 'The Allies do not agree
to the conditions of peace proposed by me and accordingly the present
negotiations are at an end.' I pointed out that this would leave the
President free to consider the question afresh and to determine
whether the United States should continue to fight for the principles
laid down by the Allies. My statement had a very exciting effect upon
those present. Balfour then made a forceful speech to the effect that it
was clear that the Germans were trying to drive a wedge between the
President and the Allies and that their attempts in this direction must
be foiled.

It was then suggested that France, England, and Italy confer
together and submit tomorrow drafts of the proposed answers to the
President's communication asking whether they agree to his terms of
peace, stating where they can agree with the President and where they
disagree. I then offered to withdraw from the conference so that they
would feel at liberty to discuss the matter between themselves. They all
stated that they had no secret from America and that they wished me
to remain. Accordingly it was agreed after further discussion and after
the reading of the terms agreed upon by the inter-Allied naval

conference now in session in Paris for the naval armistice that we should meet Wednesday afternoon to consider draft answers by the Allies to the President's communication transmitting correspondence between the President and Germany.

French Prime Minister and Italian Prime Minister are not at all in sympathy with the idea of the League of Nations. Italian Prime Minister will probably submit many objections to fourteen points. French Prime Minister, George and I agreed to meet Wednesday morning without Italian Prime Minister for the purpose of further discussion. . . .

> *FRUS,* 1918, 1 (Washington, 1933),
> pp. 421 – 22

2   The German Cabinet considers Allied peace terms, 21 March 1919

The President of the Reich [Ebert] opens the session and gives the floor to Minister Rantzau.

Count Rantzau [Reich minister for Foreign Affairs]: Let me make a few preliminary remarks. Out enemies will submit the completed draft of the peace treaty with the words 'Take it or leave it'. The draft will diverge widely from Wilson's programme. There are three possibilities: to turn it down; to make a counter-proposal; or to examine the draft in detail and make individual counter-proposals. The latter is the right approach. Negotiators must be instructed in such a way that they can offer counter-proposals. Wilson's programme leaves untouched the question of the freedom of the seas as well as the Schleswig question and that of a German-Austrian union. I have divided the material into ten points for the time being: territorial questions; protection of minorities; reparation questions; trade policies; financial questions; general legal questions; German colonies; disarmament; League of Nations; war guilt.

I Territorial Questions [Count Rantzau gives some further information on this point.]
Erzberger [Reich Minister]: We must demand first of all that the occupied territories be evacuated on the day the peace treaty is concluded. This demand should be backed up energetically by the press. The Allied soldiers, anxious to return home, are our natural allies on that score. Very well, let us insist on a referendum in

Alsace-Lorraine, with the possibilities: autonomy, autonomy within France, autonomy within Germany (possibly autonomy within a French or American protectorate). . . .A special agreement must be made about the hauling and marketing of potash.

Rantzau: In this question our enemies are unanimously opposed to our demand.

Gothein [Reich Minister]: . . .Annexation of the Saar territory to France would be against England's interests, since its coal would compete with England's. This conflict should be exploited. . . .

Prime Minister: Our demand that the occupied territories be evacuated before the referendum will be countered with our own conduct after Brest Litovsk in Lithuania, etc. . . .

Bell [Reich Minister for Colonial Affairs]: Even if evacuation of occupied territories cannot be obtained, the demand should be raised. At the very least, it will prevent the occupation from dragging on for years. Alsace and Lorraine should vote separately. The Germans expelled from there should also be given a vote. It is very important to protect the German industrial concerns in Alsace-Lorraine. . . .

Reinhardt [Minister of War]: It is desirable to speak up against coloured occupation troops. The term 'blacks' is too narrow, since Moroccans and Turcos are not black according to French terminology. . . .

Count Rantzau: It would be valuable if public opinion pressed for lifting the occupation before peace is concluded.

David [Reich Minister]: Yes, propaganda for it should be started right now. But we won't get anywhere. The year 1871 will be referred to. Conditions of occupation should be clarified: personal and economic communication; mail; precise guarantees for the safety of our people. English and American occupation troops. As to the question of autonomy for Alsace-Lorraine, we are in a favourable position because we did grant some autonomy which threatens to be lost in centralized France. . . .

Reinhardt: It is doubtful whether we will get coloured troops withdrawn since the Americans are in the same position as the other Allies.

Ebert: We want to urge immediate evacuation of the occupied territories, possibly withdrawal of coloured troops; the nature of the plebiscite should be determined and treaties on economic questions, especially potash and iron ore, drawn up. As there is little hope of regaining Alsace-Lorraine, the economic questions weigh even more heavily in the balance.

II Protection of Minorities [Rantzau gives further information.]

Gothein: We must advocate protection of national minorities on general principle, without stressing special German interests. The referendum should be organized by small districts—not whole regions, which would be very dangerous for Pozen.

Erzberger: Protection of national minorities should be limited to the inhabitants, not the temporary residents.

Schiffer [Reich Finance Minister]: Austria is making efforts to guarantee continued Austrian citizenship for Austrians living outside the country. This might be considered.

Lewald [State Undersecretary]: Far-reaching regulations for the protection of national minorities are being incorporated in the constitution. This should be stressed.

III Reparation Questions [Rantzau gives further information.]

Erzberger: We must base our arguments on the note of 5 November, 1918. After the formal exchange of notes, according to international law, a treaty was concluded. Belgium will have to be completely rebuilt. This does not hold for Northern France. . . .The principle for the method of payment must be: small quotas, extending over a long period of time. . . .There is the possibility that in the long run changes will be made, anyhow. Payment must be in kind, not in money.

David: I agree that we should rest our case on the note of 5 November, but the enemies will have a different interpretation. The note says 'German attack', not 'German attacks', which means that Germany waged an aggressive war and must make good total damage.

Dr Bell: We must take a stand on the guilt question. One might explain that the march through Belgium was motivated by erroneous assumptions. (1) This was an emergency in which ordinary rules did not apply, and (2) Belgium had a secret agreement with the Entente. We have since realized our mistake. We are, therefore, responsible for payment of damages.

Noske [Reich Defence Minister]: I still think that in extreme emergencies one fends for oneself as best one can. I cannot even recognize German guilt in Belgium. Nor in U-boat warfare, either—it was a countermeasure to starvation blockade. I agree that payments should be spread out over a long period.

Count Rantzau: We can justify submarine warfare by the hunger blockade. Other guilt questions will be taken up under Point 10.

Count Bernstorff [Envoy]: The enemies. . . .will say: 'Besides

Wilson's points, it must be taken into account that Germany must be punished'. We can reply: '. . .You only wished to fight in order to abolish autocracy and militarism and that has been eliminated'. But we won't get anywhere and the big guilt question will still be raised.

Gothein: . . .England and America show understanding for our inability to bear great burdens.

Giesberts [Reich Minister for Postal Affairs]: We cannot scrape up four billion a year. The standard of living of the German workers and the social welfare measures must be safeguarded. This we must emphasize as a precondition, with reference to the internal political struggle (Bolshevism, etc).

Landsberg [Reich Minister of Justice]: . . .The question of guilt and reparations cannot be separated. The march into Belgium resulted from an emergency, but was not self-defence. Emergency conditions do not relieve us from responsibility for damage, so we should consent to making restitution. The payments should be small.

Ebert: What is the extreme limit for our capacity for reparation payments?

Rantzau: Does this imply an authorization to break off negotiations if demands endanger our very existence?

Erzberger: Let us maintain, according to the note of 5 November, that reparations be limited to damage in occupied areas. No other demands should be recognized. . . .

Count Rantzau: I agree. The Reich reparation commission has estimated that on that basis we would have to pay 20 to 25 billions. This takes into account deliveries since armistice and perhaps colonies given up. This sum is within reason. Payments should be in kind. . . .

Schiffer: The principal consideration is what we can pay. Granting that domestic obligations and obligations towards neutrals must be met, hardly any resources are left for payment. . . .

Bell: Our negotiators must be clear as to what is the limit of our capacities. This should not enter in the negotiations, however, since this would damage our prestige. . . .

Count Bernstorff: From the legal point of view, we should stick to our interpretation, but we won't be able to put it across, since the English would then not be entitled to reparations, which they keep mentioning in every political statement.

Reinhardt: Just rebuilding occupied territories will be very costly, from what I know of destruction; that alone will exceed our capacities.

Ebert: There is agreement that the note of 5 November in its most favourable interpretation should serve as our starting point. . . .

VII German Colonies [Count Rantzau gives further information].

Bell: Emphasis should be on the fact that proposal for League of Nations contradicts not only point 5, but also Wilson's proclamations that we had as much right as others to colonies. . . .Loss of colonies would be fatal, would make us purely a continental power. . . .New Guinea is perhaps our most valuable colony, so let us try to retain it. There is but slight hope for Southwest and East Africa. The greatest effort should be put forth for Cameroons and Togo. . . .The value of the individual colonies has been very carefully estimated. The total value of 30 billion must, of course, be kept strictly secret.

Ebert: Willingness to accept mandates as a solution should be shown only as a last resort.

> *The Political Institutions of the German Revolution, 1918 – 1919* eds. Charles B. Burdick and Ralph H. Lutz (Stanford. Cal., 1966), pp. 268 – 75

3 Conversation between Wilson, Clemenceau, Lloyd George and Orlando, 27 March 1919

Mr Lloyd George: Have you read the memorandum I sent you dealing with the general conditions of the Peace?

M. Clemenceau: I intend to give you a reply in writing; but it must first be translated into French for the President of the Republic.

President Wilson: [American President]—I trust that, in principle, you are agreed with Mr Lloyd George as to the moderation which must be shown toward Germany. We do not want to destroy Germany and we could not do so: our greatest mistake would be to furnish her with powerful reasons for seeking revenge at some future time. Excessive demands would be sure to sow the seeds of war.

Everywhere we are obliged to modify frontiers and change national sovereignties. Nothing could entail greater dangers, for these changes are contrary to long-established habits; they transform the very life of populations, and affect their feelings at the same time. We must not give our enemies even an impression of injustice. I do not fear, in the future, wars prepared by the secret plots of governments, but rather conflicts created by discontent among the peoples. If we are ourselves guilty of injustice, such discontent is inevitable, with the consequences which are bound to follow. Hence our desire to negotiate with moderation and equity.

Mr Lloyd George: May I cite a precedent from history? In 1814 after the defeat of Napoleon, Prussia, represented in this matter by Blücher, planned to impose crushing terms on France. Wellington, a man of sound sense, took the opposite view and his attitude was supported by Castlereagh, previously one of France's bitterest enemies. They both felt that it would be a grave mistake to try to destroy France, since her presence was necessary for both civilization and the European order. This was the attitude towards France of the representatives of England, and if their advice had not prevailed, France would have been half destroyed, with no other result than to deliver all of Europe into the hands of the German Powers.

Germany has received as severe a lesson as any known in all history. The fall of the Napoleonic Empire in 1814 is not comparable, for the campaign in France was a glorious conclusion to the Napoleonic Wars, while the Germans, last November, capitulated without even attempting to make a last stand.

M. Clemenceau: I said yesterday that I entirely agreed with Mr Lloyd George and President Wilson on how Germany should be treated; we cannot take unfair advantage of our victory; we must deal tolerantly with peoples for fear of provoking a surge of national feeling.

But permit me to make a fundamental objection. Mr Lloyd George has excessive fears of possible German resistance and refusal to sign the treaty. I may point out that, apprehensive no doubt of atrocious reprisals of which we are incapable, they surrendered without waiting for the entrance of our troops. This time we must expect them to resist; they will dispute. They will dispute on every point, they will threaten to refuse to sign, they will play up such incidents as that which has just occurred at Budapest and which can occur tomorrow in Vienna; they will contest or refuse everything that can be refused. You may have read in yesterday's papers the interview given by Count Bernstorff. He speaks with the arrogance of a conqueror. But excessive fears must be avoided. We must reckon with every possible danger; but since the victory was gained at such a cost, we must also be assured of its fruits.

After all, the resistance of the Germans did not always come up to expectations. You took their entire battle fleet; yet they were very proud of it, and their Emperor had told them: 'Our future is on the sea'. The Germans would put up a desperate resistance, it was thought, if deprived of their fleet; you remember Marshal Foch's [Supreme Allied Commander] remarks on this point when we were drafting the Armistice terms. In fact, however, nothing happened. At this moment we are seizing their merchant fleet, in order to feed them, it is true. But they hardly count on our sending them food, for today's *Berliner Tageblatt* writes that if we did not, Germany would manage to live despite the blockade.

I come to President Wilson's maxim, which I accept, but apply to the Germans with a grain of salt. President Wilson warns us against giving the Germans a sense of injustice. Agreed, but what we regard as just here in this room will not necessarily be accepted as such by the Germans.

People are surprised that France should oppose the immediate admission of Germany to the League of Nations. Yesterday once again I received another dossier on the atrocities committed in France. Unfortunately, we have come, to our cost, to know the Germans, and are aware that as a nation they submit to force in order that they themselves may impose force on the world. I shall remind Mr Lloyd George of a conversation we had at Carlsbad, seven or eight years ago: I confided to him my apprehension over Europe's future and referred to the German danger. Mr Lloyd George hoped that Germany would behave herself; unfortunately events undeceived him.

The Germans, a servile people, must have force to sustain an argument. Shortly before he died Napoleon said: 'Nothing permanent is founded on force'. I am not so sure; a glance at the great nations of Europe and the United States themselves is enough to give one pause. What is true, is that force cannot establish anything substantial unless it is in the service of justice. Every effort must be made to be just toward the Germans; but when it comes to persuading them that we are just toward them, that is another matter. We can, I believe, save the world for a long time to come from German aggression; but the German spirit is not going to change so fast. Witness the German social democrats who claimed to be brothers of our socialists and yours: we saw them in the service of the Imperial Government and today they are in the service of Scheidemann [German Prime Minister] surrounded by the former bureaucratic personnel of the Empire, with Rantzau at the head.

Note that no one in Germany draws any distinction between the just and unjust demands of the Allies. It is the assignment of Danzig to Poland which they are resisting most stubbornly. Nevertheless, to right the historical wrong against the Polish nation, we are bound, if we bring this nation back to life, to give it the means to live. We cannot forget the crimes against Poland committed by Germany in particular, after the great crime of its partition: and this during the nineteenth century and, so to speak, by scientific methods. We remember the children who were whipped for having prayed to God in Polish, and the peasants expropriated and driven from their lands to make way for tenants of the German race.

All of us, perhaps, have on our conscience similar expropriations in a more or less distant past; but these acts occurred under our very eyes, and those responsible are here before us. Among them we find the social democrats, who supported their government during four years of war.

I respect Mr Lloyd George for the spirit of fairness shown in his expressed desire to give Poland the smallest possible number of German subjects. But I cannot approve his statement while discussing the matter of communications between Danzig and the interior, that all considerations of strategy should be set aside. If we followed this advice, a sad heritage would be left to our successors. Some deviations from the principle of self-determination are inevitable, otherwise the principle itself cannot be safeguarded.

I am haunted by one case, that of Austria. It is said that we should all disarm; I am willing to agree. Believe me, the spirit of conquest formerly characteristic of the French people is now dead for ever. But if we reduce our armaments and if, at the same time, Austria's 7 million inhabitants are added to Germany's population, the increased strength of our German neighbours becomes dangerous. Does it violate the right of peoples to tell the Austrians: 'We only ask you to remain independent; do what you like with this independence; but you must not join a German bloc nor participate in a plan of German revenge.'?

My principles are the same as yours; I am considering only their application. May I say this to President Wilson: do not believe that these principles of justice that satisfy us will also satisfy the Germans. I know them: since 1871 I have forced myself, almost every year, to visit Germany; I wanted to know the Germans and, at various times, I hoped a means could be found to bring our two peoples together. Their idea of justice, I assure you, is not ours.

After expending the greatest effort, and suffering the greatest sacrifices in blood in all history, we must not compromise the results of our victory. The League of Nations is proposed as a road to the security we need: I accept this method; but if the League of Nations cannot buttress its orders with military sanctions, we must find this sanction elsewhere. May I point out that, at sea, this sanction is ready to hand: Germany no longer has a navy. We must find an equivalent on land. I have no preference for any particular method. I beg you to understand my state of mind, just as I am trying to understand yours. America is far away and protected by the ocean. England could not be reached by Napoleon himself. You are sheltered, both of you; we are not.

No man is further removed from the militaristic spirit than I. I am ready to do anything to find a solution that will be better than the military solution. But we cannot forget that in our great crisis the military did much to save us. Let us not err by refusing their advice at a time like this. If the danger and the ordeal came, they would say 'It is not our fault that you did not listen'.

One last word. We are right to fear Bolshevism among the enemy and to avoid stimulating its progress, but we must keep it from spreading among ourselves. There is a sense of justice as between the allies which must be satisfied. If this feeling were violently thwarted, either in France or in England, grave danger might follow. Clemency toward the conquered is good; but let us not lose sight of the victors. If a revolutionary movement should develop somewhere, because our solutions appeared to be unjust, let this not be amongst us. My intention is merely to offer a word of caution.

Mr Lloyd George: In many respects I am in agreement with M. Clemenceau, but some of his positions seem to me full of danger. I know something of the Bolshevik peril in our countries; for several weeks I have been combating it myself and I congratulate my colleagues for having had less trouble here than I have had. I am fighting Bolshevism, not by force, but by seeking a way to satisfy the legitimate aspirations which may have given it birth.

As a result, trades unionists such as Smillie, Secretary of the Miners' Union, who might have become formidable, have in the end helped us to avoid a conflict. The English capitalists, thank God! are frightened; this makes them reasonable. But to return to the conditions of peace, the accusation most likely to provoke an explosion of Bolshevism is not that we ask too little of the enemy, but that we ask too much. The English workman has no desire to overwhelm German people with excessive demands. It is rather in the upper classes that an unbridled hatred of the Germans will be found.

Besides, a marked change of attitude has occurred in this matter, since the renunciation by Germany of her former political regime. If our conditions are viewed as too moderate, I shall have great difficulties in Parliament; but not from the working classes.

I cannot agree with M. Clemenceau about the view of military men. Their aid is indispensable in time of war. But in the realm of the statesman, they are the last persons I would consult. I admire and like Marshal Foch very much; but where political questions are at issue he is just a child. On the question how to guarantee the most complete security to the nations, I would not take his advice. Let us not forget how Moltke, assuredly an eminent military authority, dragged Bismarck further in 1871, perhaps, than he himself was prepared to venture. In the end Germany fell a victim to the concept of the strategic frontier, which led her to mutilate France.

Similarly we had a school of officers who sought for the Indian Empire a so-called scientific frontier. Gladstone did not believe in scientific frontiers. But Disraeli, applying this doctrine, permitted Afghanistan to be occupied, and we were later forced to withdraw in disastrous conditions. Since then Afghanistan, respected by us, developed into the most useful kind of buffer State. This brings us back to the discussion I have just mentioned between Wellington and Blücher.

I have received a letter from General Smuts [South African commissioner to the conference], a fair-minded man whose loyalty to us I wish to recall. He is one of the best generals who fought against us in the South African War. He invaded Cape Colony with a few hundred men; he had thousands when he surrendered to us. During the present war I need only recall his role in helping us to suppress the uprising fomented by Germany in South Africa.

His letter, as he himself says, is not a pleasant one. He says much about Danzig; he believes that our proposed conditions are by no means the act of a statesman. I confess I have myself grave fears about Danzig. We are about to give two million Germans to Poland. The Poles are bad at government and it will be a long time before they learn to conduct matters in the western manner. There will be disturbances; the Germans in Poland, if they revolt, will be defeated; if Germany wants to intervene, will you dispatch troops to keep the Germans in Poland under the yoke? The Poles, it is true, will say: why did you give us these territories if you won't help us keep them? Public opinion, in both America and England, would certainly not support us if we intervened in such conditions. Both the League of Nations and the treaty signed by us will be flouted. I have no use for a treaty whose subsequent execution could not be assured. If you are not determined to assure the performance of this clause, why insert it in the treaty?

In any case, we are preparing to impose on Germany a very onerous peace: no colonies, no fleet; she will lose 6 or 7 million inhabitants, a large part of her natural wealth; almost all her iron, a considerable proportion of her coal. As a military power, we reduce her to the status of Greece and, as a naval power, to that of the Argentine Republic. And on all these points, we are in entire agreement. In addition, she will pay, according to estimates, £5,000 or £10,000 million. Even if our conditions are made as light as possible, no civilized nation has ever been forced to shoulder anything comparable. If to this are added secondary conditions which could be interpreted as unfair, the result may perhaps be the straw that breaks the camel's back.

What has France resented most: the loss of Alsace-Lorraine, or the obligation to pay 5 billions of indemnity? I know your answer in advance. During my first trip to Paris, what impressed me most was the statue of Strasbourg draped in mourning. We must not, by any fault of ours, drive Germany to raise such statues in her cities. . . .

> Paul Mantoux, *Paris Peace Conference 1919* : *Proceedings of the Council of Four* (Geneva, 1964), pp. 24 – 9

4   President Poincaré argues for indefinite occupation of the Rhineland as security for payment of German reparations

Letter from the French president to Clemenceau, French prime minister, 28 April 1919

My dear President,
Before any definite decisions are taken, I think it might be useful to sum up certain observations which the proposals put forward suggest to me, and which I have acquainted you with from time to time. You will thus be able to communicate my opinion, if you think fit, to the Allied and Associated Governments.

The amount of claim which the Allies and Associated Powers will have to bring against Germany cannot be definitely assessed until after the Commission set up during the peace preliminaries has made its calculations. But it would already appear from the work of the Delegations that the annual payment will very likely spread over some thirty years at least. It would therefore be fair and logical for the military occupation of the left bank of the Rhine and the bridgeheads to last for the same length of time.

In the first place, in favour of this occupation, the serious considerations can be quoted which were set out in the two memoranda submitted by Marshal Foch to the Allied and Associated Governments.

The Marshal thinks, as do the military authorities, that the Rhine is the only barrier which really guarantees, in the event of another German attack, the common defence of England, Belgium and France. It is therefore to our interest not to abandon this barrier before Germany has fulfilled all the terms of the Peace Treaty.

There is, moreover, something quite unusual in the idea of renouncing a security before the amount secured has been completely paid.

Seeing that the occupation is to terminate in the event of payment in advance, the logical counterpart of this clause is for the occupation to continue in any case until the total liquidation of the debt.

After the war of 1870, the Germans occupied various French provinces until they received the last centime of the indemnity imposed on France, and M. Thiers only succeeded in obtaining the evacuation of the territory by discharging in advance the milliards which the conqueror exacted.

Occupation as security for a debt which represents reparation for war losses is in no way contrary to the principles proclaimed by President Wilson and accepted by the Allies. It has not, of course, any connection with annexation. It does not interfere with the national sovereignty of the defeated nation; it does not involve the inhabitants in a change of their native land; by its very definition it is temporary and dependent upon the duration of the debt which it guarantees; it merely constitutes a safeguard, a means by which the creditor assures payment without resorting to force.

One is at a loss to understand how this occupation could be shorter than the period fixed for annual payments. The figure of fifteen years is purely arbitrary, and it is equally arbitrary to make provision for three successive stages of evacuation during these fifteen years, when on the expiry of this time-limit, France and her Allies may still be Germany's creditors.

It is argued that even when the occupation ceased, it could be resumed in the event of non-payment. The option to renew occupation may look tempting today on paper. But it is bristling with drawbacks and risks.

Let us imagine ourselves sixteen or seventeen years ahead. Germany has paid regularly for fifteen years. We have evacuated the whole of the left bank of the Rhine. We have returned to our side of the political frontiers which afford no military security. Imagine Germany again a prey to Imperialism or imagine that she simply breaks faith. She suspends payment and we are obliged to reoccupy. We give the necessary orders, but who will vouch for our being able to carry them out without difficulty?

In the first place, Germany by her customary methods of propaganda will be sure to misrepresent the facts and to assert that it is we who are the aggressors, and as it will actually be our troops who are returning to German soil, we shall easily figure as the invaders.

And, further, shall we be sure of finding the left bank free from German troops? Germany is supposedly going to undertake to have neither troops or fortresses on the left bank and within a zone extending 59 km east of the Rhine. But the Treaty does not provide for any permanent supervision of troops and armaments, on the left bank any more than elsewhere in Germany. In the absence of this permanent supervision, the clause stipulating that the League of Nations may order enquiries to be undertaken is in danger of being purely illusory. We can thus have no guarantee that after the expiry of the fifteen years and the evacuation of the left bank, the Germans will not filter troops by degrees into this district. Even supposing they have not previously done so, how can we prevent them doing it at the moment when we intend to reoccupy on account of the default?

It will then be simple for them to leap to the Rhine in a night and to seize this natural military frontier well ahead of us.

The option to renew the occupation should not therefore from any point of view be substituted for occupation.

It is objected that prolonged occupation will constitute a heavy military drain. Marshal Foch thinks, on the other hand, that the defence of the Rhine will require fewer troops than the defence of our political frontier, and assuredly he is best qualified to speak on this matter. Besides, for the present, it is not a question of our being compelled to occupy; but of compelling Germany to accept this occupation. The Allies will always be free to abandon it if they think fit.

It is also objected that a prolonged occupation may embitter relations between the troops and the inhabitants and cause trouble. If the objection held good, it would apply equally well to an occupation lasting for fifteen years as to an occupation guaranteeing a debt. It would be even more valid in the former case, since this occupation, which fixes an arbitrary time-limit, does not appear to have any clearly defined object, whilst the second, which constitutes a security for payment, is easily grasped by everyone and particularly by the inhabitants of the locality occupied. It should be added that on the one hand those inhabitants are among the most friendly in Germany and have never cherished the same feelings of hostility against the Allies as the Prussians; and on the other hand, the French troops will have enough tact, once the Peace is signed, not to treat these people as enemies. If there were a risk of friction, it would be more likely to occur early because of war memories; but as time goes on, the relations between the armies of occupation and the civil population are bound to improve.

In brief, everything calls for the type of occupation which represents the natural consequence and the security for the debt. The one should cease when the other is liquidated. Neither sooner nor later.

No one esteems more highly than I the offers of alliance which have been generously extended to France by the President of the United States and the Prime Minister of Great Britain. The permanent alliance of our three nations in defence of justice and liberty will be a fine and splendid thing. But the valuable assistance which our friends are in a position to render us in the event of German aggression cannot unfortunately ever be instantaneous. Besides it will not directly affect the security for the debt. It will thus be no substitute for occupation.

I am fully confident that the Allied and Associated Governments will take this situation into consideration and that they will be willing to confer on France, who has suffered so heavily, the one safeguard which in my opinion can guarantee effectively the payment of our debt.

Believe me, my dear President,
                              Yours very sincerely
                                 (sd) Poincaré

                              David Lloyd George, *Memoirs of the
                              Peace Conference*, I (New Haven, 1939)
                              pp. 281 – 4

5   Smuts encourages Keynes to denounce the Treaty of Versailles

Letter from General J.C. Smuts, South Africa's commissioner at the Peace Conference, to J.M. Keynes of the British delegation, 10 June 1919

My dear Keynes,
Thank you for your note. I was sorry to note that you had cut the painter. Not that you did not have every reason. But it is never advisable to act under the impulse and influence of such a strain as you

had been passing through. However, it is done.

And now as to the future, I think it would be very advisable for you as soon as possible to set about writing a clear, connected account of what the financial and economic clauses of the Treaty actually are and mean, and what their probable results will be.[1] It should not be too long or technical, as we may want to appeal to the plain man more than to the well informed or the specialist. Anything technical which you may wish to write should be dealt with separately from this more popular, but still accurate, statement for public guidance. And when you could let me have a copy I shall be very grateful to you. Our actual course we need not decide just yet. Indeed, I have not yet made up my mind on the matter. The Treaty will in any case emerge as a rotten thing, of which we shall all be ashamed in due course. But it is necessary to have a formal Peace in order that the world may have a chance; which it will not have so long as the present state of affairs continues. And it may well be that with peace, and the better knowledge of what it all means, a great revulsion will set in and a favourable atmosphere will be created in which to help the public virtually to scrap this monstrous instrument. I am still considering both the time and the manner of doing the thing, as very much is at stake, and no tactical mistakes should be made. But I want every preparation for the attack to be made in advance.

> *Selections from the Smuts Papers*, IV,
> eds. W.K. Hancock and Jean van der
> Poel, (Cambridge, 1966), pp. 222 – 3

6   The German army looks to the resurrection of Germany, 28 June 1919

Letter from General Stülpnagel, chief of the operations section of the High Command, to General von Seeckt, head of the High Command.

In my opinion it is absolutely essential that an officer corps with monarchical convictions and of the old stamp should be preserved for the miserable creature of the new army. Counter-moves are naturally on the way. I have been informed that *Herr General* [Seeckt] has handed in his resignation. After the decree of the war minister no other step was feasible. . . .I am hoping that within the foreseeable

1. *The Economic Consequences of the Peace*, by J.M. Keynes was first published in December, 1919

future the resurrection of the monarchy, a struggle with Poland and perhaps with France too will be possible, and I therefore consider it my duty to ask *Herr General* to remain in the army for these tasks and for these aims.

> F.L. Carsten, *The Reichswehr and Politics*, 1918 – 1933 (London 1966), p. 30

7 The United States and the League of Nations

Letter from Raymond B. Fosdick, assistant secretary general of the League of Nations, to Sir Eric Drummond, secretary general, 25 November 1919

Washington 25 November 1919

The Labor Conference will adjourn this coming Saturday November twenty-ninth, and most of the delegates are slated for immediate return. I am sorry to have to report that they are going home in a spirit of bitterness and disillusionment — glad to get away from Washington, and vowing, many of them, never to return. This feeling is so widespread among the delegates and its repercussions will so soon be felt in Europe, that I think I ought to describe, somewhat at length perhaps, the various factors which have led up to it.

1 The Labor delegates undoubtedly thought that they were coming to a country where the idea of international cooperation, as embodied in a League of Nations, was warmly and enthusiastically sponsored. President Wilson's work in Europe, and the emphasis which had been placed upon the new order in international relations, gave them the right to believe that inasmuch as they represented the first tangible beginning of the new machinery, they and their work would be received in America with generous hospitality. Instead they found a country that was confused and torn with doubts about the whole conception of a League of Nations. Their work was conducted in Washington, which was the storm center of the debate. They saw the League kicked about the political arena with the apparent approval of many powerful interests and newspapers, and finally defeated in a debate that was wholly partisan in character, the result of which was applauded in many parts of the country.

They were not in a position to see or to understand the silent forces in America, represented in thousands of homes and communities that are looking and working for the League. All that the delegates could know is that loud and vociferous interests shrieked hysterically against American cooperation in any international movement and apparently won the fight. Consequently, these delegates are going home convinced that either America's early belief in a League of Nations was hypocritical and insincere, or that President Wilson's work in Europe was a false pretense. They are utterly disillusioned about America and they believe that light and leading cannot be looked for here. I am sure that among the European delegates there would scarcely be a single vote that would favor another international meeting of any kind in Washington.

2 Another factor in this feeling of bitterness is the environment of industrial conflict in which the meetings of the Conference were held. By an unhappy coincidence, the meetings were staged in the midst of the two greatest strikes in America's history— the steel strike and the coal strike. The drastic methods to which the Government resorted to break these strikes have made a most unfavorable impression upon the Conference. The novel use of the injunction as a weapon of industrial warfare, the employment of the State constabulary in Pennsylvania to break up meetings of strikers, and the generally hostile attitude of the press toward the attempts of the Unions to obtain recognition, have given the delegates from Europe the impression that America is the center of industrial Bourbonism.

Moreover, the delegates have seen the great confusion of thought that exists in America in regard to industrial unrest, by which liberalism in any form is made synonymous with radicalism, and labor unionists, mild socialists or any persons who dare to think along unusual lines, are indiscriminately dubbed 'anarchists', 'reds' and 'Bolsheviks'. They have seen a great popular wave of 'heresy hunting' sweep over the country, accompanied by raids and lynchings. They have been holding their meetings in an environment that was distinctly hostile to the very program which they were invited here to discuss.

3 The hostility and indifference of America to the Labor Conference has been distinctly shown in the press. The *Washington Post*, which is perhaps our most important local paper here at the Capitol, has followed the conference in attack after attack, calling the representatives 'waifs', 'strays', 'reds', etc. Two or three New York and Chicago papers have been almost equally bitter. The *Washington Post* is far too extreme to be typical of the attitude of the American press as

a whole, but it is the paper which is most widely read by the delegates. Moreover, the delegates are convinced, I believe, that there has been a conspiracy of silence among those papers which did not positively attack them. Many prominent papers have scarcely mentioned the Conference. Personally, I do not believe that this belief has any foundation. The news of the Labor Conference has been literally crowded out of the papers by the industrial situation and the Treaty debate. It is true, however, that quite apart from any feeling of hostility, the American newspapers have not treated the Conference with any degree of seriousness, and that little interest has been displayed by the reading public.

4 The Conference has been attacked not only by the press, but by public officials. The speech of Senator Sherman, of Illinois, in protesting against the influx from Europe of the 'dangerous radicals and anarchists' assembled at Washington, was bitterly resented by the Conference. This speech was followed by others of like tenor, and just before it adjourned, the Senate passed a reservation to the Treaty excluding the United States from participation in the Labor Conference except upon such terms as Congress itself might name. Inasmuch as the Conference was meeting at Washington under the urgent invitation of the President and with the approval of Congress, this last step was regarded as a crowning insult.

5 Another factor in the bitterness with which the Conference is adjourning, is the utter lack of courtesy on the part of the United States Government in welcoming and entertaining the delegates. It is now well known among the delegates that Congress refused to supply the necessary funds and that money had to be obtained from Europe. The illness of the President made it impossible for him to take any action along the line of official entertainment, and the State Department, because of its fear of the Senate, refused to participate. Consequently, there was scarcely any official recognition of the Conference. Some two weeks after the Conference opened, the Vice President came to the hall one afternoon and shook hands with the delegates, and later the Navy Department arranged a trip down the Potomac to Washington's tomb. But apart from these two incidents, there has been no offical act of hospitality. Invitations to a reception to the Conference, extended by a Republican Senator, were subsequently withdrawn — an act which increased the strain of an already strained situation. The Conference has been snubbed officially and socially, and I doubt if any international gathering was ever held under more unhappy auspices.

I have written at length because I know that you will hear much of this in Europe. I confess, too, that I have written with a deep sense of humiliation. Under the circumstances I am forced to the opinion that the League should take careful thought before scheduling another international meeting of any kind in Washington.

> Raymond B. Fosdick, *Letters on the League of Nations* (Princeton, 1966) pp. 73 – 7

8   The British Cabinet sums up its policy on Russia, 29 January 1920

The trend of our policy was summed up towards the end of the meeting in the following sense:

(a) There can be no question of making active war on the Bolsheviks, for the reason that we have neither the men, the money, nor the credit, and public opinion is altogether opposed to such a course.

(b) There can be no question of entering into Peace negotiations with the Bolsheviks until they have demonstrated their capacity to conduct an orderly, decent administration in their own country and their intention not to interfere, by propaganda or otherwise, in the affairs of their neighbours, nor until they can show that they represent the governing authority of the areas for which they claim to speak. A hint might be given to the Bolsheviks in a public speech that when they have accomplished this, and only then, should we be prepared to treat with them.

(c) The Border States surrounding Russia must themselves take the full responsibility for deciding as between peace and war. Not the slightest encouragement, however, should be given them to pursue the policy of war, because if we were to give that advice we should incur responsibilities which we could not discharge. . . .

(d) We should continue our policy of giving material support to enable the Border States to defend themselves if attacked by the Bolsheviks.

> Cited in: Martin Gilbert, *Winston S. Churchill*, IV, Companion, Part 3 (London 1977), p. 1020

9   Excerpt from the Theses on the National and Colonial
     Question adopted at the Second Congress of the Communist
     International July – August 1920

3 The imperialist war of 1914 demonstrated with the greatest
clarity to all enslaved nations and oppressed classes of the entire world
the falseness of bourgeois-democratic phraseology. Both sides used
phrases about national liberation and the right of national self-determination to make good their case, but the treaties of Brest-Litovsk and
Bucharest on one side, and the treaties of Versailles and St Germain on
the other, showed that the victorious bourgeoisie quite ruthlessly
determine 'national' frontiers in accordance with their economic
interests. Even 'national' frontiers are objects of barter for the
bourgeoisie. The so-called League of Nations is nothing but the
insurance contract by which the victors in the war mutually guarantee
each other's spoils. For the bourgeoisie, the desire to re-establish
national unity, to 'reunite with the ceded parts of the country', is
nothing but an attempt of the defeated to assemble forces for new
wars. The reunification of nations artificially torn apart is also in
accordance with the interest of the proletariat; but the proletariat can
attain genuine national freedom and unity only by means of
revolutionary struggle and after the downfall of the bourgeoisie. The
League of Nations and the entire post-war policy of the imperialist
States disclose this truth even more sharply and clearly, everywhere
intensifying the revolutionary struggle of the proletariat of the
advanced countries and of the labouring classes in the colonies and
dependent countries, accelerating the destruction of petty-bourgeois
national illusions about the possibility of peaceful coexistence and of
the equality of nations under capitalism.

4 From these principles it follows that the entire policy of the
Communist International on the national and colonial question must
be based primarily on bringing together the proletariat and working
classes of all nations and countries for the common revolutionary
struggle for the overthrow of the landowners and the bourgeoisie. For
only such united action will ensure victory over capitalism, without
which it is impossible to abolish national oppression and inequality
of rights.

5 The world political situation has now placed the proletarian
dictatorship on the order of the day, and all events in world politics are
necessarily concentrated on one central point, the struggle of the
world bourgeoisie against the Russian Soviet Republic, which is

rallying round itself both the soviet movements among the advanced workers in all countries, and all the national liberation movements in the colonies and among oppressed peoples, convinced by bitter experience that there is no salvation for them except in union with the revolutionary proletariat and in the victory of the Soviet power over world imperialism.

6 At the present time, therefore, we should not restrict ourselves to a mere recognition or declaration of the need to bring the working people of various countries closer together; our policy must be to bring into being a close alliance of all national and colonial liberation movements with Soviet Russia; the forms taken by this alliance will be determined by the stage of development reached by the communist movement among the proletariat of each country or by the revolutionary liberation movement in the undeveloped countries and among the backward nationalities. . . .

11. In regard to the more backward States and nations, primarily feudal or patriarchal or patriarchal-peasant in character, the following considerations must be kept in mind:

(a) All communist parties must support by action the revolutionary liberation movements in these countries. The form in which this support will take should be discussed with the communist party of the country in question, if there is one. This obligation refers in the first place to the active support of the workers in that country on which the backward nation is financially, or as a colony, dependent.

(b) It is essential to struggle against the reactionary and medieval influence of the priesthood, the Christian missions, and similar elements.

(c) It is necessary to struggle against the pan-Islamic and pan-Asiatic movements and similar tendencies, which are trying to combine the liberation struggle against European and American imperialism with the strengthening of the power of Turkish and Japanese imperialism and of the nobility, the large landlords, the priests, etc.

(d) It is particularly important to support the peasant movement in the backward countries against the landlords and all forms and survivals of feudalism. Above all, efforts must be made to give the peasant movement as revolutionary a character as possible, organizing the peasants and all the exploited wherever possible in soviets, and thus establish as close a tie as possible between the west European communist proletariat and the revolutionary peasant movement in the East, in the colonies and backward countries.

(e) A resolute struggle must be waged against the attempt to clothe

the revolutionary liberation movements in the backward countries which are not genuinely communist in communist colours. The Communist International has the duty of supporting the revolutionary movement in the colonies and backward countries only with the object of rallying the constituent elements of the future proletarian parties – which will be truly communist and not only in name – in all the backward countries and educating them to a consciousness of their special task, namely, that of fighting against the bourgeois-democratic trend in their own nation. The Communist International should collaborate provisionally with the revolutionary movement of the colonies and backward countries, and even form an alliance with it, but it must not amalgamate with it; it must unconditionally maintain the independence of the proletarian movement, even if it is only in the embryonic stage. . . .

> Cited in: Jane Degras, *The Communist International 1919 – 1943 : Documents.* I, (London 1956), pp. 140 – 4

10   Britain at the Washington Conference, 1921

Letter from Balfour, foreign secretary, to Lloyd George, prime minister, 11 November 1921

4 From the discussions which took place at the Cabinet before my departure I formed the clear impression that the ultimate aim of the British Empire Delegation at the Washington Conference is to secure the largest possible limitation of armaments consistent with the safety of the British Empire. It is clear, however, that if satisfactory and durable results are to be achieved in regard to naval disarmament, which mainly affects the British Empire, the United States of America and Japan, an agreement must also be reached in regard to certain political problems which have arisen in China and the Pacific.

5 First and foremost among these latter problems is that of the Anglo-Japanese Alliance. Evidence continues to reach me, from those Delegates and officials who arrived in Washington before us, in confirmation of previous reports to the effect that adherence to the Alliance in its present form will be very unpopular in the United States of America, and will render the conclusion of a satisfactory and enduring arrangement for the limitation of armaments extremely difficult to negotiate. Further it is undeniable that, with the collapse

of the Russian Empire and the elimination of Germany from the Pacific, the conditions which brought the Anglo-Japanese Alliance into existence have disappeared for the time being, though it would perhaps not be prudent to assume that they will never be re-created. On the other hand, we are bound to give the utmost consideration to the feelings of an ally who has loyally stood by his engagements and rendered us valuable support in the late War, and we cannot contemplate any action calculated to alienate, much less to outrage, Japanese sentiment. Finally, the utmost weight must be given to the strong views expressed at the recent Imperial Meetings in regard to the importance which Australia and New Zealand attach to the maintenance of the Anglo-Japanese Alliance in some shape or form.

6 In order to harmonize these partially conflicting elements in the problem, I have devised a formula in the shape of a draft tripartite agreement between the British Empire, the United States of America, and Japan, dealing with the preservation of peace and the maintenance of the *status quo*. . . .The object of the scheme is:

(a) To enable the Americans to be parties to a tripartite arrangement without committing themselves to military operations:

(b) To bring the existing Anglo-Japanese Alliance to an end without hurting the feelings of our Ally:

(c) To leave it open to us to renew a defensive alliance with Japan if she should be again threatened by Germany or Russia:

(d) To frame a Treaty which will reassure our Australasian Dominions:

(e) To make it impossible for American critics to suggest that our Treaty with Japan would require us to stand aside in the case of a quarrel between them and Japan, whatever the cause of the quarrel might be.

DBFP, First series, XIV, No. 415

11   Japan at the Washington Conference

Admiral Kato Tomosaburo (Washington) to navy vice-minister (Tokyo), 27 December 1921

Generally what has governed my thinking at the conference has been the need to improve the bad relations which have until now existed between Japan and the United States. That is, I should like as far as possible to set to rights the many anti-Japanese opinions in America.

. . .At the first plenary meeting on 12 November we heard [naval] proposals which I had not expected. I was surprised and realized that important developments were afoot. Judging from the prevailing atmosphere, there can be no denying that Secretary Hughes's speech was very welcome to the delegates. [After a period of doubt] I concluded that we could not in any circumstances oppose the American proposals on principle. If we were to oppose them, Japan would pay dearly for it later. We had to accept the principles while we treated the details as a separate issue. So I assembled the important people in our mission and announced my conclusions. . . .

Since the recent world war it would appear that the feelings among politicians about defence have generally been the same throughout the world. That is to say, security is not the exclusive preserve of soldiers and war is not something which can be made by soldiers only. It is difficult to achieve one's objectives if one does not operate on the basis of total mobilization of the state. Thus, however well one arranges munitions, one cannot put them to practical use unless one can exploit industrial power, encourage trade and really maximize the national strength. Frankly, one has to admit that, if one has no money one cannot make war. . . .We cannot find any country apart from the United States which can supply us with a loan. . . so there is no other course open to us but to avoid war with her. . . .

I felt that we had to agree in principle with the American proposals. What could happen if there was no success over naval limitation and competition in naval shipbuilding continued on the lines laid down in the existing programmes? Though Britain has not the power any longer to expand her great navy, she would certainly do something. Although American public opinion is opposed to expansion of armaments, America has the power, if she once feels the need, to expand as much as she wants. On the other hand, if we think about Japan, our 8 – 8 fleet will be completed in 1924. (Britain is a separate case at the moment). Despite the fact that Japan would continue her new building between 1924 and 1927, the United States would not ignore Japan's new building without herself making a fresh plan. Japan must make up her mind that the United States would do this. While Japan was experiencing the greatest financial difficulties in completing her own 8 – 8 programme, she could not cope with further American naval expansion. It would be difficult for us to pursue a plan to expand the 8 – 8 fleet after 1927. Thus, the gap between American and Japanese naval strength would widen more and more and we could do nothing to narrow it. Japan would therefore be seriously threatened.

Though we are not satisfied with America's so-called 10.10.6 proposals, it would still be the best policy to accept them when we consider
what would happen if naval limitation was not achieved.

It seems to me to be necessary to arrange for a secret committee in
the Diet on some occasion and to explain to them the meaning of all
this. We should not mention it in public session. This view may seem to
be rather a cowardly course to take; but there is no alternative to it
since it is an inevitable necessity for Japan. . . .

In these circumstances Japan agreed on the 10.10.6 ratio. If we had
held to our original demands, we might have accomplished our
wishes; but judging from the state of opinion at the time, we could not
hope to get Britain and America to agree. If we had pressed our views,
they would merely have adopted the method of referring the matter to
the full public assembly. I do not need to tell you the hostile attitude
American public opinion would have taken towards Japan.

> Ian Nish, *Japanese Foreign Policy*,
> 1869 – 1942 (London, 1977),
> pp. 289 – 91

12   Lloyd George and Briand discuss an Anglo–French alliance, 21 December 1921

M. Briand [French prime minister] asked the Prime Minister whether
he might give him a sketch of a proposed Alliance between France and
Great Britain.

Mr Lloyd George said that he would be very glad to consider such a
sketch. He had already had his attention called to the conversations
which had taken place between Lord Curzon and the French Ambassador in London. Might he ask M. Briand a few questions on that
subject? Was it the idea that the guarantee of the Alliance should go
beyond that concluded in Paris in 1919?

M. Briand said he had in mind a very broad Alliance in which the
two Powers would guarantee each other's interests in all parts of the
world, act closely together in all things and go to each other's
assistance whenever these things were threatened.

Mr Lloyd George said that opinion in Great Britain was hardly
prepared for so broad an undertaking as that. So far as the western
frontier of Germany was concerned, it would be possible to give France
complete guarantee against invasion. The British people were not very
much interested in what happened on the eastern frontier of
Germany; they would not be ready to be involved in quarrels which

might arise regarding Poland or Danzig or Upper Silesia. On the contrary there was a general reluctance to get mixed up in these questions in any way. The British people felt that the populations in that quarter of Europe were unstable and excitable; they might start fighting at any time and the rights and wrongs of the disputes might be very hard to disentangle. He did not think, therefore, that this country would be disposed to give any guarantees which might involve them in military operations in any eventuality in that part of the world. On the other hand, he repeated, public opinion would readily give a guarantee against a German attack upon the soil of France.

M. Briand said that he conceived of an Alliance on a larger scale than Mr Lloyd George had outlined. He quite understood that there was no passion in the hearts of the British public for giving unqualified support to countries in Eastern Europe. But from the French point of view the first result of a firm understanding would be to reduce the military burden [?s] on France and make them more proportionate to her power to carry them. This was the earnest wish of at least three-fourths of the population of France and their belief was that it could only be done by means of a close compact between France and Great Britain. It was not impossible to imagine other nations coming into the compact including Germany herself. He thought that there was much to be said for some arrangement similar to the Quadruple Pacific Treaty just concluded in Washington. That would not bind the Powers to very strict military obligations but would provide for their taking counsel together in a crisis in the event of threats to their interests and the 'status quo'. Such an arrangement might include three or four Powers but the nucleus of it should be a complete Alliance between Great Britain and France, around which other nations would gather. He repeated with emphasis that Germany should be a party to the Pact.

Mr Lloyd George said that English public opinion was hardly prepared at the present moment to contemplate such an extensive alliance, but there would be a majority in Parliament and in the country for a plain guarantee to France against invasion, although in point of fact the guarantee would be opposed by a stronger minority today than two years ago. But Monsieur Briand contemplated something which went beyond the two countries. If we could draw in Germany, so much the better. He would like to consult his colleagues on M. Briand's suggestion and resume the conversation when they met at Cannes.

DBFP, First series, XV, No. 110

13   Reparations and War Debts : Cabinet Minutes, 22 December 1921

[*Forthcoming visit of M. Briand*]

The Cabinet were informed by the Chancellor of the Exchequer that when arrangements had been made for the forthcoming Conference with M. Briand it had been contemplated as possible that the representatives of the Unites of States of America, France and Great Britain would have entered upon a general discussion of the various large outstanding economic questions, including the question of inter-allied debts. At such a discussion it would have been possible for Great Britain in the event of the United States of America agreeing to a cancellation of her European indebtedness, to have similarly cancelled the debts owed to her by the Allies, and also possibly to have foregone any claim to further reparation from Germany, except claims in respect of actual damage sustained. A policy of this character would have left France in a position to obtain from Germany reparation for her devastated regions. M. Loucheur [French minister of reconstruction] had been willing to entertain proposals of this character, and it was not out of the question that he might have been willing, as part of a general settlement, to forego the French pension claim against Germany.

As a result of tentative enquiries made in responsible quarters, it was, however, certain that any suggestion to the United States Government to enter upon discussions of this character would meet with a very hostile reception. While certain of the mercantile and trading classes in the Eastern States might be favourable to some general arrangement, the view of the great majority of Americans was that the debts should be paid, and that the failure to pay them was the primary cause of the present distress in the United States. The attitude of the Finance Committee of the Senate was of a similar character, and in a recent discussion on the subject of the funding of Allied Debts, that Committee had laid down that such funding should be subject to the condition that there should be no cancellation, either of interest or principal, and that there should be no acceptance by the United States Treasury of the Bonds of one country in satisfaction of the American debt of another. In these circumstances, American participation in any general discussion must be ruled out and the Allies must turn to the smaller problem of German reparation.

The position as regards German reparation was that on 15 January and 15 February next, Germany would have to find two instalments amounting to a sum of 30 to 35 millions sterling, and it was pretty clear that the utmost that in the present circumstances the German Government could produce would be £10 to £12 millions. In the main the money would have to go to Belgium by reason of her priority. It must be borne in mind that France was at present receiving reparation coal on very lucrative terms, and in fact she was only being debited in the accounts of the Reparation Committee for coal at a price of 8/4 per ton. Notwithstanding the great size and extravagant cost of her Army of Occupation, the amount received by her in respect of German coal was more than sufficient to pay for the cost of the Army of Occupation.

If Germany defaulted on the instalments, the question arose whether she should be granted a moratorium. Undoubtedly her inability to pay was due to a very large extent to her own action. As a result of the generous subsidies given by the German Government, the State Budget showed a deficit, while the German manufacturers were in receipt of enhanced profits, some of which they were converting into foreign credits. Herr Rathenau [German reconstruction minister] was of the opinion that these credits were not more than enough to finance German industry, but while doubts might be felt on this point, it was quite clear that it would be most difficult for the German Government to lay their hands upon the actual money. The real fact was that the German Government was a very weak Government, in fear of Bolshevism on the one hand, and a revival of Prussianism on the other. Any moratorium granted to Germany should be upon conditions, such as the cessation of all subsidies, the balancing of the State Budget, the stoppage of note printing, the calculation in gold of customs duties, the reconstitution on more independent lines of the Reichsbank, and the raising of the internal price of coal in Germany.

The experts were unanimously of opinion that if the Allies were to insist on Germany making considerably heavier payments than she could at present afford to make, she would before the winter collapse into a hopeless state of chaos. M. Loucheur had admitted that France did not desire the collapse of Germany. When asked whether in the event of default the French Government would occupy the Ruhr he had, speaking for himself, deprecated such occupation, but this might not, of course, be the view of the French Government, which might be forced by French public opinion into violent action.

It was quite clear that M. Briand would suggest that Great Britain should lend Germany the money to enable her to satisfy the coming instalments. This, in effect, would be equivalent to Great Britain paying Germany's reparation, which she was not in a position to do, but even if she could find the money on this occasion, she would undoubtedly be pressed to take the same course in the case of future instalments. M. Briand would also no doubt press Great Britain to give up some part of the 38 million pounds which she had received under the August Agreement. The money represented a contribution towards the cost of the British Army of Occupation, and it would be most objectionable to hand any part of it over to France, as by so doing undoubtedly a deficit would be created in next year's Budget. It would be possible to say to France that if she would agree to the moratorium, Great Britain would be prepared to waive her claim to any part of the excess values under the Rathenau-Loucheur Agreement.

Some discussion then took place as to the possibility of marketing a portion of the 'A' Bonds, it being represented that even if these Bonds were sold at a very substantial discount, they would still fetch cash which would be very acceptable to the French Government. On the other hand it was pointed out that these Bonds might be of great value in the future, and that it would be mistaken policy to part with them for a more or less nominal figure at the present moment.

The suggestion was then made that the difficulties of the French Government were largely attributable to the fact that France had not adopted a proper financial policy. She was still maintaining a very expensive army, fleet, and air service, and was engaging in costly adventures in the Near East. So long as she refused to economize, it would be mistaken policy for Great Britain to deal tenderly with her on the reparation question.

Attention was also drawn to the instability of M. Briand's position, and it was pointed out that if he returned from England empty handed, he would probably fall; particularly in view of the strong opposition which had been raised to his Angora policy. The view was expressed that if M. Poincaré were to return to power, it might be possible to come to some more satisfactory settlement with him than with M. Briand.

A discussion next took place on the question of Anglo-American indebtedness and the view was expressed that the moment was not yet ripe for making any definite proposals on the subject to the American Government. It was pointed out that if Great Britain once started paying interest on the debt she would have to continue to pay, and that the effect of such payment would be to enable the American Government to reduce taxation and so place the American manufacturer in a favourable position as regards his British competitor. It was pointed out that Great Britain was at present materially assisting the American Government at the Washington Conference and by the Irish settlement and that it would be a mistaken policy to initiate any payment of interest except under the greatest pressure.

A suggestion was made that France might be willing to disarm if she could be given a defensive alliance with Great Britain, but it was pointed out that the French Government were opposed to such an alliance, and it was suggested that if M. Briand threatened to occupy the Ruhr if Germany defaulted, that it might be sufficient to threaten her with isolation and the termination of the Entente.

M. Briand might ask that the difficulty should be considered at a Meeting of the Supreme Council, but it was pointed out that France would be in a minority on the Council in wishing to occupy the Ruhr.

The suggestion was then made that in order to help France, an effort should be made to persuade Belgium to postpone her priority in favour of France, provided Great Britain made some similar contribution; but it was pointed out that the present attitude of the Belgian Government on the subject was very uncompromising. It was then urged that a National Economic Conference should be summoned forthwith to consider the whole European situation, and that this suggestion would give M. Briand the time which he much needed to make his arrangements.

In connection with this last suggestion, reference was made to the enormous importance to Great Britain of the economic reconstruction of Europe and especially of Eastern Europe. It was clear that the rehabilitation of Russia could only be properly effected by Germany, and proposals had been made that the Allies should facilitate the task of Germany in this respect and that a substantial proportion of the German profits derived from a revived Russia should be earmarked for reparation purposes. Herr Stinnes [German industrialist] and Herr Rathenau were strongly in favour of a scheme on these lines, and it was proposed that the British Ministers should discuss the whole situation with M. Briand and M. Loucheur. It was, however, pointed out that before any scheme of this character could be brought into operation, the consent and cooperation of the Soviet Government would be necessary and it would clearly involve some foreign control of the Russian Railways and Customs and the making of definite guarantees in respect of the Russian debt.

The Cabinet agreed:

(i)   That in the conversations with M. Briand and M. Loucheur the Prime Minister should be perfectly free to examine all aspects of proposals for dealing with the problem of German reparations and *inter alia* a scheme for the formation of a syndicate of the Western Powers (and possibly the United States) for the economic reconstruction of Russia, subject to possible conditions, e.g. recognition of Russian debts, the control of Russian Railways and Customs and diplomatic recognition of the Soviet Government.

(ii) That before diplomatic recognition of the Soviet Government was agreed to, the Cabinet should be consulted and that in the meantime Ministers were in no way committed.

The Secretary of State for the Colonies wished his view recorded, that while he regarded a tripartite trade agreement as premature at present, he had no objection to it in principle. He dissented, however, from any decision being taken at this stage, and, in the absence of several colleagues, to accord diplomatic recognition to the Soviet Government.

The Secretary of State for India also wished it to be recorded that in his view any scheme concerning Russia must depend on the cessation of the organized activities conducted under the auspices of the Russian Government against the British Empire — activities against which he had already protested.

Note: The Secretary of State for Foreign Affairs, who had left the room before the latter part of the above discussion had taken place and who had received no intimation that the question would be raised, asks to have his view recorded that the Foreign Office should be consulted before a decision on any of the above subjects is taken and more especially to reserve his opinion as to diplomatic recognition of the Soviet Government — a matter vitally affecting the foreign policy of the Empire and our relations with our Allies.

Cited in: C.J. Lowe and M.L. Dockrill.
The Mirage of Power, 3, *The Documents*
(London. 1972). pp. 733 – 8

14 Cecil's proposals for a Draft Treaty of Mutual Guarantee, with comments by the British Foreign Office, 1922

Lord Robert Cecil was Britain's representative at the League of Nations.

1 The High Contracting Powers hereby agree that if any one of them is attacked, all the others will forthwith take such action as may

have been agreed upon under Article 4 of this Treaty, or if there is no agreement, as may be most effective for the defence of the Party attacked, provided that this obligation shall not come into force unless the naval, military and air forces of the party attacked shall have been reduced in accordance with the terms of the Treaty.

2 In consideration of the undertaking contained in the immediately preceding Article, each of the High Contracting Powers shall forthwith reduce its naval, military and air forces in the manner and to the extent set out for each High Contracting Power in the annex.

3 It shall be the duty of the Permanent Armaments Commission to take into consideration any circumstances in the International situation, which may seem to it likely to disturb the peace of the world, and to advise the council of the League as to what steps, if any, should be taken to deal with such circumstance in accordance with the general purpose and objects of this Treaty.

4 In the event of any of the High Contracting Powers regarding themselves as menaced by the preparations or action of any other state whether party to this Treaty or not, it may so inform the Secretary General of the League of Nations who shall forthwith summon a meeting of the Council of the League, and if the Council by not less than a three-quarters majority shall be of the opinion that there is reasonable ground for thinking that the said preparations or action do constitute a menace as alleged they shall make such representations to the Governments creating the menace, in respect of such preparations or action as they may think right, and shall direct the Permanent Military Commission of the League or a Committee thereof to submit plans for assistance to be given by the High Contracting Powers to the party menaced. Such plans if approved by a three-quarters majority of the Council shall forthwith become binding on the High Contracting Parties. Providing that neither under this nor any other article of this Treaty shall any of the High Contracting Parties not being a European state be bound to furnish any naval, military or air force in Europe, or not being an American state in America, or not being an Asiatic state in Asia, or not being an African state in Africa.

5 Each of the High Contracting Parties agrees to receive such naval, military and air representatives of the League of Nations as the Council may desire to appoint and undertakes to give to these representatives such facilities and information regarding armaments as the Council may from time to time require. If it shall at any time appear to a majority of the Council that the naval, military or air forces or preparations of any of the High Contracting Parties are in

excess of those agreed to under the annex of this Treaty, the Council shall so inform the party in question and if a majority of the Council is not satisfied within six months that the naval, military and air forces of the said party have been brought into accordance with this Treaty, they shall suspend the said party from all its rights under this Treaty under such conditions as the Council shall think right and may take any other measures including, if thought right, a recommendation to the High Contracting Powers that penalties similar to those provided in Article 16 of the Covenant shall be put in force against the said party. . . .

Hurst [Legal Adviser to the Foreign Office, minuted on 31 July 1922]: The main difficulty about any scheme for disarmament or. . . .intended to facilitate disarmament, is political.

France at present obstructs the cause of disarmament. . . .If France is regarded as refusing to disarm because no other course is consistent with her safety, because at any moment she may be left single-handed to face a resurrected Germany, and single-handed because the failure of America to ratify the Help-to-France Treaty of 1919 has lost her the aid she was promised by Great Britain and the United States of America and because Article 10 of the Covenant of the League has turned out to be a broken reed, it is obvious that any scheme which helps the cause of disarmament by helping France to disarm deserves benevolent consideration at the hands of His Majesty's Government.

If on the other hand France is regarded as profiting by the disappearance of the German menace to aid her in securing the hegemony of Europe in the manner that Louis Quatorze and Napoleon strove for it, it is obvious that any scheme which may lull other Powers into a sense of false security by weakening their own forces and trusting to the protection of an ill-formed confederacy is very dangerous. History shows that self-seeking among confederates is too rife for confederacies to provide any protection against determined aggressors.

If the latter of these views prevails—viz, that there is no genuine desire in France for peace and disarmament—an attractive disarmament scheme is particularly dangerous in gatherings in the Assembly of the League at Geneva which are the happy hunting ground of the crank and the enthusiast. The scheme now put forward by Lord Robert Cecil should be obstructed and opposed unless it is considered that France will honestly accept and loyally abide by and fulfil any scheme of this sort to which she puts her name.

Cecil's scheme is dependent for its successful working on a feeling of confidence among all the States who join that every other State will play the game.

Do the circumstances of Europe today justify any such feelings? Could Poland for instance, feel confident that if she reduced her forces as desired and were attacked by Russia, France would send her battalions across Europe to help her?

A treaty of this sort can have no sanctions; if the obligations entered into were not carried out the State attacked would be left in the lurch. It is noteworthy that though this scheme provides that a State arming in excess of the amount allowed may be subjected to an economic blockade, no attempt is made to provide a similar penalty in the event of a State which fails to move to support another who is attacked.

There must be effective machinery to ensure that States will move in each other's support when a 'casus foederis' arises and when one of their number is attacked. Without it that sense of security is not going to be engendered which alone can render disarmament genuine and safe.

At the same time the scheme is not one lightly to be set aside; if the rest of the League is content to accept it, it would ill become an island power which is least exposed to the risks which beset the powers on the continent of Europe and least dependent on external assistance to frustrate its adoption. If France is regarded as genuinely anxious for peace in Europe the scheme merits at the least sympathetic consideration at Geneva. If it is thought to merit more there are some details in the scheme which require further consideration.

Villiers [minuted, on 3 August 1922]: . . .I do not believe that at the present moment of chaos and unrest in Europe, public opinion here will agree to any far-reaching measure of disarmament, still less to binding ourselves to come to the rescue with such armed forces as we have of, say, Hungary threatened by Czechoslovakia. That some scheme such as adumbrated by Lord Robert Cecil will eventually be adopted can hardly be doubted by anyone who believes in human progress. But the time has not come yet—it may come in our grand-children's days, but not in ours.

At Geneva our attitude should be one of mild approval and benevolence, coupled with a determination to shelve any such proposals *sine die*.

Cited in: Ruth B. Henig, *The League of Nations* (Edinburgh, 1973), pp. 48 – 50

15 Seeckt calls for the partition of Poland between Germany and the Soviet Union, 11 September 1922

General von Seeckt was head of the Army Command.

Poland's existence is intolerable, incompatible with the survival of Germany. It must disappear, and it will disappear through its own internal weakness and through Russia — with our assistance. For Russia Poland is even more intolerable than for us; no Russia can allow Poland to exist. With Poland falls one of the strongest pillars of the Treaty of Versailles, the preponderance of France. . . .Poland can never offer any advantages to Germany, either economically, because it is incapable of any development, or politically, because it is France's vassal. The re-establishment of the broad common frontier between Russia and Germany is the precondition for the regaining of strength of both countries. 'Russia and Germany with the frontiers of 1914!' should be the basis of reaching an understanding between the two. . . .

We aim at two things: first, a strengthening of Russia in the economic and political, thus also in the military field, and so indirectly a strengthening of ourselves, by strengthening a possible ally of the future; we further desire, at first cautiously and experimentally, a direct strengthening of ourselves, by helping to create in Russia an armaments industry which in case of need will serve us. . . .

In all these enterprises, which to a large extent are only beginning, the participation and even the official knowledge of the German government must be entirely excluded. The details of the negotiations must remain in the hands of the military authorities. . . .

> F.L. Carsten, *The Reichswehr and Politics*, 1918 – 1933 (London, 1966) pp. 140 – 1

16 Baldwin and Poincaré on Anglo-French differences, 19 September 1923

. . . I [Baldwin, British prime minister] said that it was perhaps better that I should explain to him at the outset certain conditions which might fail to come to his knowledge from any other quarter, and I dwelt upon the two reasons which in my view had been the cause of difficulties between the two countries, namely, the unhappy breakdown of the agreement come to by President Wilson on the Tripartite Alliance and the feeling in England that France had lost confidence in the British Government. I asked him point blank therefore whether or not he felt disposed to trust me implicitly as France had trusted England at the time of Sir Edward Grey [foreign secretary, 1905 – 16] as it would be valueless for me to continue were he not prepared to believe me. . . .

I dealt with the temperamental difference between the two nations showing how this had been greatly discounted before the war by the common fear inspired by Germany's attitude; how that fear had been largely removed together with the natural necessity of self-preservation; and how English people were puzzled by the impression that France apparently no longer wanted England to be with her. . . .

M. Poincaré [French prime minister] replied at some length and in terms no less sincere, for all of which I thanked him and then passed to *The present state of public feeling in England*, which counted for a great deal. Despite a commonly expressed view I assured him that it was not possible to manufacture English opinion by means of newspapers, as was said to be the case to a great extent in France. . . .

M. Poincaré, I said, must at all costs be apprised of the situation in England. English temperament was peculiar in certain respects and was doubtless difficult to French understanding; but the average Englishman pre-eminently disliked the military occupation of a civilian district; it antagonized and roused him. This might appear difficult to understand but was nonetheless a fact which had to be reckoned with, and no British Government would be able to cooperate fully in order to make the Entente what it ought to be as long as the military character of the occupation of the Ruhr remained unchanged. I expressed the belief that no other Government in Great Britain could be found more willing or desirous to work together with France; and that after his (M. Poincaré's) disagreement with Mr Lloyd George and with Mr Bonar Law in January last the British public would feel that the responsibility lay not with ourselves but with the French Prime Minister if I too found it impossible to work with the French. This might not be fair but it would be so, and I reminded him that I was not expressing my own views but endeavouring to state the currents of English opinion which it was necessary to bear in mind. . . .

Practically the whole of England, I continued, desired a settlement at the expense of Germany. As to this principle there could be no doubt, but rightly or wrongly, there was considerable scepticism as to the wisdom of the methods employed. The present position indicated a prospect of some agreement with the Germans, and in this connection I recalled that only last Saturday (15 September) the Foreign Office in London were pressing Germany, and not for the first time, to abandon passive resistance and to try to come to terms. . . .

In concluding my remarks I touched upon the reported French impression that England favoured a quick settlement in order to advantage certain speculators in London. This, I said, was totally inaccurate. England wanted a settlement firstly because, rightly or wrongly, she attributed the greater part of her unemployment to the present disorganization in the trade of the world, and secondly because, rightly or wrongly again and seeking order and peace, she feared that until this great question was disposed of there would be the probability of disorder and fighting in a Europe which had already suffered far too much. . . .

M. Poincaré at the outset associated himself unreservedly with the views which I had enumerated and expressed his appreciation of the frankness which I had extended towards him. Although he made no pretence of understanding British public opinion he had thought that the two countries were not so greatly at variance as was commonly supposed, that there was in fact in England a certain following of his methods. The French Government he assured me was no more the master of the Press than were other Governments, but he believed that his Ruhr policy was approved by at least 99 per cent of the population of France and was therefore formulated entirely on public opinion. British public opinion would thus appear to be in error if it supposed that the French Government was not unanimously supported by its own public.

He emphatically agreed that the two countries must not be allowed to drift apart, and that the causes of misunderstanding must be examined and removed. M. Poincaré was disinclined to attribute the first cause of discord between France and Great Britain to Germany's default although a certain wave of rancour may have animated France, but on the other hand French opinion was perfectly convinced that the pact as drafted was valueless and that without a military occupation France would have found herself in a worse plight than before 1914. The real motive of France's action must be sought elsewhere and he laid weight upon the fact that every time the Allies had met since the Treaty of Versailles French claims had been jeopardized until she found her share of reparations dwindling away. When Germany asked for a moratorium France demanded guarantees but

Mr Lloyd George had objected, as had also Mr Bonar Law [British prime minister] and yet if the British Government had assented to this no military occupation need have followed, since a united action could have effected the desired result subsequently brought about by France and Belgium under a military occupation. Germany had in fact calculated upon a divergence of policy between the Allies and had organized passive resistance against France and Belgium as soon as they occupied an essentially industrial area and had thereby forced them to bring into play legitimate rights of defence. It was due to this fact, in his view, that all the trouble had arisen, not because of the actual occupation of the Ruhr but because of the resistance set up by Germany. Passive resistance, he said, had now reached its culminating point. Germany was weary of it. The Reich could not maintain the position or continue the cost. So much had M. Poincaré believed in the sudden collapse of this resistance that he declined Lord Curzon's [foreign secretary] offer of intervention at Berlin because Germany would then have capitulated on Great Britain's demand and not under French pressure, and this refusal he justified by citing M. Stresemann's [German Chancellor] subsequent efforts to negotiate, though adding that the French and Belgian Governments were committed to decline all advances pending the termination of passive resistance.

M. Stresemann, he said, sought to establish the failure of the occupation and to reap the harvest himself for bringing about its end which in any case was inevitable.

M. Poincaré then went on to say that in order to continue opportunities for the useful interchange of personal views it was essential that no alien factor should be allowed to intervene and, in this connection, he alluded to the danger of allowing question of Reparations to be discussed at the meetings of the League of Nations. France, he said, could not tolerate a discussion on this subject at Geneva for the present.

Dealing with the more pertinent points which I had raised, M. Poincaré explained that he had already replied to Lord Curzon in the Yellow Book as to his plans on the cessation of passive resistance; he would be quite prepared to allow a certain latitude subject to conditions, in order to allow Germany to stabilize her position. He referred to the danger of M. Stresemann's scheme of a loan on private property which seemed to him capable of providing funds, in certain circumstances, for the continuation of passive resistance. As to M. Stresemann's policy in general, M. Poincaré was entirely prepared to act in conjunction with Great Britain, but there could be no question of a practical solution before Germany had shown herself prepared to discourage passive resistance and to desist from subsidizing labour, for by this means she was dissipating her resources and violating the Treaty.

Finally, M. Poincaré again assured me of the value he attached to personal conversations in the first instance, as opposed to conferences, and asserted that the further one was driven to the necessity of imposing conditions upon the Germans before negotiating with them, the wider became the rift between oneself and one's Allies and friends. For this reason, and as soon as the cessation of passive resistance was assured, the French Government welcomed the prospect of consulting with its allies either through the channel of its ambassadors or by the means of more personal conversations, from which fact I concluded that for the present at any rate M. Poincaré had formulated no definite plan for the future.

After a further interchange of courtesies we agreed upon the Press communiqué which was immediately issued and we parted with renewed assurances of confidence and cordiality.

DBFP, XXI, No. 367.

17 Canadian views on the British Empire and British foreign policy, 1923

Second meeting of the Imperial Conference, 3 October 1923

Mr MacKenzie King [Canadian prime minister]: The British Empire, again, is not a single community, homogenous, concentrated, with uniform neighbours, problems, needs. It is a league of peoples plus an Empire; it covers all the Seven Seas; it includes communities of every conceivable stage of civilization, every variety of resources, every range of neighbours, every combination of problems and interests. The more advanced of these communities have developed rapidly in numbers and trade and international intercourse; they have developed relations with other countries varying with their situation; they have developed distinct problems in external as well as in home affairs, a distinct national consciousness, distinct Parliaments and Governments to control their affairs. Some problems are distinct and primarily concern only one or a group of these Empire States; some are of common interest or common menace, and concern the whole Empire and it alone, some are of still wider implications and concern all or a great region of the world, whether organized in permanent

Leagues of Nations or in temporary conferences, or not organized at all.

Given then these conditions — given wide scattered communities within the British Empire growing steadily in numbers, in intercourse with the world, and in the habit of self-government; given the growth of problems and difficulties especially with neighbouring countries; given the diversity of conditions and of interest and knowledge which makes these problems in many cases distinct in each country — it is inevitable that each of these communities should seek to control those foreign affairs which concern it primarily.

This is obviously true, and has long been true of the United Kingdom. Its foreign affairs have been of such overshadowing importance — it is on the verge of a crowded and troublesome and uneasy continent, it is the greatest trading nation in history, it has dependencies, protectorates, coaling-stations, in every quarter of the globe — that they have in the past been practically identical with the foreign affairs of the whole British Empire, and are still, and must long remain, immensely more important and complicated than the distinctive foreign affairs of any other part of the Empire.

It is increasingly true also of the Dominions. In this field Canada has naturally been most active, as the oldest federation and as the community which, next to the United Kingdom, is in most intimate and constant intercourse with powerful neighbours, pre-eminently with one great neighbour. It is unnecessary to review the process by which Canada has steadily widened the range of foreign affairs with which she deals through her own Parliament and Government; trade, tariffs, immigration, boundary disputes as to power, navigation or fisheries and other questions which half a century ago were considered beyond her jurisdiction, are now unquestionably matters for her own decision as my opening observations concretely indicated.

Clearly, then, as regards this wide and growing range of foreign affairs, the Dominions, or some of them, now possess control, and determine the policy to be followed. . . .

Need for Consultation on Fundamental Issues

Each part of the Empire, then, has its own sphere. But at certain points the arcs cut, the interests become common. There are issues which are of fundamental concern to all parts of the Empire; and with these all parts of the Empire must deal; the Governments of the Empire must confer; the Parliaments of the Empire, if need be, must decide.

It is true that there is no clear cut and enduring line of demarcation between these fields, between those foreign affairs which are of primary concern to one part of the Empire and those which are of joint concern. No foreign question affecting one part of the Empire is without its influence on other parts, however small and indirect that influence may be, but it is equally true that no domestic affair of one part of the Empire, no foreign problem of any foreign country, is without some bearing on the fortunes of the rest of the Empire and the world. It is a question of degree. Again, issues which were primarily of concern to one part may grow to vast proportions and afford a menace or an opportunity that has substantial concern for all parts; if so, it can then be dealt with by all concerned. In drawing the lines there will inevitably be difficulties, but goodwill and commonsense and experience will settle these as they have in the past.

Again, were it considered desirable to establish a unified foreign policy on all issues, it would not be practicable.

No scheme has been worked out, no scheme, I venture to say, can be worked out, by which each part of the Empire can be not only informed but consulted as to all the relations of every other part of the Empire with foreign countries, and a really joint policy worked out. The range is too vast, the situation too kaleidoscopic, the interests too diverse, the preoccupation of each Government with its own affairs or its own existence too absorbing, to make this possible. We must face facts. It is possible to consult on matters of overwhelming and enduring common interest; it is not possible to consult on the great range of matters of individual and shifting concern.

A further questionable feature of the Empire one-foreign-policy theory is that it ignores the necessity for associating the Parliament and peoples in the decision of foreign policy. Granted that a measure of secrecy is essential in the course of negotiations, granted that the conduct of affairs must rest largely with an experienced and specialized executive department, still it is true that it is not desirable for any Dominion or for the Empire that vital issues of foreign policy should be determined decisively in a small executive or Conference group. The problem of foreign policy is not settled when provision is made for bringing Prime Ministers together. Each Prime Minister must on important issues secure the backing of his Parliament and his people. . . .

Near Eastern Crisis, September, 1922

In referring to the Lausanne Conference, perhaps I should say just a word or two about the circumstances surrounding the manner in which we were asked if we would like to associate ourselves with the British Government in its policy towards the Near East, and, in particular, if we would participate by sending a contingent. I mention this because I think it shows the great necessity for our working out, with a little more care and caution than has thus far been exercised, the means by which communications are to pass between the different Governments concerned. The first intimation that I had that Canada was being asked to participate in a situation as serious as that in the Near East was when a press reporter came and showed me a despatch which he alleged had been given out by the British Government and asked what Canada was going to do in this matter. I did not wish to embarrass the situation by saying I had not received any communication from the British Government whatever on the situation in the Near East, and I fell back on a phrase I had frequently used in a previous political campaign, that it was not a one-man Government, that when I had had a chance of conferring with my colleagues we would decide what action we would take. I then communicated with Ottawa — I was away at the time in my own constituency — to find out if any communication had been received from the British Government, and none had been received at the time I communicated. This was on Saturday. On Sunday morning I came down immediately to Ottawa; I went to my office and ascertained that a communication had been received at noon on the previous day by the Governor-General's Secretary, the communications coming, of course, in that way. It had to be deciphered, and it came to my office during the latter part of Saturday afternoon. But in the meantime the entire press of the country, the Saturday afternoon press, had the alarmist appeal that there was likely to be war in the Near East and that New Zealand had already undertaken to send a contingent. When I called my colleagues together on the following Monday we all felt that until we had more in the way of information it would not be wise to say to what extent we were prepared to associate ourselves with the policy of the British Government. As to participation in any war by the sending of troops, as a Government we felt that Parliament must decide on that point, and I communicated accordingly. Lord Curzon spoke on Friday of the despatches and telegrams which we had been receiving from the Foreign Office. I am inclined to think that there is a doubtful value to be attached to them. They have been helpful in some particulars, but, if I may cite this case, a reference to the despatches will indicate that a couple of weeks prior to the telegram being sent, to which I have just referred, one despatch indicated that the crisis in the Near East seemed to have passed, that there was not much danger of any trouble arising of a serious character. That was the last despatch I had to place before the Cabinet before the telegram referring to possible participation in a war. These despatches come in in a bundle a week or two after the events to which they refer, and actually the information we had at that time on the Near East situation would seem to indicate that there was no crisis.

Lord Curzon: You get telegrams.

Mr Mackenzie King: Since then, Lord Curzon, we have been receiving telegrams in regard to the Lausanne Conference and some other questions. At that time we did not; at that time we were not receiving daily telegrams. We were receiving the printed despatches which came by mail and which reached us a couple of weeks afterwards, sometimes even later.

Lord Curzon: You know, of course, Mr Mackenzie King, that the particular manifesto to which you are referring was not a normal occurrence, and that it was issued without the knowledge or approval of the Cabinet.

Mr Mackenzie King: So I understand. I have no desire to do other than just present to the Conference some of the embarrassments we had at the moment, and I raise the point more with a view of indicating what we may wish to consider later on very carefully, namely, the best means to be adopted as between Governments concerned of being informed on questions which are likely to be of real concern to us all.

I want, however, at this moment to say a word about the great care that should be exercised in respect to issuing any statements from the British Government or departments of Government to the peoples of the Dominions over the heads, so to speak, of the Government concerned. I think whatever is to be done with regard to our affairs must be done through our own Government. It will certainly create all kinds of difficulties were a practice to be adopted of having memoranda or appeals sent out from any department of the British Government to the Dominions which had not received in the first instance the authorization of the Government of the Dominion concerned.

Now just a word in conclusion about the general attitude towards Europe.

The Dominions are undoubtedly concerned in the present situation. Their material interests, their humanitarian interests, their interest in the preservation of peace and of fair and honest dealing among nations, make it impossible to say we are not concerned. In fact, no part of the world, whether within or without the Empire, can be without concern, though there may be, and are, wide differences in degree.

The practical question, however, is whether any effective remedy for the situation is within our reach, and whether our peoples are agreed upon the value and necessity of this remedy. Because our interests are prejudiced by the situation it does not follow that it can be set right at once, or that the setting right is to come from outside. This is particularly true in view of the fact that much of the disturbance is internal rather than international, civil war, class war, the war of social creeds. The question for consideration is the practibility of any specific proposal, the balance of losses and gains, interpreting both, of course, in no narrowly materialistic sense.

As to the diagnosis of Europe's trouble, the British Government, supported by the dominant public opinion of the country, appears, while blaming Germany for much stupidity and lack of good faith, to place the main responsibility for the present unsettlement upon the chauvinistic ambitions and unscrupuluous intrigues of France. I cannot say there is any clear Canadian opinion on that point. A large portion of what may be called, in the general sense, liberal opinion is inclined to agree, and believes that the policy France has pursued is calculated to ensure neither her own security nor Europe's welfare. But there is also, so far as the question has been considered at all, a strong sympathy for France. . . .

> *Documents on Canadian External Relations*, 3, 1919−1925, ed. Lovell C. Clark (Ottawa, 1970), no. 234.

18 Britain considers financial pressure on France, 14 November 1923

Foreign Office to Treasury

Foreign Office, 14 November 1923

Sir,
The Lords Commissioners of the Treasury are aware, from the telegrams which will have reached them from this Department, of the course of the abortive negotiations for the summoning of a conference,

at which the United States Government would be represented, to deal with the question of reparations and German capacity to pay. A paraphrase of the latest telegram on the subject which has been received from His Majesty's Ambassador at Rome is transmitted herewith.

2 It will be seen that Signor Mussolini expresses his readiness to follow his Majesty's Government in facing France on this question of reparations, provided His Majesty's Government give a clear lead and enter into a clear understanding with him. The implication so expressed is one which deserves careful consideration. Before contemplating any line of policy which may bring His Majesty's Government face to face with decided French opposition on an important issue, it behoves His Majesty's Government to examine the question of the form of pressure which it might be possible to bring to bear upon the French Government to induce them to adopt an attitude more in harmony with the interests and sentiments of Great Britain. From this point of view it may be opportune to consider, in all its bearings, the problem raised by French indebtedness to this country, and to weigh the advantages and disadvantages of using the financial lever in dealings with the French Government.

3 The Secretary of State would accordingly be glad if he could be furnished, at any early date, with the considered opinion of the Treasury as regards the position of His Majesty's Government in respect of their holding of French Treasury bills and the possibility of exerting pressure upon the French Government through the medium of these bills, in respect of which the French Government periodically apply for renewal.

4 It might be well, in the same connection, to examine the credits or other financial assistance on which, in the normal course of business, French private firms or public or semi-public bodies are able to rely in the London market.

5 The Lords Commissioners will doubtless also bear in mind the reports which have reached His Majesty's Government as to the very considerable advances which the French Government are alleged to be making to certain of the Central European and Balkan States. . . .

6 A fuller report on this aspect of the question has been called for from His Majesty's Ambassador in Paris.

I am, & c.

W. Selby

Foreign Office Papers (Public Record Office, London), FO 371/8661 XK 6583

II
Détente, 1924 – 8

1924 was a turning point in the first postwar decade. The restoration of economic and financial order beginning with the Dawes Plan reparations settlement generated political confidence. The Dawes Plan signalled a substantial revision of Versailles since France lost the right to impose sanctions in the event of Germany defaulting on reparations and payments were sharply reduced. Before accepting the Plan the French prime minister, Edouard Herriot, had talks with the British prime minister, Ramsay MacDonald, in June 1924. Herriot asked for a British guarantee for France. Skilfully MacDonald fobbed him off with vague talk of 'constant collaboration' and insisted on settling reparations first (**19**).

The Dawes Plan was then endorsed at the London Reparations Conference in July-August 1924 and French troops were withdrawn from the Ruhr in the following year. Britain in fact abandoned any idea of an Anglo-French military alliance. Austen Chamberlain, foreign secretary in the Baldwin government of 1924 – 29, argued that Britain was an 'honest broker' working for a Europe in which Germany 'would take her place as an equal' (**21**).

The Locarno treaties of October 1925 were acclaimed as the start of real peace. In reality French politicians had few illusions about the value of Locarno (**24**). Marshal Foch warned his government against a premature evacuation of the Rhineland (**26**). The lunch between the French and German foreign ministers, Aristide Briand and Gustav Stresemann, at Thoiry, a small French village near Geneva, on 17 September 1926 aroused hopes of Franco-German reconciliation (**27**). There is no accurate record of their conversation. Stresemann's account which is published here differs in important respects from that of Briand's interpreter. Although both versions may be inaccurate, the gist of the discussion is clear and undisputed. A comprehensive Franco-German settlement was broached. Stresemann asked, *inter alia*, for the evacuation of the Rhineland and the return of the Saar. In exchange he offered the commercialization of part of the German reparations bonds under the Dawes Plan so that France would immediately receive substantial payments.

Nothing came of Thoiry. The collapse of the French franc in the summer of 1926 had encouraged Stresemann to think that he could buy an important revision of the peace treaty but the French government weathered the storm and stabilized the franc. French suspicions of Germany were justified. Germany was evading the Versailles disarmament provisions (20). Weimar's political and military leadership was in agreement on foreign policy goals: a favourable reparations settlement, recovery of Danzig, abolition of the Polish Corridor, regaining of Polish Upper Silesia, *Anschluss* with Austria, evacuation of the Rhineland and its remilitarization, return of the Saar (22, 25). Hitler's foreign policy programme was largely in the mainstream of German revisionism (23). Where he differed however from Weimar leaders was in his emphasis on the necessity for the conquest of territory in the east. Germany's 1914 frontiers were not sufficient. By contrast German military leaders wanted cooperation with the Soviet Union, not war.

Locarno did not lead to a real détente. Attempts to strengthen the League came to nought. The Draft Treaty of Mutual Assistance was rejected by Britain in 1924. A second attempt — the Geneva Protocol for the Pacific Settlement of International Disputes — was rejected by Britain and the United States in 1925. Even the League's work for financial reconstruction in Europe served to feed Anglo-French rivalry (29). The Kellogg-Briand Pact of August 1928 outlawed war but did not contain any enforcement provisions. Nine years after the armistice disarmament was beset with political and technical difficulties (28). The failure of the Geneva disarmament conference of 1927 showed that the powers were unable to agree on a limited measure of naval disarmament. A short-lived bilateral Anglo-French accord on naval disarmament — the Anglo-French Compromise of 1928 — alienated the United States. By November 1928 the British Foreign Office had reached the conclusion that a conciliatory approach to the United States was a *conditio sine qua non* for the settlement of all outstanding issues — disarmament, reparations, inter-allied debts, European security (30).

19   MacDonald and Herriot conclude a 'moral pact of continuous cooperation', 21 – 22 June, 1924

Mr MacDonald: [British prime minister]. . . .Before undertaking an engagement I must assure myself of the support of all the Dominions. I am anxious to warn you loyally and to be frank with you. There may be a difficulty. Another difficulty is that, just as M. Herriot may say that M. Poincaré is not dead, I for my part have to count with Mr Lloyd George. . . .As for the treaty of mutual guarantee, I must not hide from you that all my experts of the navy, army, air force and Foreign Office are opposed to it. . . .I can assure you besides, confidentially, that Sweden, Denmark and Holland are equally hostile to it. . . .To save the situation I suggest that France, Belgium and Great Britain first of all proceed to an examination of the situation together; if we begin by the treaty of mutual guarantee, that will bind our hands and prejudice the question when the United States calls a disarmament question. For my part I see a great advantage in broadening the question. . . .

M. Herriot: [French prime minister] I understand the situation in which Mr MacDonald finds himself, but since we are speaking as good friends, I must explain to him the situation of France. . . .My country has a dagger pointed at its breast, within an inch of its heart. Common efforts, sacrifices, deaths in the war, all that will have been useless if Germany can once more have recourse to violence. . . .France cannot count only on an international conference, and the United States are a long way off. . . .Can we not try to find a formula of guarantee against a danger of such a sort that it would render the Dawes Report useless. I speak to you here from the bottom of my heart, and I assure you that I cannot give up the security of France, who could not face a new war.

Mr MacDonald: . . .I shall do all that lies in my power to avoid a new war, for I am certain that in that case it would not be only France but all European civilization which would be crushed. . . .I do not wish to take an easy way which offers itself to me to join in an offer to France of a military guarantee of security. I should only be deceiving you; none of the Dominions would support me, a reactionary Government would replace mine, and finally France would only have false security. . . .

M. Herriot: . . .I ask permission to continue the conversation on this point, because it is the subject which touches my heart most, and which imposes upon me the greatest of duties.

Mr MacDonald: This is what I think: we are going today to settle the questions raised by the Dawes Report; but in doing so we are only taking the first step in the conclusion of a long series of agreements. When we have got the Dawes Report out of the way, I am quite ready to go to Paris to pay you a visit and spend a couple of days talking to you on the question of debts and security and so on. . . . The general perspective which opens before my eyes is that of a new method of settling questions between allies; that of a friendship and a constant collaboration. . . . We must assure our well-being, but we will work also to resolve the great moral problems of the peace of the world. Let us therefore settle first the question of the Dawes Report; then we will go on to that of inter-Allied debts, then to the problem of security, and we will try to remove from Europe the risks of war which threaten it. . . .

M. Herriot: I thank Mr MacDonald warmly for what he has just said. In effect, the most important result of our interview is a sort of moral pact of continuous cooperation between us for the good of our two nations and in the general interests of the whole world. I will do all that is possible and even the impossible to respond to his appeal. . . .

> Cited in: David Marquand, *Ramsay MacDonald* (London, 1977), pp. 339 – 40

20 Germany evades the disarmament clauses of the Treaty of Versailles, 1925

Letter from General J.H. Morgan, British military representative on the Inter-Allied Council, published in the weekly journal *Die Menschheit*, 20 February, 1925.

. . . why does the Reichswehrministerium persistently refuse to disclose its recruiting returns?. . . . These alone can establish how many men are being called up for training by the Reichsheer [Regular Army], and for five years they have been constantly refused. Why? The reason given is that they are a matter of 'inner service' which does not concern us. But is it no concern of ours to know how many men are being trained in the use of arms? And if there is nothing to conceal, why conceal it?

In the second place, why do the Reichswehrministerium refuse to show us those registers of armament production which were snatched from under our very noses at Spandau? They alone can serve to establish what your gun establishment was in 1919 and what it is now.

Thirdly, why does the Reichswehrministerium insist on retaining control of the vast network of military establishments, artillery depots, munition depots, supply depots, remount depots, which supplied the needs of the old army and are altogether superfluous for the needs, the legitimate needs, of the new? Your Government does not expropriate these, it does not alienate them, it does not sell them, it does not convert them — it either leaves them idle or lets them to a tenant at will. They are available for the mobilization of a vast army at almost any moment. A trifling sum of 200,000 gold marks is all that appears in the *Reichshaushaltsplan* Budget for 1924 as the proceeds of a sale of some two or three of them. What is being done with all the rest?

Fourthly, why is the Reichswehrministerium paying no less than twenty-two officers in the Ministry alone, without taking account of the generals in the Wehrkreis commands, as lieutenant-generals and major-generals? Why are all the captains in the Reichsheer with over two years' service drawing the pay of majors, and the oberleutnants drawing the pay of captains? Why is your Government maintaining an establishment of *Feldwebels* and *Unteroffiziers* [Sergeants major and sergeants or corporals] sufficient for an army thrice, and more than thrice, the Treaty strength? To a soldier there is only one explanation of these things and that is that this army is, and is destined to be, a cadre for expansion.

What of your 'Security Police'?. . .they are, by one statute after another, made interchangeable with the Reichsheer in pay, promotion, pensions, grades, and a dozen other things, so that the two forces match one another even as the wards of a lock match the key which fits it. Behind every Reichsheer soldier there stands, like a silhouette, a 'police official'.

As to your army expenditure — and I have studied your Budget — I will only say this: if your army is really as small as your Government say it is, then your Government is the most extravagant Government in the world; and if your Government is not extravagant, then your army is far larger than it ought to be. Your Reichsheer, in theory small in stature, projects in reality a gigantic shadow across the map of Germany, and the shadow is the greater reality of the two. That shadow is the old army. Everything that an ingenious brain could devise and a subtle intellect invent, down even to giving the companies of infantry of the new army the numbers and badges of the regiments of the old, has been done to ensure that, at a touch of a button, the new army shall expand to the full stature of its predecessor. The proofs in my possession are overwhelming.

Your Government tells us repeatedly that our work is done and that there is nothing left for us to find out. They tell us that the Treaty of Versailles had been loyally executed. How then do they explain the astounding paradox that every time a store of hidden arms in a factory is revealed to the Commission by a pacifist workman, the workman, if discovered, is immediately arrested and sentenced to a long term of penal servitude?. . . .If. . . .the military clauses of the Treaty 'are part of the law of Germany', these unfortunate workmen were merely assisting in the execution of the law. If these concealments of arms are not approved by the German Government, why are the workmen who disclose them ruthlessly punished and the factory owners who conceal them allowed to go free?

> Brigadier-General J.H. Morgan, *Assize of Arms*, 2 vols. (London, 1945) pp. 268–70

21 Britain as honest broker

Sir Austen Chamberlain, foreign secretary, to Lord D'Abernon, British ambassador in Berlin, 19 March 1925

Foreign Office, 19 March, 1925

My Lord,
The German Ambassador called upon me this afternoon immediately after M.de Fleuriau,

He explained that he had sought the interview in order to ascertain what progress was being made. Germany had made her proposals for security and arbitration in the hope thereby she might facilitate the solution of the more immediately urgent questions, which, for her, were disarmament and the evacuation of Cologne, but these questions seemed to make no progress. Germany was not told wherein her defaults existed or what it remained for her to do. She thought that she was entitled to the publication of the report of the Military Control Commission and to be given the opportunity to make good any defaults, and thus to secure evacuation; but it seemed to his Excellency that the whole movement had become stagnant.

I observed that to me, on the other hand, it seemed that very remarkable progress had been made since the German proposals were first put forward. I would even venture to say that part of the progress was due to the emphasis which I had laid, in my speech in the House of Commons on the eve of my departure for Geneva, on the high importance attached by His Majesty's Government to the new step taken by Germany. It had, in my opinion, opened up new and better possibilities, and, provided that there were patience and goodwill, I was not unhopeful of their resulting in a real success; but if this result was to be achieved, the German Government must have confidence in the good faith of the British Government and in their desire to make these new proposals succeed, and they must have patience in dealing with immediate difficulties so that the larger hopes which seemed to be within our reach might not be shipwrecked on some smaller point before we could bring them into port.

Round and about the two positions thus stated the conversation continued for a considerable time. I find that Herr Sthamer habitually comes to me with a particular idea, and that whatever may be the turn of our conversation, he reverts to this idea again and again. So it was on this occasion, and I could only insist again and again on the need of patience and goodwill lest their contraries should wreck a great scheme of durable peace and goodwill upon temporary and comparatively minor difficulties. Her Sthamer expressed his confidence in the good faith of the British Government, but accompanied it with profound suspicions of the French. I observed that I, who stood a little further away from the danger point than either of them, could perhaps appreciate the genuineness of the fears and suspicions of each, even though I did not fully share them, and that my part was to be a moderator and a reconciler. I did not underrate the difficulties of such a role. Any chance of success might easily be destroyed by unwisdom either in Paris or Berlin, but I would beg Herr Sthamer to believe that I was working heart and soul to found upon the German proposals a restoration of the concert of the Great Powers in Europe and a lasting peace for our countries. I believed that this might be achieved if there were sufficient wisdom in our respective Governments.

Her Sthamer enquired whether he might consider that I interpreted my role as that of 'the honest broker', and I accepted the description, though I said I preferred my own word 'moderator', and that I was making it my business, with perfect loyalty to my allies, as I wished him clearly to understand, to work for an arrangement which would close the war chapter and start Europe afresh as a society in which Germany would take her place as an equal with the other great nations. Herr Sthamer said that he should report what I had said to his Government, that he appreciated my attitude and had perfect confidence in me, but, as so often throughout the interview, he reverted to the point which he had first mentioned, and his parting words were of fear lest German public opinion, failing to obtain any satisfaction in regard to Cologne and disarmament, might force the German Government to withdraw its overtures and reject the policy of concession and goodwill.

Austen Chamberlain Papers (University of Birmingham) AC 52/156

22 Stresemann's foreign policy goals, 1925

Letter from Gustav Stresemann, German foreign minister, to the ex-Crown Prince, 7 September 1925

On the question of Germany's entry into the League I would make the following observations:

In my opinion there are three great tasks that confront German foreign policy in the more immediate future—

In the first place the solution of the Reparations question in a sense tolerable for Germany, and the assurance of peace, which is an essential premise for the recovery of our strength.

Secondly, the protection of Germans abroad, those 10 to 12 millions of our kindred who now live under a foreign yoke in foreign lands.

The third great task is the readjustment of our eastern frontiers; the recovery of Danzig, the Polish corridor, and a correction of the frontier in Upper Silesia.

In the background stands the union with German Austria, although I am quite clear that this not merely brings no advantages to Germany, but seriously complicates the problem of the German Reich.

If we want to secure these aims, we must concentrate on these tasks. Hence the Security Pact, which guarantees us peace and constitutes England, as well as Italy, if Mussolini agrees to collaborate, as guarantors of our western frontiers. The pact also rules out the possibility of any military conflict with France for the recovery of Alsace-Lorraine; this is a renunciation on the part of Germany, but, in so far, it possesses only a theoretic character, as there is no possibility of a war against France. . . .

The question of a choice between east and west does not arise as the result of our joining the League. Such a choice can only be made when backed by military force. That, alas we do not possess. We can neither become a continental spear-head for England as some believe, nor can we involve ourselves in an alliance with Russia. I would utter warning against any utopian ideas of coquetting with Bolshevism. When the Russians are in Berlin, the red flag will at once be flown from the castle, and in Russia, where they hope for a world revolution, there will be much joy at the Bolshevization of Europe as far as the Elbe; the rest of Germany will be thrown to the French to devour. That we are perfectly ready to come to an understanding with the Russian State, in whose evolutionary development I believe, on another basis, and my contention that we are not selling ourselves to the west by joining the League, is a matter on which I would gladly enlarge to Your Royal Highness in a personal talk. The great movement now stirring all the primitive people against the colonial domination of the great nations, will in no way be influenced to the disadvantage of these peoples by our joining the League. The most important thing for the first task of German policy mentioned above is, the liberation of German soil from any occupying force. We must get the stranglehold off our neck. On that account, German policy, as Metternich said of Austria, no doubt after 1809, will be one of finesse and the avoidance of all great decisions.

I beg Y.R.H. to allow me to confine myself to these brief indications, and I would also ask you kindly to view this letter in the light of the fact that I am compelled to use the greatest reserve in everything I say. If Y.R.H. could give me the opportunity for a quiet talk about these matters that will soon come up urgently for decision, I am gladly available at any time.

> *Gustav Stresemann, His Diaries, Letters and Papers*, edited and translated by Eric Sutton, II (London (Macmillan) 1937), pp. 503 – 5

23 Hitler, Mein Kampf, 1925

. . .German-Austria must return to the great German mother country, and not because of any economic considerations. No, and again no: even if such a union were unimportant from an economic point of view; yes, even if it were harmful, it must nevertheless take place. One blood demands one Reich. Never will the German nation possess the moral right to engage in colonial politics until, at least, it embraces its own sons within a single state. Only when the Reich borders include the very last German, but can no longer guarantee his daily bread, will the moral right to acquire foreign soil arise from the distress of our own people. Their plough will become our sword, and from the tears of war the daily bread of future generations will grow. . . .

. . .As opposed to this, we National Socialists must hold unflinchingly to our aim in foreign policy, namely, *to secure for the German people the land and soil to which they are entitled on this earth.* And this action is the only one which, before God and our German posterity, would make any sacrifice of blood seem justified: before God, since we have been put on this earth with the mission of eternal struggle for our daily bread, beings who receive nothing as a gift, and who owe their position as lords of the earth only to the genius and the courage with which they can conquer and defend it; and before our German posterity in so far as we have shed no citizen's blood out of which a thousand others are not bequeathed to posterity. The soil on which some day German generations of peasants can beget powerful sons will sanction the investment of the sons of today, and will some day acquit the responsible statesmen of blood-guilt and sacrifice of the people, even if they are persecuted by their contemporaries.

And I must sharply attack those folkish pen-pushers who claim to regard such an acquisition of soil as a 'breach of human rights' and attack it as such in their scribblings. One never knows who stands behind these fellows. But one thing is certain, that the confusion they can create is desirable and convenient to our national enemies. By such an attitude they help to weaken and destroy from within our people's will for the only correct way of defending their vital needs. . . .

The folkish movement must not be the champion of other peoples, but the vanguard fighter of its own. Otherwise it is superfluous and above all has no right to sulk about the past. For in that case it is behaving in dynastic considerations, and the future policy must not be directed by cosmopolitan folkish drivel. In particular, we are not constables guarding the well known 'poor little nations', but soldiers of our own nation.

But we National Socialists must go further. *The right to possess soil can become a duty if without extension of its soil a great nation seems doomed to destruction.* And most especially when not some little nigger nation or other is involved, but the Germanic mother of life, which has given the present-day world its cultural picture. *Germany will either be a world power or there will be no Germany.* And for world power she needs that magnitude which will give her the position she needs in the present period, and life to her citizens.

And so we National Socialists consciously draw a line beneath the foreign policy tendency of our pre-War period. We take up where we broke off six hundred years ago. We stop the endless German movement to the south and west, and turn our gaze towards the land in the east. At long last we break off the colonial and commercial policy of the pre-War period and shift to the soil policy of the future.

If we speak of soil in Europe today, we can primarily have in mind only *Russia* and her vassal border states.

Here Fate itself seems desirous of giving us a sign. By handing Russia to Bolshevism, it robbed the Russian nation of that intelligentsia which previously brought about and guaranteed its existence as a state. For the organization of a Russian state formation was not the result of the political abilities of the Slavs in Russia, but only a wonderful example of the state-forming efficacy of the German element in an inferior race. Numerous mighty empires on earth have been created in this way. Lower nations led by Germanic organizers and overlords have more than once grown to be mighty state formations and have endured as long as the racial nucleus of the creative state race maintained itself. For centuries Russia drew nourishment from this Germanic nucleus of its upper leading strata. Today it can be regarded as almost totally exterminated and extinguished. It has been replaced by the Jew. Impossible as it is for the Russian by himself to shake off the yoke of the Jew by his own resources, it is equally impossible for the Jew to maintain the mighty empire forever. He himself is no element of organization, but a ferment of decomposition. The Persian empire in the east is ripe for collapse. And the end of the Jewish rule in Russia will also be the end of Russia as a state. We have been chosen by Fate as witness of a catastrophe which will be the mightiest confirmation of the soundness of the folkish theory.

Our task, the mission of the National Socialist movement, is to bring our own people to such political insight that they will not see their goal for the future in the breathtaking sensation of a new Alexander's conquest, but in the industrious work of the German plough, to which the sword need only give soil. . . .

. . .I should not like to conclude these reflections without pointing once again to the sole alliance possibility which exists for us at the moment in Europe. In the previous chapter on the alliance problem I have already designated England and Italy as the only two states in Europe with which a closer relationship would be desirable and promising for us. . . .The military consequences of concluding this alliance would in every respect be the opposite of the consequence of an alliance with Russia. The most important consideration, first of all, is *the fact that in itself an approach to England and Italy in no way conjures up a war danger*. France, the sole power which could conceivably oppose the alliance, would not be in a position to do so. *And consequently the alliance would give Germany the possibility of peacefully making those preparations for a reckoning with France, which would have to be made in any event within the scope of such a coalition*. . . .

> Adolf Hitler, *Mein Kampf*, trans. by Ralph Mannheim, intro. by D.C. Watt (London, Hutchinson, 1969), pp. 3, 596 − 8, 607.

24   France and Locarno, 1926

Foreign Affairs Committee of the French Chamber of Deputies: Minutes, 12 February 1926

The meeting began at 10.10 a.m. under the chairmanship of M. Franklin-Bouillon. . . .

M. Soulier: renewed the tributes addressed to M. Paul-Boncour. His report was not only the work of an eminent jurist. . . it was also that of a prudent man who sees the strength and weaknesses of the Treaties. One weakness was revealed when M. Briand reported to the Foreign Affairs Committee. . .he remained enclosed in a kind of armour: the Prime Minister would not agree to the release of papers. Now we cannot judge the agreements if we do not know how they were negotiated. . .there were three essential points: the Rhine, East Central Europe, the colonies. For the Rhine, the door has been closed; England and Italy held it closed with us. After the Treaties, these two powers have abandoned us; they have not sided with Germany, but they are in a trench between Germany and us. They watch the barrier as Olympian and disinterested witnesses. We are at a turning point, the end of the regime of Louis XIV.

As regards East Central Europe, before Locarno there was no doubt among our allies; we were at their side unreservedly; nor was there any doubt on the matter in Germany. Today, although the Polish press has praised the Treaties, a Warsaw newspaper and the German press, which is more significant, affirm that all is changed, that Germany does not guarantee the frontiers of eastern Germany as those of the West. . . .

M. Soulier concluded by asking that the Foreign Minister should speak to them on the negotiations leading to the Treaty. . . .

The Chairman: . . .said that he spoke not as Chairman but as one of the Committee's members in drawing the attention of his colleagues to the gravity of the situation. He would vote for the acceptance of M. Paul-Boncour's report. . .but though he accepts the report and the Treaty itself, his conscience compelled him to say that he would vote for them without conviction. One could not refuse to conclude this Treaty. Nor could one not ratify it. It was an experiment. But there was not one German in a million who was inspired by the spirit of Locarno. It would be folly not to vote for the Treaty but it would be greater folly to believe in it. Germany was unanimous in wanting a union with Austria; the recovery of Danzig; she was almost unanimous in the return of the Hohenzollerns, on the rectification of the Italian and Czechoslovak frontiers. . . .Having fought the Treaty of Versailles he considered that we should be vigilant. France's misfortunes came from the fact that her leaders knew only the officials of other countries. None of them has penetrated the mind of an Englishman, a German, an Italian. France negotiated at Locarno under the pressure of English policy which is dominated by ignorance and lack of foresight. We are asked to follow the blind. We are oppressed by political and financial pressures. It's a dramatic. Terrible situation (*strong signs of approval*). . . France was as threatened today as in 1914.

M. Milhaud: maintained his approval of the report and of the Locarno policy. . . .The Rhine problem, he said, dominated everything; it conditions French policy and the life of Europe. If France were to collapse a second time on the Rhine, the fate of the world would be changed.

. . .The men who created Locarno have remade or tried to remake what France did in 1830, and afterwards, in support of Belgium and her neutrality. Was England. . .afflicted with blindness, as M. Franklin-Bouillon suggested?. On the contrary, he believed that she was vigilant. . .M. Milhaud did not ignore pangermanism. But the more certain he was of the irrestible will of Germany, the more he supported the Treaty of Locarno, which fixed the status quo on the Rhine. We must not disarm; but along with our military strength there is a justice which generates alliances. . .Locarno takes nothing from us. Doubtless the English do not want us to stay at Mayence. . . .But the Treaty has closed Germany's claim to Alsace and Lorraine: it gives us England's diplomatic complicity. As long as England remains conscious of her European duties there will be nothing to fear. . . .However no promise of diplomatic support can dispense us from having sufficient military forces.

The Chairman: considered, like M. Albert Milhaud, that we could only follow a policy of reliance on England. But this common policy was not constant and far-sighted. England often saw clearly but too late. . . .If Lord Grey had not hesitated in 1914 the war would have been avoided. We should practise the policy of entente as leaders, not as followers. At bottom Locarno was England's device for escaping from the pact of guarantee. The Geneva Protocol was correct: the world's nervous system was not on the Rhine but in Poland. There a conflict. . .is certain. Now no attempt has been made to remedy the danger. When the conflict erupts it will be necessary for England to intervene: but too late this time again. There is only one thing that will count, France's effort. . . .

M. Soulier: believed in the traditional policy of England, but also in her blindness. The Treaty of Locarno was bad for England since it paved the way for German hegemony. . . .

M. Barthélemy: England pays cheaply for her contribution. Germany wins equality. Italy becomes a guarantor: she protects us. France has security on the Rhine. It's a substitute, it is said, for the Pact of Guarantee. . . .We French. . .are abandoning our position as victors. Doubtless the time has come for us to do so. . . .

M. Chaumieé: . . .what he liked in the Treaty of Locarno was the announcement of a postwar policy. Attitudes will change. . . .One of the benefits of Locarno is to do away with the formulas which kept alive a war mentality. The world must be educated as children are educated. . . .

Assemblée Nationale, Service des Archives, 13 Legislature, 50 seance

25 Germany's aims, 1926

Memorandum from General Stülpnagel, chief of the operations section of
the High Command, to the German foreign ministry, 6 March 1926

The immediate aim of German foreign policy must be the regaining
of full sovereignty over the area retained by Germany, the firm
acquisition of those areas at present separated from her, and the
re-acquisition of those areas essential to the German economy. That is
to say:

1 The liberation of the Rhineland and the Saar area.
2 The abolition of the Corridor and the regaining of Polish Upper
Silesia.
3 The *Anschluss* of German Austria.
4 The abolition of the Demilitarized Zone.

These immediate political aims will produce conflict primarily with
France and Belgium and with Poland which is dependent on them,
then with Czechoslovakia and finally also with Italy. . . .

The above exposition of Germany's political aims. . .clearly shows
that the problem for Germany in the next stages of her political
development can only be the re-establishment of her position in
Europe, and that the regaining of her world position will be a task for
the distant future. Re-establishing a European position is for Germany
a question in which land forces will almost exclusively be decisive, for
the opponent of this resurrection of Germany is in the first place
France. It is certainly to be assumed that a reborn Germany will
eventually come into conflict with the American-English powers in the
struggle for raw materials and markets, and that she will then need
adequate maritime forces. But this conflict will be fought out on the
basis of a firm European position, after a new solution to the Franco-
German problem has been achieved through either peace or war.

> *Akten   zur   deutschen   auswärtigen
> Politik*, 1918 – 1945, Serie B: 1925 – 33
> vol. 1, i (Göttingen, 1966), pp. 343 – 5.

26 Foch opposes early withdrawal from the Rhineland, 1926

Letter of Marshal Foch, Commander in Chief of the Allied armies, to the
French government, 8 March 1926.

During the session of the Chamber of Deputies on 23 February when the Treaty of Locarno was being discussed, Colonel Fabry cited a passage from Monsieur Stresemann's speech at Cologne: 'we would despair of the spirit of Locarno if it did not bring for us Germans the full evacuation of the Rhineland as soon as possible'. . . .

From now on it seems that we will be faced with demands for the early evacuation of the Rhineland. Before considering this eventuality it is necessary to affirm our right to maintain the occupation for 15 years.

The purpose of this occupation is to serve 'as a guarantee for the execution of the Treaty of Versailles by Germany' (Article 428).

This guarantee covers not only the military clauses but also reparations which extend well beyond 15 years.

Now, can one consider that Germany has satisfied her obligations in this respect, after only the first year of the operation of the Dawes Plan? . . .

What kind of a situation would France face in the event of an early withdrawal?

She will find herself:

1 With her frontier of 1815. This frontier is not protected. Several years will be needed to fortify it adequately.
2 With a much smaller army, the organization and establishment of which are not yet settled, and of which a large part is devoted to overseas operations, Syria, Morocco.
3 With arms supplies. . .greatly reduced.
4 With an empty treasury, a large debt, and difficult credit.

It is high time, therefore, that the government and especially the Ministry of War, addressed themselves to the business of dealing with this military inferiority which in present conditions would, as a result of the abandonment of the Rhine, put France at the mercy of a German attack — which is feasible even with existing forces.

Without these indispensable military precautions our security, which until now has been based on the line of the Rhine and which has allowed us our operations in Syria and Morocco, will no longer exist the day when we evacuate this line.

II

. . .In rejecting the heresy which entrusts France's security to the relative pacifism of Germany, one cannot overlook the fact that Germany, though deprived of her colonies, has a population of over 65 millions, with a rapid rate of growth, which will lead to overpopulation and a threat to a neighbouring country such as ours, with a smaller population and a low birth rate. This situation will one day dictate the conduct of the German government and bring it back to its tradition of a predatory nation.

Consequently, however secure our legal rights might seem, we will be threatened by a new invasion. . .if we do not have on the day when we leave the Rhine sufficient forces to enforce our rights on our own frontier. The preparation and consolidation of these forces must be a first priority. . , .

Moreover the 15-year occupation period under the Treaty of Versailles has been recognized as necessary for the consolidation of the new states of Central Europe. By reducing it we will risk the collapse — without our being able to intervene — of the free Europe that our victories established.

Finally while we are on the Rhine, peace is assured. . . .Germany, after the savage devastation that she unleashed on the invaded countries, will never start a conflict on her own soil.

III

The policy of the early evacuation of the Rhine is the policy that Germany will certainly seek to pursue through the League of Nations once she is a member. For the possession of the Rhine has always given her freedom of action. By abandoning it we will give Germany the ability to dominate and subjugate central Europe — beginning with Austria.

A similar tendency is to be feared on the part of England, our Ally of yesterday. She shows herself as tenacious in her policy of reducing French power as she is blind to the consequences for her Empire.

Italy. . .only partly supports France. . . .

Belgium has been freed from the neutrality whose violation brought about England's intervention. Relying on her own resources, ruled by a Socialist government and divided by a Flemish movement, she has just cut back her military strength to such an extent that one can question the effectiveness of her intervention — assuming that she would intervene on our side.

Czechoslovakia includes within her frontiers powerful minorities with external ties. She could in the event of conflict be reduced to a passive role, seeking above all to keep her integrity as a nation. And it is the same for Romania.

Only Poland continuing the policy of recent years, would be forced by the dangers which threaten her existence to support us.

IV

To sum up: while we are on the Rhine, peace and our security and the maintenance of the new Europe are fully assured. Germany cannot absorb Austria.

The day when we leave it to return to our 1815 frontiers and distance ourselves from the successor states, France will lose her predominance in the centre of Europe. . . .

This change must be delayed as long as possible. In addition the military frontier that we should have to hold after withdrawal . . .demands fortifications and a long-term reform of our military forces. . . .

In conclusion:

1 There can be no question of France withdrawing from the Rhineland before the expiration of the 15 years stipulated in the Treaty of Versailles.

2 As a matter or urgency we must create the conditions which will guarantee France's security when the day comes for withdrawal.

3 Without such preparations evacuation will mean a national disaster coming on the heels of the financial crisis. Security, foreign policy, reparations will all collapse with the abandonment of the Rhine. France will be weaker than in 1913, for in the face of a Germany strengthened by the return of the Rhine, she will have neither the army, nor the reserves, nor the supplies, nor the allies, nor the financial strength of that time; moreover she will not have the 1,500,000 men whose loss will be felt for many years to come.

> Archives nationales, Paris, *Painlevé Papers*, 313 AP -13, dr. 2

27 Stresemann and Briand discuss Franco-German rapprochement at Thoiry, 17 September 1926

Herr Briand [French foreign minister] let me know through Professor Hesnard that he was going to propose to me that the occupation of the Rhineland should be wholly terminated, that the Saar should be given back to Germany, and Military Control abolished. He would begin the conversation by quite openly laying his cards on the table and explaining his views. Professor Hesnard asked me to reply with equal candour to the question that Briand would put to me — namely whether we would in that case be ready to meet the economic needs of France in the matter of the issue of bonds. The political interview started according to plan.

Herr Briand began the interview with the expression of his conviction that partial solutions were useless, as always involving the possibility of danger in the future. His purpose was to discuss a comprehensive solution of all the questions at issue between Germany and France, and he asked me to say openly whether we could come to terms with France in the economic sphere, if this question should be solved. In this connection he was not merely thinking of the return of the Saar, but the termination of the entire Rhineland occupation.

Stresemann [German foreign minister]: The questions you raise have long been before my mind. I would recall that last March in Geneva you proposed a meeting that had to be again and again postponed, and has now fortunately taken place. As I was counting on this meeting, I have taken the trouble to sound public opinion in Germany on these matters. Not from any tactical considerations, but as a matter of plain fact, I must tell you that the question of the realizability of the Railway bonds by facilitating transfer arrangements, has met with stronger opposition than I expected. In the Foreign Committee it was contended from German National quarters that the way would thus be blocked for later loans to be raised by the German State Railways, which would be forced to issue new preference shares, and that German influence would so be still further weakened. Even on the Democratic side a man of Dernburg's authority stated that it would be better to sacrifice the political advantages such as would be entailed in the suspension of the Rhineland occupation, than to lay hands on the essential structure of the safeguards provided under the Dawes Plan. I should like to say quite openly that we are naturally anxious for a revision of that Plan. Our attitude is that there is something yet remaining of Germany's obligations, which is now embodied in the railway and industrial bonds as a German obligation, and we should be sorry to see a part of these bonds withdrawn from their destined application. The Reich Minister for Trade and Industry (Dr Curtius) and the Finance Minister (Dr Reinhold) attacked me very sharply in the Cabinet, and their Secretaries of States and officials generally are wholly opposed to such a solution. I must therefore be prepared for a stiff contest in Berlin, if I fall in with your proposal. I can only deal with the situation thus: an understanding on this basis seems to me solely possible if, in connection with the occupation of the Rhineland, there is no question of reducing the periods laid down by two years or so, etc., but that, when our agreement is in order, the troops will be removed with all the speed that is technically possible. If, then, I assume that our Cabinets agree, and that the work of the technical experts can begin at once, and within the first months of the coming year we have agreed with the other nations on the whole procedure, then all troops must have left the Rhineland by 30 September, 1927 (Briand nodded agreement). I may also make clear that the issue before us now is not the reduction in the periods of occupation, but an immediate suspension of the occupation as a whole, with an understanding in this regard.

Briand: Of course. Everything would be arranged, and as quickly as possible. But you know that the financial needs of France are very great. What, in your opinion, are the possibilities in regard to the issue of bonds?

Stresemann: As far as the Saar is concerned, the repurchase of the Saar mines is provided for in the Versailles Treaty. We reached agreement in the value of the Saar mines after a long dispute, and on a basis of about 300 million gold marks. That would be the first question to come into consideration. What quantity of bonds would be taken up by the world market, if they were provided with a certain priority, I would not venture to predict. I have seen a figure of 4 milliards mentioned in French newspapers. That seems to be quite reckless. Moreover, such preferential treatment would also be impossible from Germany's point of view. I cannot myself imagine that the world market would take up more than 1½ milliards. And that figure would, in my opinion, be the maximum which Germany could undertake, though on this point I must leave the last word to the Minister of Finance. Mr Chamberlain left me no doubt that, as indeed I had always assumed, no preferential treatment of France was in contemplation, so that of the sum that it might prove possible to issue, 52 per cent would stand at the disposal of France. From this transaction, therefore, there would accrue to France a capital sum of 750 plus 300 millions—about one milliard, in fact. But I cannot go into details, these being matters which we cannot deal with, but must leave to our technical experts.

Briand: You are perfectly right. I will discuss these matters tomorrow in Paris with a few of my friends, to prepare them for the decision of the next Cabinet. On two occasions already I have addressed the Foreign Committee on a comprehensive solution of this kind, and have always met with general agreement. I am, however, extremely tired and overstrained, and must get a week's holiday. Then I will put these matters before the Cabinet, and about the beginning of October I will send a technical expert to Berlin who will discuss details with someone appointed for the purpose on your side.

Stresemann: Excellent. The sooner we can dispose of the matter the better. And now what about the removal of Military Control?

Briand: A discussion is going on today between Massigli [Chef de Section in the Foreign Ministry in Paris], Weissman [State Secretary in the Prussian Ministry of State], and Pünder [State Secretary in the Reich Chancellery]. I believe there are still a few small matters to be settled. Perhaps you would see what you can do to help them reach agreement. Then I will at once instruct the French representative on the Ambassadors' Conference that the Military Control Commission is to be withdrawn.

Stresemann: It is regrettable that there should still be small details not yet settled. The business should be taken out of the hands of officials, and ended without more ado. What are the points remaining?

Briand: I have given express instructions that the business is to be dealt with in a generous way. These officials are impossible. When I first attacked the question of removing the Military Control, I was confronted with piles of documents from the French War Ministry regarding German derelictions. I threw these papers into a corner, and asked what matters of importance still remained outstanding, as I had no intention of going into all these trivialities. A file of documents was then put before me. At last I succeeded in getting the matter narrowed down to essentials. Military men are in themselves ready to obey and to carry out orders: but they must be given clear orders and instructions. I had a talk today with Herr Weismann, and also with Herr Pünder and Massigli. If there are still some small outstanding points, it is better they should be settled. I shall then be most ready to issue instructions to the Ambassador, and support the removal of a Military Control. . . .

Stresemann: If we are in agreement about the withdrawal of the troops from the Rhineland, the return of the Saar territory, and the abolition of Military Control, it is important that we should come to an understanding over Eupen and Malmedy.

I then gave Briand a detailed statement of the negotiations with Belgium, referred to the pronouncement by Vandervelde on 9 July, and the statement of Delacroix [Belgian member of the Reparations

Commission], and asked what was the French Government's attitude to this matter. . . .

At the conclusion of the interview, which then went on to consider the means for realizing our ideas, I said to Briand: If our agreement comes into force, we will assist in the stabilization of the French franc. I will do so gladly, for it is only in our interest that stable relations should subsist all over Europe. But I do not want to stabilize Poincaré. Don't you think he may remain, if we now give him the chance, by taking these steps to maintain the franc?

Briand: I don't think Poincaré can last long, and regard his Cabinet merely as a transition Cabinet. Moreover, it will be certainly said in France that an understanding between France and Germany was only possible for the sake of foreign policy, and everyone knows that you would not have undertaken any eventual concessions from regard for Monsieur Poincaré. It is, by the way, a delightful bit of historical *esprit d'escalier* that Germany's entry into the League and the Franco-German understanding should occur just at the moment when this man is Premier of France.

Briand then gave a description of Poincaré's personality and said in the course of it: He has never lived among men. He has always lived among documents, first at the *Palais de Justice* and now in politics. He is persistent in following his ideas to their conclusion, and knows every sentence of every Note. But he does not know the feelings of the French people, and he knows nothing of the spirit that must inspire a new age. . . .

We then discussed collaboration on the Council of the League. Briand proposed that there should be a preliminary meeting before the December session between Chamberlain, himself and me. We must not present an appearance to the Council of working against each other, we must come to an understanding beforehand.

The ensuing talk related to conditions in Czecho-Slovakia, the position of England in relation to her colonies, and the Russian question.

Relations with Czecho-Slovakia: Attitude of Beneš: his intentions were good, and he looked towards Western Europe.

Relations of England to her colonies: Difficult economic situation in England. Victory of the Liberals in Canada meant a weakening of England at the Imperial Conference.

Russia: Briand did not think that the Bolshevik regime would last much longer. There were diverging aims everywhere. Ukraine and Georgia wanted to declare themselves independent. He had been told in local Soviet circles that there were strong dispositions in Russia to join the League. The only man of importance was Trotski.

We then discussed the possibilities of economic cooperation in the reconstruction of Russia.

> *Gustav Stresemann, His Diaries, Letters and Papers*, edited and translated by Eric Sutton, vol. 3 (London, Macmillan, 1940), pp. 17 – 26.

28 Disarmament: A British view, 1928

British Foreign Office memorandum, 31 January, 1928

Since the last meeting of the Cabinet Committee on Reduction and Limitation of Armaments, there have been some developments which it may be well to summarize, in order to be able to survey the position in which we find ourselves on the eve of the resumption of serious discussion at Geneva.

In the first place, it will be remembered that the Cabinet Committee held its former sittings in November, before the meetings of the Preparatory and Security Committees at Geneva in December. It was then (in November) hoped that these meetings would be of a purely formal character, and that the actual problems of security and disarmament would not be tackled. This hope proved to be justified and we were not involved in discussion of the Disarmament issues on which we had already found ourselves at variance with other governments. But against the possibility of such discussion, instructions were given to the British Delegate, which were summarized thus: 'To state once more, though without controversy, our naval proposals, putting in the forefront the proposed reduction in the size and power of capital ships: to use our influence with the French Government to make military disarmament practicable; and to confirm the international agreement, so far as it has been reached, upon the Air Forces, with a view to establishing a basis of equality between the principal Air Powers of Europe'. Little difficulty was anticipated in regard to the Air. The two formidable issues were (1) limitation of warships and (2) limitation of trained reserves. In regard to these two points the conclusion really was that on the former we could make no concession and that in regard to the latter we must, partly for tactical reasons, maintain our view that in the absence of any limitation of trained reserves there could be no effective disarmament calculated to affect the general sense of security and so reduce the chance of hostilities.

It was hoped that an adjournment of the discussion for some months — an adjournment which was happily secured — would give time for reflection and for discussion between the governments, and it is time now, on the eve of the resumption of the sessions at Geneva, to review the result of such discussion as has taken place.

On the naval question, there are the discussions which Admiral Kelly had with the French naval authorities in Paris in November last (already circulated to the Committee). These show, that, although the French are prepared to make a slight advance, this does not, in the view of the Admiralty, alter the situation materially, and the Admiralty memorandum on those discussions concludes: 'It does not appear that there is any reason to modify our attitude on the question of disarmament. The above should show that it is only her present feeling of insecurity that prevents France from agreeing to the British method of limitation, and that as regards sound principles we are on firmer ground than she is.'

Further in regard to the naval question, there is the interview between Lord Cushendun and the French Ambassador on 19 January, at which the latter was unable to indicate any further concession on the part of his Government, though he promised to discuss the matter with them during his impending visit to Paris. We have not heard that he has brought anything back with him.

From the above it seems that, on the naval question, the French may make a small advance towards our position, but the Admiralty are clear that this is not sufficient, and are also insistent on maintaining our point of view. The situation therefore is not materially different from what it was in November.

As regards the military question, the situation has undergone, if possible, even less change. Colonel Temperley's conversation with Colonel Réquin (circulated to the Committee) shows that, although the French views on limitation of expenditure, and on control, may be modified, their attitude in regard to the main issue — trained reserves — remains immovable. This is only confirmed by Lord Cushendun's interview with M.de Fleuriau.

If, therefore, our hope was that an adjournment of the Preparatory Committee till March might give time for the governments to reach agreement on the main points at issue, it must be confessed that that hope has been deceived.

It remains, therefore, to consider in these circumstances what will be the probable course of events and what would be our best objective.

There seem to be three immediate alternatives:

1 The Preparatory Committee might meet on 15 March, and after thorough discussion—which is certain to pass through acrimonious phases—it might be able to agree on the preliminary draft of a convention, for what that might be worth. That is on the assumption that those who have so far opposed our naval proposals become reconciled to them. The rather faint chance of this would be strengthened if we could find some way of making those proposals more palatable to their opponents, but for the moment the Admiralty memorandum must be taken as their last word on the subject, and therefore the prospect of agreement cannot but be regarded as slight. No doubt our opponents may be 'bluffing' to some extent, and only a discussion at the Committee itself would reveal how far they would ultimately be prepared to go. But once embarked on a discussion we run the risk of bringing about the second alternative which, on present information, seems more likely to arise, viz.:

2 The Preparatory Committee would meet and after discussion would have to record its failure to produce an agreement.

It is quite unnecessary to point out that the results of this would be, at best, regrettable. The failure of a League enterprise entrusted to a special League Committee would produce a very bad effect. For it would be a very definite failure, and a distinct check to the policy of 'Disarmament' and all that is implied thereby. The work would be broken off, and it is difficult to see how it could be re-started in the immediate future. In the second place, the deadlock would arise out of a public difference between the French and ourselves, in which we should have the support, on some points, of only a few undesirable Allies. On principle it is obviously most undesirable to quarrel with the French: on this particular issue it is regrettable that we cannot hope that M. Paul-Boncour will do much to smooth the asperities of debate or help us find a way to friendly disagreement.

Apart from this unpleasant aspect of a disagreement at Geneva, there is the probability, or rather the certainty, that it will at once bring up the whole question of German (and other ex-enemy) disarmament. The Germans are never tired of insisting that by the Covenant the Members of the League are bound to disarm, and that by the Preamble to the Military Clauses of the Treaty of Versailles, by the Allied reply to the observations of the German Delegation to the Peace Conference and by the declaration made at Locarno, German disarmament is only a first step towards general disarmament. They will say that if the latter cannot be achieved — and the breakdown of negotiations would for the moment dash all hope of success — it follows that the former can no longer be insisted on. There is a great deal to be said against this argument, and the point will be dealt with later, but for the moment it is necessary to point out that we shall encounter this difficulty from the German side, and that it may give a good deal of trouble.

Then, from the general European point of view, we must consider that a breakdown of the negotiations may be laid at our door. We have saved the French on former occasions, from their own folly, it is difficult to avoid suspecting that they look to us to perform the same service again. It has been instilled into us that the French Government, for home political reasons, are forced to push ahead with disarmament: they quote public opinion in France as demanding that something should be done, and that quickly, and if we suggest caution or throw doubt on the possibility of achieving anything really material in a hurry, they shake their heads and make obscure and nervous allusion to their impending general election. Knowing next to nothing about French politics or the French electorate, it has always surprised me, after all that has happened, that disarmament should be a good election cry in France. Amongst M. Paul-Boncour's followers, I can imagine that there are some extremer socialists, who are pacifist in the same way that kind-hearted people in this country are mildly in favour of being as nice as possible to everyone when they direct their attention to foreign politics. I don't know that he looks for any support to the Communists — I imagine he is very far removed from them. If one were very cynical, therefore, one might be tempted to think that he would be rather embarrassed in May if he had returned from Geneva having agreed to any real scheme of disarmament, but that it might suit his book very well if he were able to return pointing out to his pacifists how he had striven for disarmament and at the same time reassuring the bulk of his electors by pointing out that these schemes had been defeated by the Imperialist and aggressive British Government. After all it is difficult to believe that a nation which, we are told (*vide* M. de Fleuriau, M. Paul-Boncour and French speakers *passim*), will never abandon universal military service, is waiting to throw out a government that does not bring about disarmament. Therefore when we are told that the French elections will turn to a great extent on disarmament, it is impossible not to suspect that, if this is true, there has been suppression of the fact that we are expected to play our role, and to be held up to the execration of the French elector for standing in the way of the realization of an ideal which is excellent to advocate but which might be awkward to put in practice.

It would not be very difficult for the French to represent us as the villain of the piece. If a break is forced on the naval question, it will be easy for them to make much of the fact that we are in a small minority, that that is due to our peculiar position at sea, and that really, as they had suspected all along, what we mean by disarmament was that other nations should disarm on land while we maintained our sea-power unimpaired. They will find many believers in this doctrine.

So the situation is unpleasant. Of course, as has been suggested, we can try to shift some of the blame on to the French by pointing out that any so-called disarmament convention that takes no account of trained reserves is a sham and a delusion. That undoubtedly is the fact, but there again we are in a minority, and there again the fact that we — and the Americans — are the only considerable nation that voluntarily adopts the voluntary system, can be adduced in proof that our arguments are not disinterested. If the Preparatory Committee is really committed to a 'second reading' of the Disarmament Convention in March, probably the best tactics would be to insist on taking the Convention in its present form and going through it Chapter by Chapter. That would involve beginning with land effectives. On that we could make our position quite clear; that a Disarmament Convention that puts no limit on trained reserves will not touch the problem which is the objective of all these activities, and that it is useless to talk of 'security' whilst each succeeding generation is trained to war. We could offer to proceed with the other subjects. If the French refuse, the responsibility for the breakdown is theirs. No doubt they will be able to prove to their own people, and to other conscriptionist countries, that we have been disingenuous in asking for the impossible so as to put them in the wrong. But, on the other hand, our attitude might be defensible at home, and might well receive a good measure of support (including that of Lord Cecil and the League of Nations Union). . . .

3 There is the third alternative, of adjourning the Preparatory Committee for some months. This would have the effect of postponing all the inconveniences and dangers of the second alternative. It has twice been resorted to — once in April of last year and once in December. On those occasions it was suggested in all good faith that further time for reflection and discussion between the governments might produce agreement. If this hope was sincere, adjournment was a reasonable policy and not merely procrastination. Our experience of

ten months or so, however, must make us realize that with the passage of time the rival policies do not seem to assimilate themselves to each other, and that adjournment does not seem likely to lead anywhere. . . .

The above has been written on the assumption that we are committed to work on disarmament on the present lines, whether we really think this is the best method or not. It is true that we are pledged several times over to disarm: it is not so clear that we are pledged anywhere to sign a general disarmament convention. It is true that under the Covenant the Council is to 'formulate plans' for reduction, but these are for 'consideration and action of the *several* Governments'. What we told the Germans in 1919 was that the first step towards general disarmament must be a disarmament of Germany. Germany accepted the military, naval and air clauses of the Treaty of Versailles (and may have carried them out). Without that, evidently no one could disarm. Once that was done, other nations were free to reduce their armaments to the 'lowest point consistent with national safety'. At any rate *we* have done so. After the Armistice we scrapped a large proportion of our fleet — a process which was carried still further by the Washington Treaty. We very soon reduced our army to proportions even more 'contemptible' than those of 1914. Other nations have done something of the same — how much, is a matter between them and their consciences. But it does not seem quite certain that 'plans for the consideration and action of the several governments' necessarily involves a general convention for all-round proportional reduction of armaments. Certainly we are nowhere pledged to reduction to the German level. And if German disarmament, carried to the point to which we believe it has been carried, does not produce sufficient sense of security to enable other nations to spare themselves expense which they must grudge, that is no argument in favour of freeing the Germans from restrictions which do not appear to have been severe enough.

But the League has chosen to act as if it were bound to produce a general disarmament convention. The Germans have seized on this and sought to connect general disarmament with their own disarmament in such a way that they can claim to be freed from their part of the bargain if the Allied Governments do not perform theirs. This course has been adopted with our consent, however reluctant, and we are therefore presumably committed to it, with the result that we are now faced with these three alternatives, one of which is favourable though very remote, and the other two which present obvious inconveniences, if not dangers.

DBFP, Ia, IV no. 267.

29 Monetary reconstruction in Europe ; Anglo-French rivalry, 1928

Note of conversations held in Paris between the governor of the Bank of England and the governor of the Bank of France, 27 − 28 April 1928

1 To explain why he had insisted that the Governor should come to Paris, Monsieur Moreau [Governor of the Bank of France] said that the elections require his presence in a constituency of which he is Mayor, and that in the interval between the two ballots he has been engaged with preparations for the new loan: in the early part of May he will not be available.

2 Monsieur Moreau then raised the question of Roumania, which was discussed for about two hours on the afternoon of 27 April. The Governor, in reply to what amounted to a cross-examination, made three points only; he said that:

(i)   he wished it to be clearly understood that whatever the Deputy Governor had said to Monsieur Moreau in February on behalf of the Bank of England will be implemented in the spirit and in the letter by the Bank and is endorsed by the Governor personally, without any qualifications.

(ii) if any new questions have arisen since then, which now require to be answered, the Governor could not undertake to answer them without first consulting his colleagues at the Bank, because for some time past he has been out of contact with developments in the situation.

(iii) he could however express his own personal opinion on the general questions of principle involved; for example, he could say:

  (a) that he has always held, still holds, and will continue to hold, whatever other course events may take, that Roumania is a case for the League and

  (b) that he has championed and will continue to champion the cause of Central Bank cooperation and wishes to work in harmony with the Banque de France.

3 Monsieur Moreau suggested at the start that the Governor's letter to Monsieur Burillianau [Roumanian central bank official], written

on the day after Monsieur Moreau's visit to London in February, amounted to a repudiation of the undertakings given by the Deputy Governor. When the Governor replied that he stands by everything which the Deputy Governor said, Monsieur Moreau asked what exactly the undertaking then given was now held to have been. But he quickly passed over any questions of interpretation or definition, after saying that it had never been the intention of the Banque de France to ask for the recommendation and endorsement of the Federal Reserve Bank for the Roumanian scheme. Their intention was to recommend the scheme themselves, and to ask, in the first instance, for the participation of the Federal Reserve Bank, the Bank of England and the Reichsbank severally. Monsieur Moreau said that he is already corresponding with Dr Schacht [President of the Reichsbank] on the subject. The Banque de France was now so deeply engaged that there could be no turning back, and the scheme would be proceeded with at all costs. If the Bank of England were to refuse participation, Monsieur Moreau would regard it as an unfriendly act and as confirming the suspicions which it was possible to entertain about the motives and methods of the Bank of England, not only in this but also in other questions. He would then have no further regard to the interests of the Bank of England and would always act with an eye solely to the advantage of the Banque de France. Very often, until now, he had gone out of his way to render services to the Bank of England — a fact which ought to be recognized and admitted. There was no other reason why he should take gold from America and pay the extra expenses; he might just as well have based the franc on dollars as on sterling in the Paris market; and the present strength of sterling was due mainly to the Banque de France which takes American money over London at a fixed price for sterling and allows the whole benefit of the movement to be reflected in the sterling dollar rate.

4 Monsieur Moreau said that in the entourage of the Governor of the Bank of England it had been thought, and even stated, that the Banque de France was actuated by political considerations in the Roumanian affair. He wished to remove this misconception, and he gave a detailed account of the series of events by which, between Monsieur Rist's [deputy governor of the Bank of France] meeting with Vintila Bratianu [Roumanian central bank officer] in September and the return of Monsieur Quesnay [Bank of France official] from Bucharest in the middle of February, the Banque de France had become associated with the Roumanian scheme. He had an absolutely

clear conscience on the subject and would prove his case by handing over copies of the relevant correspondence which he had had prepared for the Governor. As a matter of fact, the Quai d'Orsay, so far from initiating, had, as usual, been rather behindhand with its information and knew nothing about the whole affair until it had reached a comparatively advanced stage. . . .

10 When it was suggested that besides the difficulty of the 1913 loan the Bank of England would have to take some account of the questions of principle involved in the procedure adopted by the Banque de France (such as that two names are required to a bill, or that the Bank of England can not participate in a scheme which they would not be content to recommend) Monsieur Moreau lost patience. He said these so-called questions of principle were simply childish and he refused to take them seriously or to believe that they could honestly be thought by anyone else to have any importance whatever. They were a mere pretext and the fact of their being dragged in again at this stage revived in his mind all the unpleasant suspicions about the sincerity of the Bank of England to which he had alluded on the previous day. He then proceeded to bring a series of charges, supported by detailed accounts of what at various times had been said and done in London and New York. For example, he referred to a letter said to have been written by the Governor to Signor Stringher [Governor of the Bank of Italy] about Roumania, and he alleged that the Bank of England took part in all the negotiations between Monsieur Markovics and the private bankers about a Jugoslav Loan. He complained that the Bank of England had offended, in the case of Jugoslavia, against that principle of the open door which he had been at pains to recommend to the French bankers in the case of Roumania. He also quoted a story about the impending resignation of Messieurs Moreau, Rist and Quesnay which was said to have been circulated in order to discredit the Banque de France. All these charges were denied in toto by the Governor, who described them as 'tittle-tattle'; but it was clear to Monsieur Moreau they constitute an overwhelming body of circumstancial evidence against the good faith of the Bank of England. Other examples appeared in the private conversation of Monsieur Quesnay; as when he attributed to the Bank of England a scheme supplanting the Federal Reserve Bank in the leadership of Italian stabilization.

11 The Governor replied with a general criticism of the attitude of the Banque de France towards the Financial Committee of the League. He said that it was quite unfair to pretend that stabilization

through the League involves control on the Austrian model, or that the League imposes a cast-iron scheme regardless of local conditions. Had Monsieur Moreau chosen to do so, he might have helped to establish the League in the position of godfather to all the different countries which, in differing degrees, required help from without: and they would have all been the better for it.

Monsieur Moreau denied hostility to the Financial Committee and cited the fact that he had been consulted a dozen times about the Bulgarians and had always said that they must go to Geneva. He had no regrets about Poland, which (unlike Italy, where nothing had yet been done of what was promised) seemed to be making good progress. He maintained that never in any circumstances could Poland or Roumania have been brought to the League and he did not see that their having taken another course need prevent the Financial Committee from doing useful work in years to come, especially as in any event the period of stabilization plans is practically over. The choice whether to go to the League or not clearly lay, both rightly and inevitably, with the country concerned. Since Roumania had chosen not to go, the sensible thing to do was not to stand aside and decline responsibility for the consequences, but to render such help as could be rendered with a sound scheme, and at any rate avoid the only alternative, which was that Roumania should borrow money and spend it without any scheme at all. The line of demarcation between countries requiring League intervention and those which could do as well with some other kind of help was both arbitrary and vague. For example, it was not clear what were the reasons for differentiating in this respect between Jugoslavia and Roumania.

12 Finally, Monsieur Moreau asked whether the Bank of England would wish to be formally invited now to participate in a Roumanian credit. The Governor suggested that the formal invitation might be delayed until he had had an opportunity of writing, in 8 or 10 days' time, a personal letter to Monsieur Moreau on the subject.

> Cited in: R.S. Sayers, *The Bank of England* 1891 – 1944, vol. 3 (London, 1976) pp. 101 – 6.

30   Anglo-American relations assessed, 1928

Memorandum by Foreign Office official, Mr Craigie, 12 November 1928

Outstanding Problems affecting Anglo-American Relations
The Period 1920 – 28

It is probably safe to say that at no time since 1920 have Anglo-American relations been in so unsatisfactory a state as at the present moment. Between that year and 1923 a series of events occurred which had a profoundly beneficial effect on those relations; the Mesopotamian oil question was settled, the Irish Free State was created, the Washington Naval Treaty was signed, the Anglo-Japanese Alliance was abrogated and the debt settlement took place. In the United States the effect of these events — and particularly of the debt settlement — was to place the name of Britain higher in the esteem and regard of the American people than at any previous time within living memory. In this country there was undeniably a feeling of exasperation at the harshness of America's debt settlement terms, but with it there was a sense of gratification that British prestige should have gained immeasurably from the settlement.

As late as 1926 this earlier improvement in relations was reflected in the negotiation of an agreement under which the great mass of American war claims against this country were wiped out by a process of gradual elimination leading to a final cancelling-out of inter-Governmental accounts, The agreement, which unostentatiously removed a potential source of serious friction, showed what can be done with the United States Government when they are approached in the right way and after proper preparation of the ground.-

Taking all in all it is probable that during the years 1923 – 25 the curve of good feeling between the countries touched its highest point. Then began the differences in regard to the limitation of cruisers and other auxiliary naval craft. It had been wrongly assumed throughout the United States that at Washington the British Empire had accepted the *principle* of equality for all naval craft — i.e. 'parity' all along the line. The United States Administration of the day, anxious to make the most of their achievement of 1922, did nothing to dispel this widely held assumption. Well before the Three-Power Conference at Geneva the Big Navy party in the United States had seized on this popular misapprehension to bolster up their demands for more and bigger cruisers. During and after that conference they held this country up to criticism and obloquy on the ground that we had gone back on a principle previously accepted. The Geneva failure dealt a shattering blow to our growing popularity in the United States of America — the more shattering in that it was entirely unexpected by the great mass of Americans, from the President downwards. The Anglo-French compromise failure has turned a feeling of resentful surprise into one of irritation if not exasperation. So far as the outward manifestations of feeling in the United States are concerned, we appear to be reverting to the position of 1920. . . .

Irremovable and Inherent Difficulties

Mutual jealousy; the clash of differing national characteristics emphasized by the existence of a common language; the growing discrepancies of speech and style within that 'common' language; intensive trade rivalry; determined competition between the two merchant marines; the uneasy relationship between debtor and creditor — these are some of the permanent factors in Anglo-American relations the effect of which can at the best only be slightly mitigated by tactful handling. But there are a number of other difficulties which are not incapable of removal through the exercise of a patient diplomacy taking account of things as they are, not as we would wish them to be. If through an insufficient realization of their wider and psychological aspects, we allow these removable irritants to sap what remains of good feeling in each country towards the other, we shall be drifting towards a situation of real gravity. Except as a figure of speech, war is *not* unthinkable between the two countries. On the contrary, there are at present all the factors which in the past have made for wars between States. It is dangerous to rely too exclusively on considerations such as the newly-signed Kellogg Pact, the common-sense of the two countries, the strategical difficulties in the way of a war with the United States, etc. A more positive policy seems to be called for. Even those who despair (perhaps too easily) of the possibility of really cordial relations between Great Britain and the United States of America will admit the dangers inherent in any future policy which permitted things to drift from bad to worse.

Network of other Problems susceptible of Solution

At the present moment a number of problems of the first magnitude await a solution, all of which are interconnected and all of which intimately affect our relations with the United States. The problems are: The conclusion of a naval limitation agreement at Geneva; the controversy in regard to the exercise of belligerent rights at sea and the possible summoning of an international conference on the subject by the United States; the conclusion of an arbitration treaty with the United States; the settlement of the reparations question, which has been brought sharply into prominence by the question of the evacuation of the Rhineland; the probable trouble in the United States Senate over the so-called British reservations to the Treaty for the Renunciation of War.

The Rhineland problem depends for solution on a reparations settlement; although it is dangerous to prophesy before the forth-coming meeting of the Expert Committee, it is probable that a satisfactory reparations settlement can only be achieved with the aid and cooperation of American finance in some form or other (quite apart from possible future action by the United States Government in respect of war debts); it is not unreasonable to suppose that American aid and cooperation may be more difficult to enlist at a moment when the United States is acutely irritated over the successive failures to achieve any agreement on naval limitation; a naval limitation agree-ment could probably be more easily achieved if the belligerent rights difficulty would first have been cleared out of the way. Similarly, the conclusion of the American draft arbitration treaty would have been greatly facilitated by the elimination of belligerent rights as a likely cause of arbitral controversy with the United States. Finally, the passage of the Treaty for the Renunciation of the War through the United States Senate should afford some indication as to the probable attitude of the United States towards the inclusion of a 'special regions' clause in the new arbitration treaty.

So interconnected are these problems that a failure to solve one of them may result in all being left in a state of suspended animation. Conversely, the solution of one tends to smooth the way for the settle-ment of the next. At present they form a vicious circle, each unsolved problem delaying and complicating the solution of the others. The circle can be broken, but there would seem to be two prerequisites to success: (1) the formulation of a general policy to be applied uniformly to the solution of the whole set of problems; (2) the balancing of political considerations, based upon that general policy, against technical considerations. All the problems named above are, either directly or indirectly, Anglo-American problems. Even the solution of the reparations question may be found in the last resort to depend upon the state of the relations between Great Britain and the United States of America. The formulation of a definite policy must therefore in the main depend on the answer to this question: What is the value of good relations with the United States?. . . .

The existence of satisfactory relations between Great Britain and the United States must necessarily increase our influence and prestige in the councils of Europe. It is perhaps for this very reason that the Europeans are constantly trying to drive a wedge between this country and the United States. Instances of this tendency are numerous, and mention need only be made here of the French attitude at the opening of the Washington Conference in 1922 and the French effort to give a wrong 'twist' to the recent Anglo-French compromise by exaggerating its implications and by making calculated 'leaks' in regard to its provisions. The tendency is a perfectly natural one, but there is no good reason why we should contribute to its success. One French theory appears to be that good relations between Great Britain and the United States may eventually lead to an Anglo-German-American combination. The fear is groundless, and, indeed, appears absurd to anyone who knows the United States, for the United States would never enter into any 'combination' in the strict sense of the word. Anything in the nature of a German-American 'rapprochement' (sic), if it is to come about, will certainly not be prevented by the existence of strained relations between Great Britain and the United States; on the other hand, such strained relations would undoubtedly give it an anti-British orientation which it need not otherwise have.

Good Anglo-American and good Anglo-French relations are not mutually destructive, though there seems to be a real danger of public opinion in this country believing that they are so if the present Anglo-American deadlock is allowed to continue. Friendly relations with the United States need in no way interfere with that close cooperation with France which is such an important asset in European affairs. In the first place, the natural aloofness of the United States from Europe and the play of numerous other factors removes any prospect of Anglo-American relations ever becoming intimate or 'exclusive'. Secondly, the French need only fear the imposition of so-called 'Anglo-Saxon theories of disarmament' if, in fact, they are less devoted to the cause of disarmament than they profess to be. In the converse case only a reactionary Anglo-French policy as regards disarmament in general and as regards Germany in particular—or the appearance of such a policy—would militate against good relations between us and the United States.

In the realm of finance good relations with the United States are for this country so valuable as to be almost essential. The friendly attitude of the American banks since the war has been of great assistance in the maintenance of British credit — recent manifestation of this friendly cooperation occurred in connexion with our return to the gold standard — an achievement which would hardly have been possible without the aid of the Central Bank. . . .

Let us, however, now examine what are the alternatives to a policy designed to keep Anglo-American relations on the friendliest possible footing.

Alternative Policies

The first is the withdrawal from active cooperation with other nations in the solution of such questions as security, disarmament and reparations. This would involve a policy of 'go-as-you-please', a cooperation with this or that foreign Power to achieve a specific end but no further active promotion of agreements by general international consent. It would also seem to involve a reversal of the policy pursued since the war and a repudiation of the principles underlying the Covenant of the League, the Washington Treaties and Locarno. Such a policy would do nothing to ease the situation with the United States, where the Big Navy party would point to a definite collapse of disarmament as proving the necessity for further construction. Moreover, the policy of collaboration which has been consistently pursued by His Majesty's Government in Europe has been attended with undoubted success to such an extent that no practical alternative has been suggested by even their most vigorous critics. Difficulties are now being encountered in the Disarmament Commission which are arresting the natural development of that policy, but no hope of their solution lies in any general reorientation of the policy of His Majesty's Government in Europe. This seems to involve the corollary that we must look elsewhere for a solution, e.g., to Washington.

The second alternative is the continuation of the existing policy of cooperation with other Powers to the gradual exclusion of the United States. The justification for such a policy would be that, since the unreasonable and intractable attitude of the United States has had the effect of stultifying all attempts to secure reasonable settlements, the rest of the world — and particularly Europe — must try to set its house in order without the cooperation of America. In theory, however, the door would be left open to the United States to 'come in' at any time should she so desire. . . .

Some advocates of this policy feel that by this means the United States might be either alarmed by the prospect of 'compulsory' isolation from European affairs into adopting a less intractable policy or alternatively 'shown up' as the main obstruction in the way of progress and harmony and 'shamed' into adopting a more generous attitude. Nobody having any serious knowledge of American politics and American psychology could believe for a moment that such a policy would have either the one effect or the other.

The success of such a policy depends upon the willingness of five Powers at least — Great Britain, France, Germany, Italy and Japan — to embark upon it. Germany's cooperation would be essential. There are, however, many signs that Germany has been closely watching the course of Anglo-American relations and is inspired by the hope that any further deterioration in those relations may lead to a material and most lucrative improvement in German-American relations. At the present time Germany, far from showing any inclination to follow our lead (e.g. to adapt their American policy to ours), is taking the attitude that, as we are definitely committed to France, she must look elsewhere for the support which she still requires. This may be only a passing pretext, but the fact remains that Germany feels no longer dependent upon us as in the days of Lord d'Abernon, and is already counting on America to take our place as protector, Nor can she be considered unjustified in casting the United States for this role, if the increasing activity of the German-American elements in the United States and the enormous American investments in Germany are taken into account. With Soviet Russia tending towards more moderate courses, the prospect of a close German-Russian *entente*, backed by American money and goodwill, may not be remote if Anglo-American relations are permitted to suffer any serious or permanent setback.

Application of Policy of 'Settlement without America' to Problem under review

Assuming, however, for the sake of argument that all the Powers named above could be expected to embark upon a policy of 'settlement without America', it is well to examine how the various problems under review could be dealt with by the application of this policy.

Taking limitation of naval armament first, we find that the Anglo-French compromise is unacceptable to Italy, and the arrangement about the military-trained reservists is unacceptable to Germany. These difficulties might have been overcome if the United States had agreed to support the Anglo-French compromise, but they quite definitely cannot be overcome as part of an effort to solve the problem independently of the United States. Japan also would almost certainly refuse to accept any arrangements which, while setting a limit to her own powers of construction, left the United States free to build *ad infinitum*. . . .

Finally, there is the question whether a solution of the reparations problem is possible without American aid and cooperation in some form or other. The only entirely satisfactory solution of the reparations question would involve the reopening of the 'debts' question. Under the most favourable auspices this is a thorny subject to open with any United States Government. Two years ago there was a move- ment in the United States — weak but persistent — in favour of a modi- fication of the policy of the United States Government on this subject. The recent course of the naval limitations negotiations has definitely closed the door to any reopening to the inter-governmental debt settle- ments at the present time.

The best hope of being able to reopen the 'debts' question at some later date lies in eliminating some of the other questions which divide us. This can only be effected by giving the American people some tangible proof that we are not trying to isolate them and oppose the interests of Europe to those of America. . . .

Necessity of Firmness in Relations with the United States

This brings us back to the more positive policy of seeking to promote friendly relations with the United States by the elimination of points of difference between us. . . .

For the purpose of solving the urgent problems of naval limitation, arbitration and belligerent rights, no concession is, in fact, recom- mended which involves more than a recognition of the force of changing circumstances; no concession is recommended for which we cannot hope to secure a political *quid pro quo*: no concession is recommended today which will not be inevitable tomorrow. This is not a policy of weakness, nor does it postulate any lack of firmness in our general relations with the United States. It is a policy designed to utilize the better elements in the United States for the purpose of advancing our own world-wide interests. . . .

Purpose of Memorandum

The purpose of this memorandum has been to review some of the advantages to us of friendly relations with the United States; to draw attention to the great difficulty of solving a number of important problems otherwise than in collaboration with the United States; and to suggest that it is to our ultimate interest to approach the settlement of outstanding Anglo-American differences in a spirit, not of jealous bargaining, but of broad conciliation. . . .

DBFP, Ia, V, no. 490 (annex)

III

Disintegration, 1929 – 33

The onset of the world depression destroyed the fragile post-Locarno détente. The *dies irae* of the interwar world was Tuesday 29 October, 1929. It was the day of the Wall Street crash, the collapse of the American stock market. Although the full effects of the crash were delayed in Europe until the early months of 1931, the consequences were profound and far-reaching. Protectionism and beggar-my-neighbour policies wrecked international cooperation. In June 1931 President Hoover signed the Hawley-Smoot Act which sharply increased American tariffs. At the Ottawa Conference in August 1932 Britain and the Dominions adopted imperial preference. The World Economic Conference of 1933 marked the last attempt to deal with the depression through international action.

In the calm before the storm a new reparations settlement — the Young Plan of June 1929 — was adopted at the first Hague Conference in August 1929. Germany's repayments were scaled down and the ultimate total repayment fixed at about one third of the 1921 total. The price of German acceptance was the full and immediate evacuation of the Rhineland. The Young Plan left one permanent legacy — the Bank for International Settlements established in May 1930 to handle the transfer of reparations and to promote cooperation between European central banks.

Agreement on the Young Plan damaged Anglo-French relations. At the Hague Conference Philip Snowden, chancellor of the exchequer, belittled French claims and demanded a larger British share of German payments; Arthur Henderson, foreign secretary, announced the government's intention to withdraw from the Rhineland regardless of French wishes. Ramsay MacDonald's second Labour government gave priority to repairing Anglo-American friendship. In October 1929 MacDonald went to Washington to meet President Hoover. The talks, which were held at Hoover's fishing lodge on the Rapidan river in the mountains of Virginia, were a

valuable preliminary to the Five Power Naval Conference in London
in January 1930. Inevitably the success of the MacDonald-Hoover
talks revived French apprehensions of Anglo-Saxon hegemony (31).
At the London Conference the United States, Britain and Japan
reached agreement on a 5:5:3 ratio for all ships but France and Italy
refused to accept parity between themselves. Thus the London
Conference confirmed that Britain was no longer 'Mistress of the Seas'.

France's immediate response to the twin dangers of Anglo-Saxon
dominance and German resurgence was the idea of a Franco-German
economic entente as the basis for an economic United States of
Europe (32). Then in May 1930 Briand proposed a European federal
union (33). These initiatives were swiftly overtaken by deepening
depression and German nationalism. In the German elections of
September 1930 Hitler's Nazis gained 107 seats and became the second
largest party. Hitler's reflections on foreign affairs on the eve of his
coming to power are revealed in his letter of 4 December 1932 to
Colonel von Reichenau (38).

1931 was in Arnold Toynbee's phrase the 'annus terribilis'. His
opening sentences in the first chapter of The Survey of International
Affairs 1931 summed up the impact of the depression: 'The year 1931
was distinguished by one outstanding feature. In 1931 men and
women all over the world were seriously contemplating the possibility
that the Western system of Society might break down and cease to
work'. The collapse of the largest Austrian bank, Credit-Anstalt, and
a large German bank shook the world's financial centres. President
Hoover's one-year moratorium on inter-allied debts and reparations
was widely welcomed (34).

Against this background of growing misery and unemployment, the
Far Eastern crisis began with the Japanese occupation of Mukden on
18 – 19 September, 1931. Both China and Japan appealed to the
League but there was no prospect of collective action to stop Japan.
Western governments were too engrossed in the battle for economic
and financial recovery. In the United States elections were in the
offing and the Hoover administration would not risk sanctions, let
alone war. Moreover, as the British foreign secretary, Sir John Simon,
reminded the Cabinet the rights and wrongs in the Manchurian affair
were far from clear-cut (35). Nor is it certain that sanctions would
have sufficed to stop Japan. The Japanese Kwantung Army in
Manchuria might well have ignored directives from Tokyo.

But the Far Eastern crisis was not confined to Manchuria. On 28
January, 1932 Japanese marines attacked the Chinese at Chapei, a

suburb adjoining the international settlement at Shanghai. The Japanese attack at Shanghai involved Britain much more closely than the Japanese advance in Manchuria. Direct British interests in Manchuria were limited whereas the value of British commercial interests at Shanghai was estimated at over £63,000,000. British forces, together with contingents from Japan, United States and Italy, were responsible for defending the international settlement. The long-term threat to British power in the Far East if Japan went unchecked could not be ignored (36). Yet without American support Britain was not strong enough to intervene.

By 1933 the key issues of debts, depression and disarmament had grown into one dark maze (42). The Hoover moratorium of 1931 gave only a year's respite. The German chancellor, Brüning, said it was impossible for Germany to continue reparations payments and reparations were cancelled at the Lausanne Conference in July 1932. Arguing that without reparations she could not repay her war debt to the United States, France requested postponement of the instalment due on 15 December, 1932.

The United States would not recognize a connection between debts and reparations and refused postponement. The French prime minister, Herriot, then asked the French parliament for authority to pay the instalment. This was refused and the Herriot government fell. At Geneva the Disarmament Conference which had been called in February 1932 was deadlocked. It seemed impossible to reconcile France's desire for security with Germany's insistence on equality of armaments.

The one statesman who seemed capable of finding a way out of the labyrinth was the new president of the United States, Franklin D. Roosevelt. After taking office on 4 March, 1933 Roosevelt rapidly established himself as a world leader (42). He confirmed that the Hoover-sponsored World Economic Conference would meet in the summer of 1933 and in April he invited foreign leaders to Washington for preliminary discussions. The World Economic Conference which opened in London on 12 June, 1933 was a turning point in world politics. Great faith had been placed in Roosevelt's leadership. On 2 July Roosevelt torpedoed the conference with his 'bombshell' message rejecting a currency agreement. Britain and France had been anxious to secure an agreement on currency stabilization. With the depreciation of the dollar they feared economic losses through the export of cheap American goods. Although the hopes pinned on Roosevelt may have been extravagant, his prestige might have given the necessary push to secure a coherent economic strategy for the depression. On disarmament, a common Anglo-Franco-American front might have forestalled Hitler. On 16 May, 1933 the British Cabinet was advised that a stern warning from Britain, France and the United States would call Hitler's bluff (43). Indeed, Roosevelt himself believed that his diplomacy had influenced Hitler's famous 'peace' speech of 17 May, 1933. Despite a suggestion from his friend Felix Frankfurter that he should broadcast to Germany and become 'the rallying centre of the world's sanity' Roosevelt retreated from decisive action in foreign affairs (44). The New Deal came first.

Hitler knew that until rearmament was completed Germany was extremely vulnerable (40). Accordingly, he projected the image of a peace-loving Führer anxious to live in friendship with his neighbours, Hitler need not have feared a French attack. Militarily and psychologically France was unprepared for a preventive war against Germany (39). Following the defeat of Germany's Austro-German customs-union plan in September 1931 France sought to retain her leadership in central Europe with a scheme for a Danubian economic entente embracing Austria, Hungary, Czechoslovakia, Yugoslavia and Romania (37). A tariff agreement based on a reciprocal preferential system among the Danubian countries was recommended but the scheme ran into opposition. The Stresa conference of September 1932 concentrated on the economic problems of the Danubian area but failed to find permanent solutions. Great power rivalries were too closely involved. To counter the German military revival France turned to Italy and the Soviet Union (46). Mussolini's proposal of March 1933 for a Four Power Pact of Britain, France, Germany and Italy was accepted but the pact was never ratified. The pact affirmed 'the principle of revision of the peace treaties' and France's eastern allies protested because revision threatened their existence.

'The old Adam', in Sir Robert Vansittart's phrase, had triumphed. How far were the methods of diplomacy responsible for the failure to transform international relations? Writing to Sir Maurice Hankey, secretary to the cabinet, in October 1933, Lord Robert Cecil, British delegate to the disarmament conference, blamed secret diplomacy, the methods of the Congress of Vienna (45). Hankey disagreed and argued that secret diplomacy had achieved much. Cecil ignored the fact that at Geneva the League was notorious for its hotel-room diplomacy. The controversy generated more heat than light because neither correspondent attempted to define open and secret diplomacy. The two methods were complementary, not alternatives.

31   Naval disarmament : France versus the Anglo-Saxon powers, 1930

Memorandum for the French prime minister, André Tardieu, 13 January 1930

The Political problems of the London Conference

Technical and as secret as possible, is how the Americans and British would like this Conference.

Political and as public as possible, is how we want it.

To support this position, which France took in her Note to England. . .what is our strength, what are our arguments?

I

Our Strength

(a) for the party in power in England as well as in the United States. the London Conference has got to be a success. Whereas for the French government it will be something of a success in domestic and foreign policies — because of the anxieties of our Geneva friends — if this Conference fails in the narrow and personal form which the Anglo-Saxons intend it to have.

Hoover and MacDonald [respectively President of the United States and British prime minister] who have until now disappointed their supporters in internal policy, have staked their futures on the Conference: if it succeeds, the renewal, this year, of the House of Representatives and of a third of the Senate will be favourable to the Republican Administration, and MacDonald will be able to risk a general election.

They need a success so badly that they have already found a way to salvage something from the conference. As the conference approaches, their insistence on discussing a deferred replacement of cruisers and a reduction of their tonnage betrays their anxiety on the subject of auxiliary vessels. An agreement on battleships can be reached probably by five [Powers], certainly by three [Powers], and this. . .would mean a substantial reduction for the tax payer. . . .

The fate of these auxiliary vessels depends primarily on us, for the English figures assume that we will resign ourselves. . .to the percentage they give us. But politically we do not need success at any price.

(b) We are in a strong position since we possess the necessary resources to complete our maximum programme which. . .has spared our fleet the dead weight (battleships) carried by the other fleets, and which has provided the types of vessels which most trouble the leading naval powers.

Thus the English are ready to propose the suppression of our submarines—which they fear—in return for the suppression of their cruisers—which are an embarrassment to them.

(c) What is also a source of strength to us is that for the past three months the evolution of the negotiations has tended to weaken the starting point of the Anglo-Saxons and to confirm our own, as detailed in our Note to England.

In Washington Hoover and MacDonald discussed three political questions—the Pact of Paris (Kellogg-Briand Pact), parity, freedom of the Seas. . . .As for the third, MacDonald and Dawes [American negotiator] were to discuss it in London and it was hinted that an accord would be reached by the end of the year—before the Conference.

But these conversations have not been started and in the Commons, on his return, MacDonald declared that the Conference would not discuss the freedom of the seas and that the subject would be reserved for bilateral Anglo-American talks. Hoover confirmed this declaration.

This did not prevent Hoover, a few days later, in November, from returning to the subject when he proposed the complete freedom of foodships in wartime. Silence from the English.

Nor did this stop the Foreign Office in December from raising the subject by publishing a White Paper on England's support for the optional clause of Article 36 of the Statute of the Permanent Court of International Justice, in which it stated that for League members, there should no longer be neutrals in a war of repression authorized by the League of Nations. . . .

This public conversation in fits and starts. . .has underlined the profound disagreement of their policies beneath the apparent technical accord. . . .

II

Our Policy

We are then well placed to say no.

But we must do our utmost not to discourage America. If its imposing delegation—the first to be sent to Europe since the end of the war—returns empty-handed, we may have to wait perhaps another ten years for a third delegation. Let us recognize that in ten years America has made a few steps to meet us. Under Harding [American President] she was set on ruining the League of Nations; now she is collaborating on technical and humanitarian problems. . .this time, she comes as a suitor, which is not often; why not try to make her take a further step?. . . .

It is by trying to find a way for America to collaborate with Europe that we will bring her back to Europe and towards the League of Nations, which England would like to be free of. The League of Nations in Article 16 is deprived of sanctions; article 16 cannot be applied without England; England will only apply article 16 if she is assured of American policy on the freedom of the seas. Thus, through England, the United States weighs on Europe.

The interdependence of armaments

We must cling to the principle desperately because of our geographical and political situation.

Now we have agreed to go to London to deliberate on naval armaments alone. There the Americans and English are proposing to fix the figures by taking as a principle a security system (Pact of Paris) which is different to the security system (Covenant) on which the discussion on other armaments has been based hitherto and according to a method. . .which is different from the method prescribed by Article VIII of the Covenant. . . .For the Anglo-Saxons. . .there cannot and there must not be interdependence of armaments, for they are not all on the same moral plane, naval armaments being quite separate.

A natural sentiment for peoples protected by the sea, depending on their fleets for a quasi-absolute security and priding themselves on having always put their navies at the service of liberty and civilization.

A sentiment reinforced by the Pact of Paris. Because of the Pact England and the United States consider that a war between them would be 'unthinkable'. The naval armaments, of which they have the majority, lose in their eyes any aggressive purpose. The only possible war is a police action against an aggressor; now naval forces will be the best weapons for a policeman, since they will be able to re-establish peace in any part of the world without bloodshed (blockade); thus they are moral armaments. . . .

It is quite different for land and air forces. The English and Americans are convinced that a future war for them (police action) or between them (concerning the freedom of the seas) can only come from two continents (Far East, Europe above all). So in their view the armaments of the continental powers involve in themselves a power of aggression and domination. . .so they are immoral.

Such is the scheme of ideas of the 200 million men who share the nonconformist spirit. Relying on the promptings of their conscience, they make all their judgments in moral terms. There is no alliance between the United States and the British Empire. . .but beneath their invocation of the Pact of Paris and of parity, there is a collusion of moral instincts. . . .

. . .Faced with French strength, England is not seeking to cooperate with us but to reduce our power.

This idea that it is high time to curb French power is a national idea in England, common to Labourites, Liberals and even Conservatives. For monetary, financial and economic reasons we are envied, we are becoming a nuisance, more than that, dangerous, if we are allowed to have the army and fleet corresponding to our resources. Thus there is a complete contrast between the sentimental sympathy for the United States and its moral armaments and the distrust towards France and her immoral armaments. . . .

Let us suppose that France accepts definitive figures in London, figures such that London and Washington are henceforth assured that their monopoly has been achieved at the least possible expense, what will happen at the General Disarmament Conference in Geneva? America and England, having already excluded naval matters from the discussion, will be present more as arbiters than as parties to the negotiations. Their idea will be the levelling of European armies, hence the destruction of the system of which the French army and its allies is the centre. They will support Germany. . . .

If we claim a directing role in the unification of Europe let us not give here and now the great maritime powers the instrument of an hegemony which they will use to neutralize. . .the forces of continental Europe *in order to keep them quiet.*

It is necessary that at the General Disarmament Conference the United States and England should have to defend their naval armaments against a threat of an increase in the European tonnage. In London let us indicate a tonnage on which the final decision will form part of the negotiations on other armaments. . . .

French   foreign   ministry   archives,
Tardieu Papers, volume 41.

32   French plans for Franco–German economic cooperation, 1930

Letter from Sir William Tyrrell, British ambassador in Paris, to Sir Robert Vansittart, permanent under secretary of state for foreign affairs, 11 February 1930.

My dear Van,

I have been thinking over your letter of 3 February about the Franco-German business and Sargent's [foreign office official] Secret letter C.1002/G of 6 February on the same subject.

2 On receipt of your letter of 3 February I thought the first thing to do was to get in touch with Serruys [director of trade agreements, French commerce ministry] again and press him to come down to facts. What did he on so many occasions and Seydoux [deputy director of political affairs, French foreign ministry] in 1928, mean by holding this bogey of Franco-German economic cooperation over our heads? Were they actuated by a genuine wish to save us from future isolation, or did they simply want our help to strengthen France against German economic pressure? The reaction of Serruys to this approach was of considerable interest. He said that, put briefly, his position was as follows. We were always at the head of the group of commercial Powers who advocated European cooperation by means of the lowering of tariffs. We were the great traders and the Free Trade theorists, and it was easy to see why we wanted to lower tariffs. On the other hand there was a second theory as to the means of securing cooperation in Europe, and that was the theory advocated by France, to some extent by Germany and a number of other European Powers. This theory was based on the better organization of production. It was the Cartel or rationalization theory, and it contemplated special arrangements for special trades and special cases. It was easy to see that we were not sufficiently industrially organized to approve the second theory, and he, Serruys, and the people who thought like him, realized the folly of pressing it upon us. On the other hand we ought to realize that it was just as foolish for us to press our theory of reduction of tariffs on the French. They would never accept it, and in pressing it like we did, we were marching to defeat.

3 As he had now been asked to come out into the open, he would say that the manner in which we consistently advocated this theory and thought we could teach it to the French, as at one time our financiers like Bradbury had thought they could teach the French their methods of finance, created the most deplorable impression. If anything had

turned responsible French opinion against the tariff truce it was the clumsy interventions of Salter [director of league of nations economic and financial section] (apparently there has been a particularly tactless one quite lately) and what he called the Free Trade '*épouvantails*' who were constantly paraded by British delegations at Geneva. In Serruys's opinion neither the British theory nor the French theory could carry the day at the moment. What ought to be done was to talk in a free and friendly manner. Perhaps the French had been wrong in talking too much in the past to the Germans. But it was so difficult to talk with British officials. Many of them did not seem able to understand the continental theory or talk the continental language, and Serruys quoted Chapman in this connexion. Fountain was better. But we ought to talk, to see other's difficulties and the matters on which it was possible *through Geneva* — and Serruys was very insistent on Geneva — to make progress. Thus the results of the Conference on the Treatment of Foreigners and the Import and Export restrictions, were unfortunate, and we ought to get some definite agreement on these questions and talk over the most-favoured-nation theory and commercial arbitration and matters like that. Flandin [French minister of commerce] was a moderate and intelligent man, and one whose moderation had been much appreciated by the Germans. Our delegation to the Tariff Truce Conference ought to talk with him. He, Serruys, would do all he could to help.

4 He wished to warn me that the doctrinaire attitude of the British officials had already exhausted the patience of a number of influential people in France and apparently in Germany as well. These people were headed by Loucheur [minister of labour] and had got hold of Briand [French foreign minister], who, Serruys said, is being pushed all the time in the same direction by his chef de Cabinet, Léger. This is interesting, as unlike so many of his colleagues in the Ministry, Léger, though a man of great brilliance and charm, does not give the impression of knowing too clearly where he is going. Serruys said that Loucheur and Léger and under their influence Briand — and this was what he wanted to tell me the other day — were definitely out for the federalization of Europe on the economic basis of the organization of production, rationalization etc., and that as our attitude seemed to them so hopeless they were ready with Germany to organize Europe without us. Their ideas were still nebulous and they did not realize the difficulties and dangers, but they thought they could organize Europe behind some kind of tariff barrier which would be erected to our disadvantage and still more to that of the United States (see in this

connexion Chapman's letter to Howard Smith of 27 January, your despatch No. 292 (W 961/451/98) of 6 February). Loucheur and Co. seemed to think that such a scheme would appeal to the European agricultural countries, such as Hungary, just as much as to the industrial countries like Germany and France, since they would each receive advantages. Serruys said that the elaboration of such a scheme would necessitate first a long and difficult study of the possibilities of modifying the theory of the most-favoured-nation clause. It is of a certain significance, though it has not necessarily any bearing on our own position in this matter, that such a study has been advocated by Deputies in the Chamber within the last few weeks. Serruys said that in certain German circles the Loucheur proposals were much approved, and that he was often pressed by the Germans with whom he negotiated, notably Trendelenburg [state secretary in Reich economics ministry] in this connexion. Incidentally we have been told by the German Embassy here that there is no difficulty between them and the French on the economic side of the organization of Europe; it is on the political side that the difficulty lies.

5 With reference to the report mentioned in Sargent's letter of 6 February, I have no information of any recent negotiations here by Rechberg [German industrialist], but I know from recent speeches etc. that people like Paul Reynaud [leading French politican] well towards the Right of the Chamber, favour closer relations with Germany. As certain people in France want to get us in to strengthen them against Germany, it seems to me not impossible that there are Germans who, for the opposite reason, wish to keep us out. But on this Rumbold [British ambassador in Berlin] must advise, not I.

6 Serruys seemed to think that as to whether Loucheur or the opposite school of opinion finally obtains the victory, really depends a great deal on the attitude we now take up ourselves. If we show ourselves friendly, sympathetic, helpful and ready to listen, we may keep this movement on the right lines and one from which we shall not suffer. On the other hand if we continue to take up what the French consider to be the doctrinaire and suspicious and unsympathetic attitude, I do think there is a possibility that an attempt will be made to proceed without us.

7 My despatch on the whole question, political and economic will reach you this week.

Public Record Office, F.O.
371/14365/K5786

33 Britain assesses Briand's proposal for a European Federal Union, 1930

British Foreign Office memorandum 30 May 1930

The Memorandum for which M. Briand has kept Europe waiting all these months, is at least at first sight, a surprising and disappointing work. It is permeated by a vague and puzzling idealism expressed in such phrases as 'collective responsibility in the face of the danger which threatens the peace of Europe', 'need for a permanent *régime* of solidarity', and much else which may mean a great deal or may mean nothing at all. But M. Briand makes certain very definite proposals. The chief of these are for the agreement of all European Members of the League to draw up a Pact affirming the principle of the moral union of Europe; and for the creation of a 'European Association' of these States to express the idea of the establishment of a 'federal' system. This 'Association' is not to be taken as in any way derogating from the full political and economic sovereignty of its members, or as being in any sense directed against non-European States. M. Briand justifies his proposal by reference to Article 21 of the Covenant with its authorization of such 'regional understandings as the Monroe Doctrine'. He prescribes for it three organs corresponding to the Assembly, Council and Secretariat of the League, which he would call, respectively, the European Conference, the Permanent Political Committee and the Secretariat. These bodies would all have their seat at Geneva, and the meetings of the Conference and the Committee would normally coincide with those of the Assembly and Council of the League of Nations.

It may be noted as of first and singular importance that M. Briand insists that in the work of this proposed 'European Association' economic problems should be subordinated to political problems. This curious proposal is in direct contradiction to that made in M. Briand's September speech, in which he had insisted that the Association would be 'primarily economic' and that the economic problem was both the most urgent and the easiest to settle. Moreover, the whole point of such schemes of Pan-European organization as are identified with the names of Count Coudenhove-Kalergi [founder of the Pan-European Union] and other theorists is the rationalization and unification of European resources and their protection against extra-European competition, particularly that of the United States of America. If all idea of a Pan-European economic unit is to be dismissed as 'incompatible with the principles of the League of Nations', then all that M. Briand's proposals, if taken literally, would seem to amount to is the assertion of the principle 'Europe for the Europeans' and the attempt to remove European affairs from the immediate cognizance of the League of Nations, and to reserve them for discussion in the first place by the League's European Members, leaving to the League itself only the role of ultimate approval and supervision.

It certainly appears essential to consider sooner or later how M. Briand's proposals, if they could be carried out, would affect the prestige and utility of the League. There seems to be every reason to fear that in practice the League's work and prestige might be adversely affected. European affairs are the most interesting of the League's many political activities, and the removal of these from its general cognizance would certainly destroy much of the League's authority. Moreover, on many occasions it has been in the past of importance to draw British Dominions and Asiatic and American States into an active participation in questions which under the new proposals might be reserved as European questions. M. Briand's proposed organization could hardly fail to interfere with many of the practical activities already carried on by various organs of the League, and might well prove an embarrassing rival to it, while it is hard to see how it could, within a measurable period of time, become more efficient. In a word, if it did not actually embarrass and hamper the activities of the League, the European Conference Permament Committee and Secretariat would at best simply duplicate those activities.

It is probably more profitable to consider not what M. Briand literally says, but what his real intentions are. Two alternatives present themselves:

1 It is conceivable (though very improbable) that M. Briand was not serious when he spoke of the urgency of economic reorganization at Geneva last September; or (it may be from apprehension of British and American criticisms) he may indeed have been serious then, but has since changed his mind. In this case we are forced to take it that M. Briand is making his present proposals as a political move. He may think that the establishment of his European Association would have set a further seal on the sanctity of the present territorial and political organization of Europe established by the Peace Treaties and post-War arrangements. It would be strange if he seriously believes that all or even the majority of European Powers would be likely to accept such a plan, which would offer most of them no advantages and would in

their eyes appear to merely reinforce France's political hegemony in Europe. Perhaps, then, M. Briand calculates that the refusal, which is to be expected, of Germany, Italy and other Powers to entertain his proposals, ostensibly directed as they are towards a high moral ideal of stabilization and cooperation, may both discredit the general policy of these countries in the eyes of the world, and provide him with convincing proofs on which future French Governments can dilate, that France, alone or chief of the European Powers, thinks and works for the salvation of Europe. All this is possible, perhaps even probable; it is typical of a certain kind of French policy, but it does not fit in with what we know of M. Briand. Almost alone among French politicians he has in recent years consistently shown himself a good European, a friend of peace and of the improvement of international relations. It would be disappointing to have to fall back on the conclusion that M. Briand had been persuaded or coerced into the view that all there is for him to work for now and in the future is the maintenance of France's political supremacy. Moreover the attempt is really too barefaced to be likely to succeed. Germany, Italy and other Powers are not likely to fall into the trap, if trap there be.

2 It would be well, then, to assume that M. Briand is not animated by this cynical intention, but that on the contrary he genuinely desires to make the peoples and Government of Europe understand that they have important common interests, and that they can greatly benefit both themselves and the world at large by forgetting their traditional conflicts and animosities and by cooperating more effectively to promote these interests. If this is really his intention, he is aiming at something more positive and practical than the vague political organization outlined in his memorandum. Though he emphasizes the necessity of political association as a preliminary to all European reorganization, it may well be that what he has in mind is not only, perhaps not even primarily, further military and political security for France (though no doubt he does desire this) but also such regrouping and consolidation of European finance and industry as to assure France and the rest of Europe against the ever-growing strength of non-European and especially American competition. This is primarily what has always been meant by the 'United States of Europe' or 'Pan-Europa' and without this it is hard to see that the word 'Pan-Europa' can mean anything at all. It is difficult to believe that M. Briand, who has repeatedly expressed his sympathy for the Pan-European idea, should not have something like this at the back of his mind; indeed, it is only the economic aspect of European

reorganization which could offer any attraction to Germany, Italy and many other European States, and if Europe is ever to be brought into a closer political formation it can surely be only as a result of closer economic ties. It is true that M. Briand in his memorandum makes no proposal of the sort and even appears to veto the idea of the protection of Europe from extra-European competition, but it is interesting to observe that in the list of subjects which he draws up as appropriate for consideration by his European Association the first of the nine headings is that dealing with economics, and this is the only one of the nine categories which seems to contain anything of first importance. M. Briand under this heading puts down for discussion 'the effective realization in Europe of the programme laid down by the last Economic Conference of the League of Nations; control of the policy of industrial unions and cartels between different countries; examination of and preparation for all possible future measures for the progressive reduction of tariffs, etc.'. . . .

To sum up, what is in the first place needed is fuller information as to M. Briand's real intentions and the attitude of European Governments. As this information comes in, various questions will arise requiring close departmental consideration. In any case, it would appear both unsatisfactory and unwise to attempt to give any complete or final answer to the memorandum by 15 July, the date mentioned by M. Briand.

It is suggested that His Majesty's Government should base their policy on the following principles:

(i) We can agree to no proposals which in practice (whatever their intention) may damage the prestige and authority of the League;

(ii) If, therefore, there is to be new machinery, it should be built into the existing framework of the League;

(iii) We warmly desire to improve the cooperation between European countries for the promotion of their common interests, or will help to bring it about;

(iv) We cannot, however, help to create any political or economic group which could in any way be regarded as hostile to the American or any other continent, or which weaken our political cooperation with the other members of the British Commonwealth;

(v) We believe that in economic and technical matters much might be done which would not be open to objection in these respects which would promote British interests;

(vi) We must not antagonize Latin-America, Asia or any other section of the League. This being so, M. Briand's proposals should not

be discussed in a 'European' Conference run as a rival meeting outside
the Assembly, but rather in the Committees of the Assembly itself.

If these principles are accepted, it is suggested that His Majesty's
Government, if they reply before or on 15 July, should confine themselves to an expression of warm sympathy with the high ideals of
European cooperation and to the assurance that they will give these
and all future proposals from the French Government the fullest
consideration both on their own part and in consultation with His
Majesty's Governments in the Dominions. There might be added the
observation that, as M. Briand's proposals affect either directly or
indirectly all members of the League of Nations, His Majesty's
Government assume that M. Briand intends to place them on the
Agenda of the Assembly either this year or in 1931.

DBFP, 2nd series, I, (no. 189)

34   President Hoover's proposal for a Moratorium on War Debt and Reparation Payments, June 1931

The American Government proposes the postponement during one
year of payments on intergovernmental debts, reparations and relief
debts, both principal and interest, of course, not including obligations
held by private parties. Subject to confirmation by Congress, the
American Government will postpone all payments upon the debts of
foreign governments to the American Government payable during the
fiscal year beginning 1 July next, conditional on a like postponement
for one year of all payments or intergovernmental debts owing the
important creditor powers.

The purpose of this action is to give the forthcoming year to the
economic recovery of the world and to help free the recuperative forces
already in motion in the United States from retarding influences from
abroad.

The world-wide depression has affected the countries of Europe
more severely than our own. Some of these countries are feeling to a
serious extent the drain of this depression on national economy. The
fabric of intergovernmental debts, supportable in normal times,
weighs heavily in the midst of this depression.

From a variety of causes arising out of the depression such as the fall
in the price of foreign commodities and the lack of confidence in
economic and political stability abroad there is an abnormal movement of gold into the United States which is lowering the credit

stability of many foreign countries. These and the other difficulties abroad diminish buying power for our exports and in a measure are the cause of our continued unemployment and continued lower prices to our farmers.

Wise and timely action should contribute to relieve the pressure of these adverse forces in foreign countries and should assist in the re-establishment of confidence, thus forwarding political peace and economic stability in the world.

Authority of the President to deal with this problem is limited as this action must be supported by the Congress. It has been assured the cordial support of leading members of both parties in the Senate and the House. The essence of this proposition is to give time to permit debtor governments to recover their national prosperity. I am suggesting to the American people that they be wise creditors in their own interest and be good neighbors.

I wish to take this occasion also to frankly state my views upon our relations to German reparations and the debts owed to us by the allied Governments of Europe. Our government has not been a party to, or exerted any voice in determination of reparation obligations. We purposely did not participate in either general reparations or the division of colonies or property. The repayments of debts due to us from the Allies for the advances for war and reconstruction were settled upon a basis not contingent upon German reparations or related thereto. Therefore, reparations are necessarily wholly a European problem with which we have no relation.

I do not approve in any remote sense of the cancellation of the debts to us. World confidence would not be enhanced by such action. None of our debtor nations have ever suggested it. But as the basis of the settlement of these debts was the capacity under normal conditions of the debtor to pay, we should be consistent with our own policies and principles if we take into account the abnormal situation now existing in the world. I am sure the American people have no desire to attempt to extract any sum beyond the capacity of any debtor to pay and it is our view that broad vision requires that our government should recognize the situation as it exists.

This course of action is entirely consistent which the policy with we have hitherto pursued. We are not involved in the discussion of strictly European problems, of which the payment of German reparations is one. It represents our willingness to make a contribution to the early restoration of world prosperity in which our own people have so deep an interest.

I wish further to add that while this action has no bearing on the conference for limitation of land armaments to be held next February, inasmuch as the burden of competitive armaments has contributed to bring about this depression, we trust that by this evidence of our desire to assist we shall have contributed to the good will which is so necessary in the solution of this major question.

> Cited in: *Economic History of Europe: Twentieth Century*, ed. Shephard B. Clough *et al.* (London, Macmillan, 1969), pp. 224 – 6

35 Sir John Simon on the Manchurian crisis, 1931

Memorandum from Sir John Simon, foreign secretary, to the Cabinet, 23 November, 1931.

There has been an unsolved Sino-Japanese problem in Manchuria for over twenty years—ever since the Japanese succeeded to Russian rights in that region after the Russo-Japanese war [of 1904 – 5] The Chinese have never willingly accepted the Japanese position in Manchuria. In recent years their resistance—for the most part passive—has taken on a more active character. There have been frequent incidents and great friction eventually culminating in the affair of 18 September last. The Japanese military force guarding the zone of the South Manchuria Railway, alleging an attack by Chinese troops on the railway line just north of Mukden, carried out what was evidently a carefully prepared *coup* and proceeded systematically to drive out the Chinese authorities and establish their own authorities instead. On 21 September China appealed to the Council of the League, then in session at Geneva, under Article II of the Covenant. On 30 September the Council adopted unanimously a Resolution in which it took note of the Japanese representative's statement that his Government would continue as rapidly as possible the withdrawal of its troops, which had already been begun, into the railway zone in proportion as the safety of the lives and property of Japanese nationals was effectively assured and that his Government hoped to carry out this intention in full as speedily as may be. The Japanese Government, however, failed to carry out the assurances given to the Council which therefore met again at Geneva from 13 – 24 October. The Japanese representative now adopted the attitude that a preliminary agreement, binding

China to recognize Japan's treaty rights in Manchuria, was an essential element of security and must be a condition precedent to evacuation. The other members of the Council on the other hand maintained that evacuation must be a condition precedent to the negotiations for a settlement of the questions in dispute between the parties. On 24 October, therefore, the Council adopted a draft Resolution by thirteen votes to one (the Japanese alone voting against) calling upon Japan to evacuate within three weeks, namely by 16 November, the date fixed for the next meeting of the Council. Owing to the want of unanimity, this resolution had no juristic effect. Japanese military operations in execution of the programme above described have continued during this session of the Council as during the last. The Japanese representative has been persuaded to propose that a League Commission should visit Manchuria and China, but it is very doubtful whether agreement can be reached as to the terms of reference of this Commission. The Chinese delegate has indicated that he does not reject, in principle, the suggestion of a Commission, but that its appointment should not furnish a pretext for delay in Japanese evacuation. If the appointment of such a Commission could be secured by general consent of the members of the Council, it would undoubtedly be able to supply much useful information on points which are at present obscure or disputed between contesting parties.

There is a widespread feeling, which I believe to be justified, that although Japan has undoubtedly acted in a way contrary to the principles of the Covenant by taking the law into her own hands, she has a real grievance against China and the merits of the matter are complicated by a further consideration. This is not a case in which the armed forces of one country have crossed the frontiers of another in circumstances where they had no previous right to be on the other's soil. Japans owns the South Manchurian Railway and has been entitled throughout to have a body of Japanese guards upon the strip of land through which the railway runs. Japan's case is that, having her armed guards lawfully there, she was compelled by the failure of China to provide reasonable protection for Japanese lives and property in Manchuria in the face of attacks of Chinese bandits, and of an attack upon the line itself, to move Japanese forces forward and to occupy points in Manchuria which are beyond the line of the railway. This has grown by degrees into what is in effect an organized occupation, leading in its turn to serious fighting and bombing. But Japan continues to insist that she has no territorial ambitions in Manchuria — an expression, it will be observed, which does not necessarily imply that she is not thinking of some sort of protectorate, at any rate in Southern Manchuria. In spite of Japan's protests to the contrary, there can of course be no real doubt that she is pursuing the course of putting pressure on China by means of this occupation for the purpose of securing that the Japanese claims against China in that region may be met, e.g. the stopping of cut-throat competition with the South Manchurian Railway, which Japan asserts is already promised to her by a Protocol of 1905 and the reaffirmation by China of the rights which Japan claims to have secured by a Treaty of 1915.

It may well be that the Chinese Delegate will put into effect the threat which he has often uttered, and appeal to the Council under Article 15 of the Covenant.

Under the Article the Council must make an investigation and could decide, independently of the parties, to send out a Commission of Enquiry. It has hitherto been desired to avoid the application of Article 15 on the ground that it introduces a more menacing atmosphere. In fact, it seems difficult to see how the position is in that respect changed. Indeed, it might give a respite of six to nine months during which passion may cool. But M. Briand's own conversations with me show that he is personally anxious to keep all discussion within Article II.

DBFP, 2nd series, VIII, no. 76.

36   Britain's dilemma in the Far East, 1932

Memorandum by Sir John Pratt, foreign officer adviser, 1 February 1932
The Shanghai Situation, 1 February.

1   There are two significant items of news today (*a*) Mr Yoshizawa's [Japanese delegate to the League of Nations] statement reported in today's *Times* foreshadowing the sending of *military* (as distinct from naval) reinforcements to Shanghai, (*b*) the naval demonstration at Nanking.

2   We must expect that hostilities will continue in Shanghai as long as the Japanese forces remain there, that they will become more and more serious, and that more and more Japanese troops will be poured into Shanghai.

3   This situation may (and indeed is likely to) end in the Japanese forces destroying a large part of the native city and suburbs of Shanghai (which have a Chinese population of approximately two

million) and ousting the authority of the Shanghai Municipal Council from the whole area of the International Settlement. I gather from a recent telegram of Mr Brenan's that once this has happened the former status of the Settlement will never be restored: it will become a Japanese concession.

4 If Japan continues unchecked the British will have to retire altogether from the Far East. If it is decided that we must check Japan certain preliminary measures could be adopted – such as rupture of diplomatic and economic relations – but in the end Japan can only be checked by force. Ultimately we will be faced with the alternatives of going to war with Japan or retiring from the Far East. A retirement from the Far East might be the prelude to a retirement from India.

This memorandum was minuted by Sir V. Wellesley [deputy Under Secretary of State] and Sir R. Vansittart [permanent Under Secretary of State] and initialled by Sir John Simon, as follows: 'The dangers to which Sir J. Pratt calls attention are undoubtedly very real ones the more so since we now know that the Japanese Naval and Military Authorities are completely out of hand and the Japanese Government more or less impotent. V.W.1/2/32.'

'I agree with Sir J. Pratt's estimate both of the immediate and ultimate problems and dangers. The ultimate ones are those on his first page [paras. 1 – 4]. The conclusions must logically be these.

'(1) If Japan continues unchecked and increasingly, as she indeed seems bent on doing, our position and vast interests in the Far East will never recover. This may well spread to the Middle East. The Japanese victory in 1904 was the beginning of trouble there.

'(2) *We* are incapable of checking Japan in any way if she really means business and has sized us up, as she certainly has done.

'(3) Therefore we must eventually be done for in the Far East, unless

'(4) The United States are eventually prepared to use force.

'(5) It is universally assumed here that the US will never use force.

'(6) I do not agree that this is necessarily so. The same was said of the US in the Great War. Eventually she was kicked in by the Germans. The Japanese may end by kicking in the US too, if they go on long enough kicking as they are now.

'(7) The Japanese are more afraid of the US than of us, and for obvious reasons. At present, however, they share our low view of American fighting spirit.

'(8) By ourselves we must eventually swallow any and every humiliation in the Far East. If there is some limit to American submissiveness, this is not necessarily so.

'(9) We can therefore frame no policy and face no future till we are sure on this all-important point. To *assume* that there is no limit is a counsel of despair.

'(10) We must let the provocation proceed further than at present. At some point, however, we shall, if Sir J. Pratt is right, have to know where we stand on this vital question. When that moment comes, it will be impossible to make sure either by telephone or telegram. The moment, however, has of course not yet come.

'(11) If and when this sounding has to be taken, there will probably be a lull in Japanese aggression till we and they know the answer. R.V., 1 Feb.'

'[To] Secretary of State
'I think there is an universal tendency to go to great lengths of (5) in my annexed minute. I suggest that you should consider it in connection with Sir J. Pratt's memorandum, and put the logical sequence to your colleagues. Till this sequence has been faced (see (9) in my minute) we can have no long-range, or even short-range, policy in the Far East. We must live from hand to mouth — an humiliating process — unless we have made up, or cleared, our minds upon the answer to (6). R.V., 1 Feb' 'J.S., 3 Feb.'

DBFP, 2nd series, IX, no. 238

37 France's scheme for a Danubian economic entente rejected, 1932

French foreign ministry memorandum, 11 May 1932

Note on the scheme for a Danubian entente

The malaise caused by the break-up of the Austro-Hungarian Empire, which has been latent since the war, has greatly increased because of the world economic crisis. More and more distress signals have come from countries which were formerly complementary and whose normal patterns of trade have been suddenly broken. The authors of the Austro-German customs union plan have invoked the need to 'enlarge' the economic activity of Austria, and many similarly inspired plans have come from the pens of central European economists.

The purely financial remedies have revealed their inadequacy; the loans offered to Hungary and Austria have only succeeded in delaying the evolution of the crisis afflicting these countries. On the whole, they have acted as stimulants artificially maintaining the strength of a sick man. The two Hungarian bankruptcies and the worsening of the situation of Austria are the proof. One may even consider that the loans made to these states are tending to increase their difficulties. . .and so delay their recovery.

Moreover after the unfortunate experience which foreign creditors who invested capital in Austria and Hungary have just received, it seems difficult to secure new loans in the future if the available capital cannot count on a change in the economic climate of the debtor countries.

For these reasons, the Department considered it to be a matter of urgency to favour the efforts for a rapprochement of the states of Danubian Europe — the only way to secure a return to normal economic conditions.

Specific circumstances have moreover provided the possibility of developing the Department's interest: firstly the report of the League of Nations Financial Committee, approved on 29 January, drew the attention of interested governments to the situation of Austria and Hungary and urged the establishment of a new commercial system between these countries and their neighbours. Secondly, the urgent appeal that M. Buresch, the Austrian Chancellor, addressed on 16 February to the ministers of France, Great Britain, Germany and Italy. M. Buresch invited the great powers to collaborate in the recovery of the Austrian economy and expressed Austria's desire to open negotiations for an economic rapprochement with neighbouring states and with other interested states.

This appeal which confirmed our conviction that in the near future the countries of central Europe would find it impossible to meet their financial commitments unless they developed their own trade, determined the French government to draw up at once an overall scheme for the reorganization of economic relations between the Danubian states.

On 2 March therefore the French government sent to the British, Italian and German governments an aide-mémoire informing them of our viewpoint. This aide-mémoire proposed that a preferential system should be created between the five Danubian countries (Hungary, Austria, Czechoslovakia, Rumania and Yugoslavia). It would be for these states to undertake the necessary planning for the establishment of this system. The British, Italian and German governments were invited to concert with the French government. . . .

In the thinking of the French government such an economic

rapprochement of the Danubian states would constitute the comple-
ment to the bilateral agreements concluded on the recommendation
of the League of Nations and in conformity with the constructive plan
presented by M. Briand after the bid for an Austro-German customs
union. If these latter agreements, which are in harmony with the
policy of European mutual aid recommended by the French government, are capable in part of solving the agricultural crisis affecting the
Balkan and Central European states, it must not be concealed that
they alone are not sufficient to bring about a fundamental improvement in the economic conditions of these countries. To complete the
work of financial and economic reovery followed by the League it was
necessary to consider an overall plan for the trade of Danubian
Europe. Such a formula is moreover wholly in harmony with a healthy
policy of European cooperation. . . .

On the other hand, on the purely economic level, it must be stressed
that the French plan aims only at renewing broken links and at
suppressing artificial obstacles to the natural trade patterns of
complementary regions. It is a question in fact of lowering the barriers
erected by the protectionism of the new states and of organizing the
framework for a new economic life.

There is moreover no need to stress France's interest in seeing the
reconstitution of an economic unity which would keep Austria and
Hungary out of the German or Italian orbits as well as moderating
Hungary's hostility towards the Little Entente.

In its reply to the French Government (8 March) the Italian government declared that it fully shared the French government's preoccupation concerning. . .Central Europe. However it pointed out that
Italy had already an interest in the economy of the Danubian states
since it has a special relationship with them. . . .

While considering a general solution desirable the Italian government stated that the first priority was for agreements with Austria and
Hungary. The way was prepared by the arrangements Italy had
concluded with the governments of Vienna and Budapest (Semering
agreements).

Doubtless it was necessary for discussion to take place between the
Danubian states but, in the opinion of the Italian government,
negotiations should not take place without the direct participation of
France, Germany, Great Britain and Italy.

The result of this action could not however have an immediate
effect and in the meantime some financial help was necessary to save
the most threatened states (Austria, Hungary).

It seemed, then, from this reply that the French initiative had disturbed Italy's own efforts and all the attention of the government of Rome was concentrated on concluding agreements with Austria and Hungary designed to isolate Czechoslovakia economically and to prevent a regrouping of Danubian states.

The German government's reply (15 March) revealed an analogous policy. . . .

The British government's reply (22 March) expressed the view that mere discussions between the five Danubian states would be ineffective. The four great powers should meet without delay to examine the general lines of a plan which would serve as an agenda for discussions between the Danubian states. The programme to be discussed by the four great powers. . .should include:

1 Special assistance measures for Austria and Hungary in the form of unilateral preferences granted by neighbouring countries (Danubian or not):

2 a general reduction of 10 per cent, for example, of all tariffs between the Danubian states. . . .

As had been agreed, preliminary Franco-British discussions in London on 4 April preceded the meeting on 6 April of the four great powers.

These preliminary talks resulted in the following conclusions: the proposed conference should be confined to the Danubian states. The invitation to be addressed to the Danubian states should include the following principles:

(a) The five states should agree to a general reduction of their tariffs which would not be less than 10 per cent for each category of articles, and they should consider the possibility of suppressing the economic barriers resulting from protectionism and similar measures.

(b) It would be necessary to envisage the granting of unilateral preferences by other states for Danubian agricultural products; but these states could not ask for preferential treatment for their own exports to the Danubian states.

(c) The conference of the five Danubian states could be chaired by a neutral, while the four great powers would form a committee to follow the proceedings.

(d) As regards financial help, the French government which has always insisted on the impossibility of action of this kind in the absence of an economic reorganization, agreed to the formation of a Committee of Treasury representatives of the four powers. . . .

The meeting of the Four (5 – 8 April) which followed the Franco-British discussions discussed the main lines of the scheme to be sent to the Danubian states. Now the opinions already expressed by the Rome and Berlin governments in their replies to the French government were hardened and clarified in such a manner that the conference could not succeed. The German delegation manifested in effect a marked hostility to the introduction of an interdanubian preferential system which, according to M. von Bülow [State secretary, German foreign ministry] would only profit Czechoslovakia and involve too heavy a sacrifice for German trade.

Without taking as firm a position on interdanubian preference, the Italians. . .insisted on the calling of a conference of 9 or 10 powers.

Faced with this opposition. . .M. Flandin [French finance minister]. . .had to refuse the French government's consent to the calling of a conference since the disagreement on fundamental questions prevented agreement on an agenda. . . .

> French foreign ministry archives,
> *Tardieu Papers*, volume 85.

38   Hitler's letter to Colonel von Reichenau, 4 December 1932

Reichenau was chief of staff of the army command in East Prussia.

Dear Colonel,

Through Pastor Müller I received the letter in which the staff of Military District 1 requested that a special directive should be issued to the Party and SA leaders in East Prussia asking them during the internal political struggle of the National Socialist German Workers Party in the province to take into account the grave dangers in foreign policy. Not only do I appreciate, but most unfortunately, I myself share the concern expressed in this letter. That I will do everything possible not to cause additional harm in the province is of course obvious. Since I very much fear that many people will not understand my measures and that the result can only too easily be interpreted in the negative sense, I feel constrained, Colonel, to give you in your capacity of Chief of Staff of the Reichswehr division the picture as I see it in justification of my action. If from the very start you are acquainted with the underlying aims of my movement, and my own principal ideas perhaps you will judge it differently.

The question of the territorial security of East Prussia is bound up with the external and internal political position of the Reich as a whole which I wish to outline in a few sentences. The outcome of the World

War did not allow France to realize her cherished aims in their entirety. Hopes of a general internal collapse of the Reich were in particular not fulfilled. The aim of the Peace Treaty of Versailles, insofar as it was dictated by French efforts, was thus the maintenance of as broad a political community of interest against Germany as possible. The territorial dissection of the Reich primarily served this aim. Since almost all the neighbouring states were bequeathed some German land it was hoped to forge a ring of allied nations with a common interest round Germany. In the East, Poland, a dependent of France, was thus to take the place of Russia, a power which at that time was of declining importance (and whose future development was then in any case unpredictable). The separation of East Prussia, through the Polish Corridor, could only have the effect of increasing the desire for incorporation of the Province into Poland, which surrounds it on all sides. In fact, immediately after the Treaty of Versailles was signed propaganda on behalf of a greater Poland was focused in this direction.

Indeed because of this obvious fear it was the aim of German foreign policy to try to reduce tension in the East by establishing close relations with Russia. While fully appreciating the political and military arguments I had always taken a firm line against what appeared to me to be a dangerous experiment. The reasons for my well known attitude, which were expressed especially clearly to General von Hammerstein [Chief of Army Command] many years ago, were and are the following:

1 Russia is no state but a *Weltanschauung* which is at present confined to this territory it may dominate, but which maintains sections in all other countries that not only strive for the realization of the same revolutionary aims but which, for the purposes of organization, come under the central control of Moscow. A victory of this idea in Germany must have unforeseen consequences. The more cooperation there is on political and military grounds with the centre of this poison, the more difficult is the struggle itself against this poison. The German people today are no more immune from communism than they were in 1917. At any rate in 1918 they were not immune from revolutionary ideas as such. Officers and statesmen can only understand this problem after they have become psychologists of peoples. Experience proves that this seldom happens.

2 For this reason I contend that Soviet diplomacy is not only unreliable but that in no sense can it be compared with foreign policy as conducted by other nations. It is thus incapable of negotiating or

(contracting) treaties. 'Treaties' can only be concluded when the contracting parties are on an equal ideological footing.

3 If ever, which God forbid, we are saved in an emergency through Soviet help this will immediately mean the hoisting of the Red Flag in Germany.

4 Insofar as the growing military strength of Russia reduces the value of the Polish alliance to France so that the real support for French aims against Germany in the East seem to be in jeopardy, France will either try to detach Russia from Poland, or, if this fails, she will drop Poland and let Russia take her place.

5 Political cooperation between Germany and Russia finds an unsympathetic response from the outside world. Economic coopera- tion will in time destroy our German industrial export trade.

Because of these considerations I have never ceased for approxi- mately twelve years from proposing closer ties, on the one hand with Italy on the other with England, as the most desirable aim to strive for in foreign policy.

I believe that developments now prove me right.

France, as a result of the obvious deterioration of her Polish ally, has tried, in my opinion successfully, to commit Russia in the Far East in order to reduce tension on the Russo-Polish border. From the non- Aggression Pact, which will soon be signed between Russia and Poland, this far-reaching action of France must be considered as having reached mainly a successful conclusion. But as a result we are in the middle of a new policy of encirclement, if it is not already complete. That France's newly acquired power in capital contributes significantly to this undertaking may be taken as proved as far as Poland is concerned. I also think it will probably (be used) in the future (in favour of) Russia, who is deficient in capital.

East Prussia is lost at the very moment a certain internal political situation in Germany creates an unfriendly atmosphere in the world for a Polish attack. The proclamation of a monarchy for instance, or the restoration of the House of Hohenzollern in whichever way it is envisaged today, would only precipitate this step.

The military resources and possibilities open to East Prussia are in my opinion inadequate for resistance with long-term prospects of success. The military support which is available from the Reich however is in my view, on account of the present political situation, absolutely nil. I contend that forcing the issue of theoretical rearma- ment is the worst danger. It is conceivable that France is no longer in a position to sabotage Germany's (claim for) equality of status (in armaments). On account of this the intervening period between the granting of theoretical equality of status and the time needed for the practical technical organization of rearmament will constitute the most dangerous epoch in German history. If ever there are reasons in favour of a preventive war, it will take the form of a French attack on Germany. Only military action of this kind will create the new facts desired, and the same world which today makes us a present of its theoretical good wishes will shy away from reversing accomplished facts by force of arms.

Nothing is more desirable for France therefore than to allow a third party to take the initiative in this new action. Causes and pretexts can be manufactured at any time.

As already emphasized I see the danger of this attack to be acute, and I believe that it would be as well to reckon with its outbreak at any moment.

On the other hand at present the possibilities of active participation by Germany in such a conflict are lacking. The reason is in no way to be attributed to lack of progress in technical rearmament but rather to the complete unfitness of the German people due to their spiritual, moral and political degeneration.

The German people today are divided into two groups holding different *Weltanschauungen*: in one group every conceivable form of military service to the present State can be written off. The following picture of the mental structure of our people emerges from the last election:

Communists	6	million
Social Democrats	7.4	"
Centre	4	"
State Party etc.	1	"
National Socialists	12	"
German National Peoples Party (including Steelhelmet)	3	"
German Peoples Party etc.	1	"

This means that if war is today forced on Germany more than half the nation are by nature more or less pacifist, one part being avowedly hostile to military service and defence. The opinion of individual generals that military training can uproot again education given on the political lines of a given Party *Weltanschauung* is just childish (in the event of an immediate outbreak of war this could in any case apply for only a very short length of time). Even two years military service in peace time was not enough to put a stop to Social Democracy. To argue from the fact that in 1914 the German Social Democrat Party worker did his duty is false. For it was not the avowed Marxist who did his duty at that time but the German who, in a state of inward elation, temporarily renounced Marxism. The avowed leaders of Marxism started their work in counteracting this only in 1915 and, after glorious resistance without precedent, they finally led the people to revolution in 1918 and thus the Reich to collapse.

The Social Democracy of that time cannot in any way be compared with the German Communist Party today. Marxism, which in the year 1914 was just a theoretical concept, has in practice today conquered a gigantic part of the world. A war for Germany in her present condition would expose the nation right from the very start to such a nervous strain that, at least as far as the interior is concerned, events of the first world war would afford no analogy.

The view that in this event it would be possible to have recourse to para-military formations is, considering the despised and persecuted way of looking at things at present, noble in the extreme, but it is not only in practice meaningless but rather fraught with terrible consequences. For the precise moment of the call-up of national units to the colours and their despatch (as more or less untrained cannon-fodder) to the front would provide the occasion for handing the home front over to the Red Mob. The year 1918 would be child's play in comparison with what would then happen.

Whereas our political and military strategists thus see German rearmament as a technical and organizational task, for me the prerequisite for any rearmament is the creation of a new unity of the German people in will and spirit. Unless this problem is solved all talk of 'equality of status' and 'rearmament' is superficial and stupid chatter.

This restoration to our people of unity in *Weltanschauung*, spirit and will has been the task which I set myself fourteen years ago and for which I have struggled ever since. That the official agencies of our civil and military authorities face this problem with complete indifference, not to say stupidity, does not surprise me. It has never ever been otherwise in history. None of the great ideas and reforms of mankind has emanated from corporations. Why should it be different today? But appreciation of this historical truth does not release anyone who has once recognized the enormous extent of such an idea, from coming forward on its behalf. I must therefore, however much I may dislike it, take a stand against, and fight unremittingly, each German government which is not determined and ready to promote the inward rearmament of the German people. From this all subsequent measures will take their course.

I consider the present cabinet of General von Schleicher [German Chancellor] to be in this respect especially unfortunate, because the person who holds office faces this problem with even less understanding than any other. This problem of the inward, spiritual rearmament of the nation cannot at present, any more than in past history, be solved by an army but only by a *Weltanschauung*. If the army busies itself with it, it allows itself to appear in the eyes of many to be partisan, just as, conversely, the task itself will seem compromised in the eyes of the masses. For neither the police nor the military have ever destroyed, far less have they created, a *Weltanschauung*. Without a *Weltanschauung* no human structure can endure in the long run. *Weltanschauungen* form the social contracts and foundations on which great human organizations must first be built. I therefore, as distinct from our present statesmen, see German tasks for the future to be the following.

1 The conquest of Marxism and its manifestations to the point of their complete obliteration. Establishment of a new spiritual unity and will of the people.

2 General mental, ethical and moral rearmament of the nation on the foundation of this new unity in a *Weltanschauung*.

3 Technical rearmament.

4 Organized exploitation of the energies of the people for the purpose of national defence.

5 Attaining legal recognition by the outside world of the new situation after it has already been brought into being.

Only a far-reaching process of regeneration, instead of the present experiments and quests for new provisional solutions, can lead to a final clear solution of the German crisis. On the basis of these ideas, Colonel, I request you to judge my attitude.

I will always — this is self-evident — do all that can be done to see that necessary regard is paid to a hard-pressed province. East Prussia can only be saved when Germany is saved. That this, the one possible solution, is again postponed and rendered more difficult by the new cabinet of Schleicher, is obvious. May it not at least resort to those experiments which would, I am convinced, make the attack prepared by France seem morally justified in the eyes of the world. For the world would consider itself fortunate if its motives for non-intervention in a Polish action — which with French support could not at present be prevented at all—could be furnished with reasons attributing the moral blame to (lie with) Germany.

Yours faithfully, Adolf Hitler.

Vierteljahrshefte für Zeitgeschichte, 7, 1959, pp. 428–37.

39 General Weygand reviews French defence policy, 16 January 1933

General Weygand was inspector general of the army, vice president of the Conseil Supérieur de la Guerre.

At a time when reorganization of the military forces of France is on the agenda, as a result of estimates to be made because of the reduction in contingents during the years 1935 to 1940, and negotiations in Geneva regarding limitation of armaments, as well as budgetary difficulties of 1933, it is important to define what France requires of her national forces as a whole. If we do not settle what purpose they must serve, we run the risk of treating these serious problems, whose solution determines the future and independence of the country, from a purely subjective point of view, losing sight of the very purpose of these forces. We thus become involved in arrangements of detail, partial concessions and reductions decided without a thorough inquiry. Pared down in this manner by retrenchments, none of which seems vital to those who agree to them but whose total and incidence multiply the destructive effects, the military forces will eventually suffer very grave impairment. If such procedures continue, these forces, in spite of the admirable devotion of the cadres, will gradually become incapable of fulfilling their basic function.

. . .The old formula, 'We must have an army which corresponds to the needs of our policy', has lost none of its value. It means that an army can be organized according to just principles only if the policy, which she must see carried out, is clearly defined.

France is profoundly pacifist. This is true, this is simple, but it is just too simple to be sufficient to define her policy. The policy of a great country like ours, which through her possessions has spread over the whole surface of the globe, has to reckon with various and complex elements which are the results of her geographic and demographic situation, the nature of her frontiers and the inclinations of her neighbours, the treaties in force and the agreements made with other powers.

1 France has land frontiers of more than 1,000km, of which she shares about 300km with Italy, and which are reinforced by the barrier of the Alps; she shares 300km of frontier with Germany without natural protection to the west of the Rhine. She is the only European country to have maritime frontiers opening on the north, west and south, on three seas which are free of ice all the year round. Her eastern and southeastern neighbours openly assert a policy of destruction of the state of things established by the treaties, and of aggressive intentions towards her. They do not even leave her ignorant of the terms and conditions of the future conflict, summed up in the newly fashionable term, 'sudden war', by land, sea and air.

The result is that the first duty of the military, air and naval forces of the national defence is to defend the territory while defending themselves against these attacks. However, the new conditions of sudden attack and barbarism which one is obliged to consider, force France, who refuses to be the aggressor, to withstand the attack and consequently to have on her frontiers a defence system which is always in good order and easily alerted. This necessity creates obligations as far as the present manpower, equipment service and calling up of reserves are concerned.

On the other hand, it must be made clear that the often-used term 'defensive army', has no meaning. Even in the defensive, especially in the defensive, an army which has neither the will nor the means to manoeuvre is doomed to defeat. Consequently, the defence system must include large manoeuvring units, in addition to the fortress units.

2 The German frontier, however, is common to France and Belgium. They are linked by an agreement for their joint defence. Belgium does not have the means of protecting the 120km which stretch from the south of Luxembourg to the Dutch Limburg against invasion. France must go to her rescue without delay in order to stop the enemy on this line. . . .There she will have the advantages of having to block 120km with the support of the Belgian army instead of 350km with her own forces alone, and of keeping the enemy at a distance from the rich country of the north. The extent of territory to be covered by French strategic deployment is therefore increased by a substantial part of Belgian territory. Consequently, new large manoeuvring units, certain of which must be capable of special speed,

are seen to be indispensable on this account.

3 We have another ally, Poland. The invasion of Polish Pomerania by the Germans is a common topic of conversation. What will be the attitude of France if this manifestation of 'sudden war' surprises her in the midst of peace? Will she immediately enter Germany to make the Germans respect the treaties and to take securities there? What will her present military condition allow her to do without having recourse to any mobilization measures? If what she can do is not sufficient, what preparations should she make?

4 Other agreements link us with the nations which form the Little Entente. In what obligations will they involve us, and involve themselves? What instructions will the governments give to their General Staffs, in case of conflict, as to how to conduct the war? Against which enemy will the initial effort be made? What cooperation in the way of equipment would be useful to these countries?

8 The study of these questions, all of which are important to the organization of our national defence forces, will necessarily lead to combinations of manpower from the home territory, North Africa or the colonies. Bearing in mind the moral and material disadvantages of an unplanned augmentation, what is the maximum manpower of these overseas contingents which could be stationed in France? Also, taking into account the security of our colonies and protectorate countries, what is the minimum manpower of the forces of each nationality which must be maintained there?

If we leave questions of this magnitude without examining or solving them, we shall be led inexorably day by day, under the pressure of budgetary necessities, political influences or international black-mail, to take measures which will gradually drain our national forces of their substance. They will become merely a facade and will not be in a condition to fulfil their missions at the hour of danger.

It therefore appears absolutely essential to begin this methodical and exhaustive study without delay. Its results will be the obligatory basis for all organization or reorganization of the national defence forces. It can only be done by responsible chiefs: ministers and military chiefs, that is, by a reduced and rationally formed council of national defence.

DDF, 1st series, II, no. 203

40 Hitler's first speech to the generals, 3 February 1933

The sole aim of general policy: *the regaining of political power*. The whole State administration must be geared to this end (all departments!).

1 *Domestic policy*: Complete reversal of the present domestic political situation in Germany. Refusal to tolerate any attitude contrary to this aim (pacifism!). Those who will not be converted must be broken. Extermination of Marxism root and branch. Adjustment of youth and of the whole people to the idea that only a struggle can save us and that everything else must be subordinated to this idea. (Realized in the millions of the Nazi movement. It will grow). Training of youth and strengthening of the will to fight with all means. Death penalty for high treason. Tightest authoritarian State leadership. Removal of the cancer of democracy!

2 *Foreign policy*: Battle against Versailles. Equality of rights in Geneva; but useless if people do not have the will to fight. Concern for allies.

3 *Economics*: The farmer must be saved! Settlement policy! Further increase of exports useless. The capacity of the world is limited and production is forced up everywhere. The only possibility of re-employing part of the army of unemployed lies in settlement. But time is needed and radical improvement not to be expected since living space too small for German people.

4 *Building up of the armed forces*: Most important prerequisite for achieving the goal of regaining political power. National Service must be reintroduced. But beforehand the State leadership must ensure that the men subject to military service are not, even before their entry, poisoned by pacifism, Marxism, Bolshevism or do not fall victim to this poison after their service.

How should political power be used when it has been gained? That is impossible to say yet. Perhaps fighting for new export possibilities, perhaps — and probably better — the conquest of new living space in the east and its ruthless Germanization. Certain that only through political power and struggle can the present economic circumstances be changed. The only things that can happen now — settlement — stopgap measures.

Armed forces most important and most Socialist institution of the State. It must stay unpolitical and impartial. The internal struggle not their affair but that of the Nazi organizations. As opposed to Italy no fusion of Army and SA intended — most dangerous time is during

the reconstruction of the Army. It will show whether or not France
has *statesmen*: if so, she will not leave us time but will attack us
(presumably with eastern satellites).

DGFP, Series C, I, p. 37, n. 7.

41   Japan withdraws from the League of Nations, 1933

Uchida, foreign minister, to the secretary general of the League of
Nations, 27 March, 1933.

It is and has always been the conviction of the Japanese Government
that, in order to render possible the maintenance of peace in various
regions of the world, it is necessary in existing circumstances to allow
the operation of the Covenant of the League to vary in accordance
with the actual conditions prevailing in each of those regions.
. . .Acting on this conviction, the Japanese Government, ever since
the Sino-Japanese dispute was, in September 1931, submitted to the
League, have, at meetings of the League and on other occasions,
continually set forward a consistent view: [namely that the League]
should acquire a complete grasp of the actual conditions in this
quarter of the globe and apply the Covenant of the League in
accordance with these conditions. They have repeatedly emphasized
and insisted upon the absolute necessity of taking into consideration
the fact that China is not an organized state; that its internal conditions and external relations are characterized by extreme confusion
and complexity and by many abnormal and exceptional features; and
that, accordingly, the general principles and usages of international
law which govern the ordinary relations between nations are found to
be considerably modified in their operation so far as China is
concerned, resulting in the quite normal and unique international
practices which actually prevail in that country.

The report adopted by the [League] Assembly at the special session
of 24 February last, entirely misapprehending the spirit of Japan,
pervaded as it is by no other desire than the maintenance of peace in
the Orient, contains gross errors both in the ascertainment of facts and
in the conclusions deduced. In asserting that the action of the Japanese
army at the time of the incident of 18 September and subsequently did
not fall within the just limits of self-defence, the report assigned no
reasons and came to an arbitrary conclusion, and in ignoring alike the
state of tension which preceded, and the various aggravations which

succeeded, the incident — for all of which the full responsibility is incumbent upon China — the report creates a source of fresh conflict in the political arena of the Orient. By refusing to acknowledge the actual circumstances that led to the foundation of Manchukuo, and by attempting to challenge the position taken up by Japan in recognizing the new State, it cuts away the ground for the stabilization of the far Eastern situation. Nor can the terms laid down in its recommendations — as was fully explained in the statement issued by this Government on 25 February last — ever be of any possible service in securing enduring peace in these regions.

The conclusion must be that, in seeking a solution of the question, the majority of the League have attached greater importance to upholding inapplicable formulas than to the real need of assuring peace, and higher value to the vindication of academic theses than to the eradication of the sources of future conflict. For these reasons, and because of the profound differences of opinion existing between Japan and the majority of the League in their interpretation of the Covenant and of other treaties, the Japanese Government have been led to realize the existence of an irreconcilable divergence of views, dividing Japan and the League on policies of peace, and especially as regards the fundamental principles to be followed in the establishment of a durable peace in the Far East. The Japanese Government, believing that, in these circumstances, there remains no room for further cooperation, hereby gives notice, in accordance with the provisions of Article 1, paragraph 3, of the Covenant, of the intention of Japan to withdraw from the League of Nations.

> Ian Nish, *Japanese Foreign Policy,*
> 1869 – 1942 (London, 1977),
> pp. 299 – 300.

42   Debts, Depression and Disarmament, 1933

Norman H. Davis, chairman, American delegation, Disarmament Conference, to President Roosevelt, 7 April 1933.

Confidential

[London] 7 April, 1933

Dear Mr President: I think that I have covered very fully in my dispatches to the Secretary of State the substance of my conversations with Mr MacDonald and some of his colleagues relative to his proposed visit to the United States. Since it has now been decided that the Prime Minister is to go it is perhaps well for me to give you certain 'high spots' which may be of some assistance in the conversations which you are to have.

In our first talk after my arrival in London I discovered that the Cabinet had been quite opposed to his making the visit and that while the opposition was diminishing it still existed. The chief opposition was from the Tories, who being in the majority were afraid that the visit, if a success, would increase MacDonald's prestige, and if a failure would weaken that of the Government. Chamberlain [Chancellor of the Exchequer] was the principal obstruction because he wanted to go himself and also because he was determined to try to force a debt settlement prior to the Conference or at least to get an assurance that we would not ask for any payments during the Conference negotiations and would carry on debt negotiations concurrently with those of the Conference. . . .

I succeeded in convincing MacDonald, and I think all of them, except perhaps Chamberlain, that recovery from the depression must be put in the foreground and debts more or less in the background. While I personally think that it would be advisable for you to get authority, if possible, to prevent any serious situation arising with regard to the 15 June payments, because it would put us in a better trading position later on if we do not get in a jam at that time, I have not told them so and I have not said or done anything which could be construed as any commitment whatever.

In one of my talks with MacDonald, at which Simon [Foreign Secretary] was present, he was laying much stress upon the importance of getting beyond the 15 June payment without raising serious political difficulties. He said, in fact, that the problem was most serious because, in the present state of mind in both countries, it was as much of a political difficulty for them to get the approval of Parliament to pay as it was for you to get the approval of Congress to postpone payment, but that it was of the utmost importance to find some way to get beyond this without a real crisis. He then inquired what I thought could be done about it. I told him that it seemed to me that it ought to ease the situation in both countries if we would concentrate our efforts in pulling out of this depression; that if this were done it might possibly somewhat change the attitude of Congress and also the attitude of Parliament; that so far as the British debt was concerned I personally had always felt that after we had made a better settlement with the

French than we did with the British it would have been fair and logical to put the British debt on the same basis and that it might have been done had it not been for the Balfour note which had been a deterring factor. He then told me that when he was at Rapidan in 1929 Hoover told him he thought the British loan ought to be put upon the same basis as the French and indicated that it would be done but that nothing was ever done about it. Simon then spoke up and said that it would not solve the problem even if that were now done because it would not relieve the situation on 15 June with regard to the French. He thus indicated it might put them in an embarrassing position as regards the French if we were to do this. I then said that while I had thought at one time that a readjustment of the British debt on that basis might be one thing which Congress would be inclined to do I had no idea what its attitude would be, especially now, and furthermore that what I had said was a purely personal and unofficial view and not intended in any way as even a tentative proposal. I also said that in fact I had no idea how you would feel about even considering such an approach to the problem and could not speak for you. I mention this to you because subsequently, in the last talk which I had with MacDonald, at his request, and at which Baldwin [Lord President] Chamberlain, Runciman [President of the Board of Trade] and Simon were present, he raised this question in such a way as to try to infer that I had advanced it as a proposal. I then made it very clear that I had done nothing of the kind. Nevertheless, my reaction was that such an arrangement would appeal to all of them except Simon and to a lesser extent MacDonald who would be rather embarrassed because of the United Front Agreement.

I may say, however, that I am more than ever convinced that it would be good strategy, if you think it advisable to ask for authority from Congress, for us, of our own volition, to announce that as matter of fair play, we were going to stop this discrimination and put the British debt on the same basis as the French, making the adjustment retroactive. I am satisfied this would have such a good effect in England that it would greatly weaken the sentiment in favor of defaulting and would disrupt the united front. It would, in fact, put the British Government on the defensive. While it would not take care of the French and other payments maturing on 15 June, in case you should not get authority to deal with those as you see fit, it would relieve the tension with regard to the British payment, which is much more than all the others put together. If the British debt were read-justed as indicated it would give them a credit of something like

£900,000,000. My idea would be to apply most of this to reducing the capital indebtedness and merely to set enough aside to cover, say, the next two instalments.

Another thing which you may bear in mind is the possibility that MacDonald may not last much longer unless he can do something in the near future to strengthen his hand. I am sorry because I am extremely fond of him. He has much imagination and ability and back of his ministerial exterior he has a subtle capacity for trading.

I am inclined to think that it was not necessary for him to act in such a hurry in submitting the British Proposal recently in Geneva and that his visit to Rome was mainly with a view of strengthening his hand. If something comes of the proposal and of the proposed Four Power Pact it will help him. If not, it will do the opposite. I am satisfied it would have been better for them to have waited for us and to have put in a joint proposal which would have had a much greater chance of success.

There are many excellent features in their disarmament proposal, most of which in fact are not new. They have not laid enough stress on the strengthening of the defensive position of nations and the weakening of their powers of offense and I think it a mistake to propose a five year instead of a ten year treaty. As soon as I have had some further talks with the French and get a better line on the German situation I may make some suggestions for your consideration. I am inclined to think that the time may come within the next few weeks when you could give the necessary push to get through a real disarmament agreement which, of course, would do more to insure the success of the Economic Conference and restore confidence and good will then almost anything else.

I hope also within a few days to give you my considered views about the so-called Four Power Pact. Just now it looks as if it would not be born — certainly not without considerable change.

To return to the debt question, England and France can think of nothing but debts. Many of their papers have in every way tried to give the impression that I have been discussing debt settlements although I have scrupulously refrained from doing so and I have insisted that any negotiations about debts must be carried on in Washington. This has been done, I am sure, to keep the debt question before the public and to embarrass us. Nearly every move they make has some relation to debts. The British and French Treasuries are acting very closely together, in fact much more so than the political sides of the two Governments. I have a very strong suspicion, based upon considerable circumstantial evidence, that the British Treasury has encouraged the French in their continued failure to make the 15 December payment.

Strange as it may seem, one of the chief causes of the failure to make the payment now is due to the fact that Herriot, who is the leader of the majority political party, has stated that he would not assume the leadership of the Government again as long as it is in default on these payments. Many of his political enemies, and in fact some within his own party now, who wish to hold office and who by conviction are not opposed to paying, are refraining from giving their approval just in order to keep Herriot out of power.

It may interest you to know that you have caught the imagination of Europe to a remarkable extent. It makes me proud as an American to have a President with so much prestige and to feel that this may enable you to exercise an effective influence in coping with the critical world situation. The excessive amount of publicity which I am at present getting — much to my dislike — is largely due to the fact that I am looked upon as your direct representative.

I am sorry to burden you with such a long letter but hope it may be of some use.

With warmest personal regards and best wishes to Mrs Roosevelt and yourself, in which Mrs Davis joins me, I am,

Faithfully yours,

> Cited in: Edgar B. Nixon (Ed.), *Franklin D. Roosevelt and Foreign Affairs*, vol. 1., (London 1969), pp. 44 – 48.

43 Britain, France and the United States must call Germany's bluff, 1933

Memorandum on Germany by Brigadier Temperley, chief military adviser to the British delegation to the Disarmament Conference, circulated to the Cabinet, 16 May, 1933.

The time has come when Germany's attitude to disarmament and the attitude of the United Kingdom towards Germany ought to be reviewed. In the past there has been much sympathy with Germany and public opinion was in favour of granting her equality of status by degrees and in proportion to evidence of good behaviour; even France had realized that the end of the disarmament clauses of the Peace Treaty was in sight. . . .While no one believed that they had been kept with complete fidelity, the breaches which could be proved in open court were individually not great, though their cumulative effect was not inconsiderable. Germany had not been idle during these years and with great ingenuity had carried out a steady erosion of the disarmament clauses, in come cases with permission but more frequentlv without. . . .

Public opinion has been well aware of the continuous breaches of the treaty but was disposed to regard them as the not unexpected reaction by a high-spirited people against their penal character. It was ready to go forward, in spite of these evasions, with a first step towards equality of status, though France was naturally more hesitant. So long as Brüning could retain his precarious hold upon the Chancellorship and continue with some form of parliamentary government, there remained a certain amount of faith in Germany's pacific intentions. . . .

Within a few weeks of his arrival, Hitler has carried out a revolution and made himself complete master of Germany. The country has given itself up to a delirium of reawakened nationalism and of the most blatant and dangerous militarism. Fuel has been added to the flames by an orgy of military parades and torch-light processions and by a constant stream of patriotic wireless addresses delivered by masters of the art of propaganda, including Hitler himself. Behind all this surge and fury, Hitler has been swiftly consolidating his position. . . . The whole country has been Hitlerized and the swastika flag flies side by side with the old banner of the Reich on all public buildings and Embassies.

On the military side, Storm detachments of the Nazis and Stahlhelm have been converted into auxiliary police. As the Nazi detachments were recruited from the most desperate and violent elements of the unemployed, they do not seem particularly suitable for police work, the more so since arms have been placed in their hands. Their numbers are probably in the vicinity of 75,000. They are to undergo military training similar to that given to the militarized police. The incorporation of these troops in the police is, of course, a flagrant violation of the Peace Treaty. It is believed that the total strength of the Nazi Storm detachment is 300,000 men. . . . It has just been announced that the Chancellor has issued a decree calling up all youths of 20 years of age annually for national labour service for twelve months beginning on 1 January, 1934. This will produce an annual contingent of 350,000. The Secretary of State for Labour Service announces that every youth must do his year in the Labour Service before passing on to military service, *when conscription has been reintroduced.* . . . .The alleged objects of inculcating discipline and patriotism and providing physical training and productive work, as well as such training described as 'Defence Sport', are the merest camouflage for intensive military training. It cannot be doubted that arms will be in their hands before long and instruction will be given in their use. All this is an equally flagrant violation of the Peace Treaty. The Stalhelm has been forcibly absorbed into the Nazi Army and the military activities of these bodies will certainly be intensified. Göring [Prussian minister of the interior] has put a number of air personnel into uniform, and the formation of an Air Force seems to be actively proceeding.

On the material side it is understood that the Air Ministry have identified at least 125 fighting machines in existence or being made, exclusive of some 60 believed to be at Lipetsk in Russia. Information has been received from secret sources that an order has been given by the Reichswehr Ministerium to the Dornier works for 36 twin-engined night bombers. The cost of these orders is to be disguised under funds for employment of the unemployed. There are numerous indications in the last two months of increased activity in the German armaments industry. Reports have been received that twelve firms, which are not allowed to produce armaments, have received test orders for war material. Preparations are reported to have been made for the reopening of eight former Government arsenals.

At Geneva the German attitude has stiffened considerably. . . .The increasing insolence of the Germans has brought discussion on effectives to a complete standstill. When material is discussed, there are strong indications that the demands for samples of military aeroplanes, tanks and heavy guns will be very large.

What then is to be our attitude? Are we to go forward as if nothing has happened? Can we afford to ignore what is going on behind the scenes in Germany?. . .the intensification of military preparations under the Hitler regime, coupled with the strident appeals to force of the Nazi leaders, not only means a secret German rearmament, but creates an entirely new situation. Admittedly, it would be a good thing to get Germany bound by a Convention, as a breakdown would mean that she would commence to rearm at once. On the other hand, there is little use in a Convention limiting effectives and material, if the preparations above indicated are to proceed unchecked, while the warlike spirit is being openly roused to a fever heat against the Poles as the first objective, with France as the ultimate enemy. . . .No moment could be worse chosen than the present one to advocate drastic reductions in the rearmaments of France, the Little Entente and Poland. Moreover, the destruction of all heavy material and bombing machines belonging to the French and her Allies and to our own armed forces seems madness in the face of this direct German menace. . . .

If it is dangerous to go forward with disarmament, what then is to be done? There appears to be one bold solution. France, the United States and ourselves should address a stern warning to Germany that there can be no disarmament, no equality of status and no relaxation of the Treaty of Versailles unless a complete reversion of present military preparations and tendencies takes place in Germany. Admittedly this will provoke a crisis and the danger of war will be brought appreciably nearer. We should have to say that we shall insist upon the enforcement of the Treaty of Versailles, and in this insistence, with its hint of force in the background, presumably the United States would not join. But Germany knows that she cannot fight at present and we must call her bluff. She is powerless before the French army and our fleet. Hitler, for all his bombast, must give way. If such a step seems too forceful, the only alternative is to carry out some minimum measure of disarmament and to allow things to drift for another five years, by which time, unless there is a change of heart in Germany, war seems inevitable. German rearmament will by then be an accomplished fact and the material of the ex-Allies, which would take years of work and scores of millions of pounds to replace, may have been destroyed. This is an alternative which is unlikely to lead us anywhere. Strong combined action, however. . .should prove decisive, even though the threat of military pressure might have to be maintained for years, calling for fresh monetary sacrifices, until Germany is brought to her senses. But even this heavy responsibility should be accepted rather than that we should allow all the sacrifices of the last war to be in vain and the world to go down in economic ruin. There is a mad dog abroad once more and we must resolutely combine either to ensure its destruction or at least its confinement until the disease has run its course.

DBFP,   2nd   series,   V,   no. 127
(Enclosure)

44   Roosevelt urged to broadcast to Germany, 1933

Letter from Professor Felix Frankfurter of the Harvard Law School to President Roosevelt, 17 October, 1933.

Dear Mr President,

1 Many thanks for your kind letters of introduction to the Ambassadors and Minister Wilson [American minister in Switzerland]

2 Dodd [American ambassador in Berlin] is, of course, keeping you fully apprised on Germany. Yet I venture to send you the enclosures — a letter to *The Times* from a distinguished British soldier (Major General Sir Neill Malcolm) and Garvin's leader in the last issue of the *Observer* — as illuminating glimpses into the violence and madness now dominating in Germany. Developments make it abundantly clear that the significance of Hitlerism far transcends ferocious anti-semitism and fanatical racism. Dr Alice Hamilton is right in insisting that the attack against the Jew is merely an index to the gospel of force and materialism that explains the present rulers of Germany.

3 The air here is charged, albeit in a sober kind of way, with the kind of feeling that preceded 1914. I think I can say without exaggeration that I have followed English public opinion rather closely for more than twenty years, and never has it seemed to me to be so essentially united on any issue as it is in its present feeling towards Hitlerism. During the last few days I have seen a number of distinguished German exiles. They are men of great culture, of balanced judgment and of passionate German patriotism, but they all agree that the international behaviour of Berlin towards the Disarmament Conference is largely explained by domestic considerations — an effort to divert attention from economic difficulties, the growing fiasco of the Reichstag fire trial, and internal dissensions. They are also agreed that the forces of violence and chauvinism of the Hitler regime will be accelerated and intensified.

4 Have you thought of broadcasting in German, and saying some plain things that need to be said? Perhaps the most stark fact about the present German situation is that its people live in darkness. Not until one meets in the flesh highly educated Germans and realizes how completely they have been barred from knowledge of the outside world can one adequately appreciate how all the channels of light are shut from them. No other voice in the world would carry such weight as yours, and a broadcast from you to the world could not possibly be kept out of Germany — though a regime that reviles Goethe as not having been a

patriotic German makes idle any prophecy about its future foolish-
ness. Such a speech may do very little in Germany, and I am not at all
hopeful that it would. But by such an act you would become the
rallying center of the world's sanity.

    Ever with warm regards and good wishes,

Faithfully yours,

Felix Frankfurter.

> Cited in: Max Freedman, *Roosevelt and
> Frankfurter: Their Correspondence
> 1928 – 1945* (London, Bodley Head,
> 1967), p. 164.

45 Open versus secret diplomacy, 1933

> Correspondence between Lord Robert Cecil, British delegate to the
> Disarmament Conference, and Sir Maurice Hankey, secretary to the
> Cabinet, October – November 1933

(a) Dear Cecil,   27 October, 1933.
As a member of a service condemned to 'secret diplomacy' methods I
cannot write to the press. But to you, as an old friend, I can write, and
I do so because I really believe you are unintentionally misleading
public opinion.

I have been at the very heart of many Conferences, some successful,
others less so, and I have in one way or another been concerned with
nearly all important conferences since the war, though sometimes only
in the second degree. My experience is that much turns on method,
and that at some stages 'secret diplomacy' is just as essential as 'open
diplomacy' at others.

Take disarmament. There have only been two more or less successful disarmament Conferences, viz, Washington 1921 – 22, and
London, 1930. Both resulted in substantial reduction and limitation
of armaments, even if the results were not as complete as we had hoped
for. In both cases, all the more difficult questions were settled or
arranged by 'secret diplomacy', as you would term it. In both cases a
record was kept — even if an informal one — of these private conversations; there was little leakage, at the critical times; and at the London
Conference there was an agreed communique.

I am convinced that by no other method would the stubborn
problems involved have yielded to solution. In some cases nations took

up at an early stage an attitude *in public* from which they could not recede, and that is why some problems remained unsolved.

Geneva has resulted, so far, in no actual disarmament at all, and in my opinion that is due partly to a wrong method, i.e. public meetings before they had been prepared by private negotiation.

I only mention these two cases, but I could give any number of instances to illustrate my contention: the two Hague Conferences (evacuation of the Rhineland) 1929, and (Reparations) 1930; and Lausanne 1932, are good examples of my method as opposed to yours.

At the right stage public meetings are essential; at the wrong stage they are disastrous. Good Conference work depends on the proper blending of the two.

Yours ever,
M.P.A. Hankey.

(b) My dear Hankey,   28 October, 1933
I am rather surprised at your instances. I had always understood that the crucial point of the Washington negotiations was the public meeting at which A.J.B. [A. J. Balfour, Lord president] accepted the American proposals. That may have been 'prepared' beforehand, but certainly not by one of the 'formal secret conferences' of four or more Powers which have, in my view, done so much harm at Geneva lately.

As for the London agreement, I have always looked on that as an almost complete failure. Its actual result was to increase rather than diminish world armaments, and even the limitation of armaments was not a solid agreement. The subsequent secret attempts to improve the result have been an equal failure. Your reference to the agreed communique at the London Conference ignores, surely, the mass of press rumours and comments which found their way into the papers, especially in Paris. I am astonished at your reference to Reparations. I should have selected the whole series of conferences on the subject as among the clearest proofs of the failure of what you call your method.

But I am afraid we shall never agree on these questions for, like Lord Hartington and Mr Gladstone, we do not mean the same thing. You, as you have often told me, are not in favour of the abolition of war. You perhaps wish to limit it, but as a valuable method of evolution you approve it. It is natural therefore for you not to desire any considerable change in armaments. Consciously or unconsciously, you dislike any method which will bring the whole force of public opinion into play against the professional advisers of the various governments on military and naval affairs. We, on the other hand, who desire a complete transformation of international relations, are confident we shall never get it by a perpetuation of the methods of the Congress of Vienna. To us, such proceedings seem to be out of date and to ignore the growing interest of the electorate in the proper conduct of what is, after all, the most important function of Government.

Yours very sincerely, Cecil

(c) My dear Cecil,   31 October, 1933
You are quite correct in your understanding that A.J.B.'s [A. J. Balfour, Lord President] acceptance of the American proposals during the first days of the Washington Conference was a very important factor, but as we have seen again and again at Geneva, there is all the difference between a chorus of acceptance in principle and the conclusion of a convention. The Conference went on for some three months after Lord Balfour's declaration. There were a number of political questions that had to be cleared up before a convention could be achieved, such as the Quadruple Pacific Treaty which replaced the Anglo-Japanese Alliance; the China Nine Power Treaty; the Shantung Railway question. In addition, a great number of important details had to be cleared up for the Arms Treaty itself some of which were very difficult and controversial such as the article relating to fortifications and naval bases. All of these more difficult questions were settled by methods very similar to those of the Council of Four at Paris before they were brought out into the open. I suppose I was present myself at at least forty meetings of this kind. I can assure you that there would never have been a Washington Treaty without them. You may not like the London Agreement, but it did achieve a large measure of limitation of armaments between the three principal Naval Powers and it did stop a competition of armaments, which was a part of the object of the Conference. Again, as one who participated, I can assure you that no Treaty could have been concluded without private conferences. Whether you like them or not, you cannot get away from the fact that these are the only Conferences between great Powers that have produced any measure of disarmament and both of them were conducted on the principles I advocate. Nothing has ever been achieved, and for my part I think nothing ever will be achieved by the method you advocate.

You do not like my references to Reparations. I do not suppose I like Reparations any better than you do, but they were a thorny problem with which it has been my unfortunate lot to be associated for many years. Broadly, I think the policy of successive British Governments was to get rid of them. They were reduced at a succession of Conferences on the Dawes Plan, the Young Plan, and at the Hague and for practical purposes were eliminated at Lausanne. My contention is not that Reparations are good or bad but that the object of these Conferences was achieved; and it was achieved so far as the two Hague Conferences and the Lausanne Conference are concerned (I do not remember details of the others) by the method of private conversations. I say without hesitation that nothing would have been achieved by any other method.

You are silent I notice about the evacuation of the Rhineland. I suppose even you would concede that that was a good thing even if you do not admit that the elimination of Reparations was good. That also was prepared behind the scenes.

In your last paragraph you raise wider questions on which I could say much but on which I will not follow you. We may not agree on some of these questions, but I should have thought that on a mere question of method and procedure at an international conference we could have agreed. As a Public Servant it is my business within the limits of my sphere of action to assist the Government in carrying out its policy quite irrespective of whether at the bottom of my heart I agree with that policy or not. All I am telling you is that in my long experience certain methods have succeeded and certain methods have failed.

But though we ought to agree I fear we shall not. You have committed yourself publicly on the subject and when a man has committed himself publicly, whether at an international conference or on a mere matter of procedure, he finds it difficult to change his position. That is the moral of my tale.

Yours very sincerely, Hankey

(d) My dear Hankey,   3 November, 1933
Many thanks for your further letter.

Your argument really amounts to this: that you are convinced from your experience that private meetings have, in various cases, been of great service. It is of course impossible for me to discuss assertions of that kind and I can only meet them by saying that in my experience of international transactions at Geneva and elsewhere I have arrived at precisely the opposite conclusion; and I could, if it were worth while, give you many instances where, I am confident, no satisfactory result would have been reached without public discussion. But in the end that too would rest on my assertion and is incapable of proof.

The point of view which you seem to me altogether to ignore is that nowadays, with modern means of communication and education it is not really sufficient for distinguished Ministers and distinguished civil servants to come to an agreement unless and until they have behind them the support of their people; and conversely, in many cases, particularly those which directly affect peace, the peoples are more and more taking strong views on the questions involved in international conferences, and the fact that these views exist is an important feature in producing or preventing agreement.

Your technique was no doubt the best in the days when foreign affairs were left either to the king or a few of his most trusted advisers; but that day is past, for good or ill, and I am profoundly convinced that we have got to conform to the new political conceptions or bring great disasters on the world.

As I have said, I cannot argue with you as to the details of this or that negotiation, but I remain of opinion that secrecy, both in the London Conference and in the Reparations discussions, — whether or not it facilitated actual agreement at those conferences, as to which we shall each retain our own opinion, — did produce most unfortunate and even disastrous political consequences outside the actual ambit of the negotiations.

However, I fear it is not much use reiterating my view. I did my best to express it clearly in my letter to *The Times*, and I adhere to it, not, as you not very courteously suggest, because I have once said it and would not go back from what I have said, but because I did not say it until I had become convinced of its truth — a conviction which I still hold.

Yours very sincerely, Cecil

> British Library, *Cecil of Chelwood Papers,* Add. Mss. 51088

46   Franco-Soviet-Czech discussions at Geneva, 1933

> Letter from an adviser of the Soviet embassy in France to the deputy commissar for foreign affairs, N. N. Krestinsky, 25 November 1933.

Dear Nikolai Nikolayevitch,
Comrade Dovgalevsky [Soviet ambassador in Paris] had a heart attack in Geneva and has been ill for the past fortnight. On returning to Paris he consulted a doctor who prescribed ten days of complete rest. However he intends to return to work before this if his health permits.

On his instructions I give below a note of the discussions he had with

Paul-Boncour and Beneš [Czechoslovak foreign minister] in Geneva [foreign minister] according to his own detailed account.

Discussion with Paul-Boncour on 19 November

The discussion took place over lunch given by Avenol, Secretary General of the League of Nations. The following conversation took place on Paul-Boncour's initiative.

At the beginning of the conversation he mentioned the trade negotiations and expressed the view that it was necessary to sign an agreement as soon as possible. Although Comrade Litvinov [Soviet Commissar for foreign affairs] had promised him that he would try to speed up the process of negotiation, he had since heard that Comrade Krestinsky did not attach the same importance to the conclusion of negotiations. Comrade Dovgalevsky of course attempted to dissuade Paul-Boncour from this view.

Then Paul-Boncour said that Germany's withdrawal from the League of Nations and from the Disarmament Conference has put the conference in a hopeless position. He also mentioned the pressure which Britain and Italy were putting on France to obtain from her further concessions to Germany and an alteration of the negotiations along the lines of the Four Power Pact.

In his opinion the way out of the impasse would be for the USSR to join the League of Nations. To his question whether one could depend on the USSR joining the League, Comrade Dovgalevsky replied in the negative. In further discussions with Comrade Dovgalevsky Massigli [French delegate to Disarmament Conference] also stressed the desirability of the USSR's entry into the League.

As regards the prospects for disarmament negotiations, Paul-Boncour announced that he would oppose with all his strength negotiations within the framework of the Four Power Pact.

If Britain and Italy insist on disarmament discussions on the basis of the Four Power Pact he would stipulate as a *sine qua non* that the USSR and Poland be invited to participate in such negotiations. On this same issue Massigli also mentioned the need to invite the Little Entente powers to the talks.

Both Paul-Boncour and Massigli spoke with unconcealed annoyance of Poland in connection with the signing of the Berlin declaration. At the same time they tried to minimize its significance by pointing to the absence of a real basis for an understanding and to the non-obligatory nature of the declaration. They consider that only

Germany benefits from the declaration because Hitler has realized that since he would not succeed in achieving all his international ambitions a temporary cover in the East was needed in order to work for an immediate settlement of the Anschluss question.

Discussion with Paul-Boncour on 22 November 1933

. . .Paul-Boncour read out a telegram from the French ambassador in Washington, together with an account of his discussion with Litvinov, in which the latter formulated his views on future tactics in disarmament matters. In connection with this telegram Paul-Boncour announced that he fully shared our opinion that it would be necessary to confine ourselves to a statement of questions of principle. However there had been no public sessions and the only sign of the continuation of the conference's work were the two committees. He would therefore indicate to his representatives in the committees that they should not enter into detailed discussions but should try to emphasize the questions of principle so that if matters were reported to the General Commission the questions of principle would be the first issues to be raised in the Commission's debates.

Paul-Boncour requested us to take an active part in the work of these committees.

As for future prospects, he declared that he was an opponent of direct negotiations with Germany and concessions of any kind to it, for Britain and Italy were in effect impelling France onto the path of recognizing the rearming of Germany, as a starting-point for negotiations, He, Paul-Boncour, would fight as long as he could, but he did not conceal from us the fact that in this matter French public opinion was far from unanimous and that some influential political, trade and industrial circles were seeking for agreement with Germany. Strictly confidentially he added that had it not been for his opposition Daladier would have already conducted direct negotiations with Germany.

He considered that the only possibility of stopping the activities of these circles was to work out a positive programme of foreign policy. On the German question France could not hold out for long in taking a purely negative stance. If French public opinion were to learn and become convinced of the fact that France can carry out a positive policy by creating a firm barrier against the onslaught of Hitler's Germany, then that would pacify public opinion and knock the weapon from the hands of those who were insisting on a deal with

Germany. He sees this barrier in the form of a mutual assistance pact. He considers the question is urgent and will brook no delay.

He said. . .that after seeing Comrade Dovgalevsky he would receive Beneš and would talk to him about these matters, together with the question of establishing friendly relations between the USSR and the Little Entente.

Discussion with Beneš on 22 November 1933

The conversation took place over a cup of tea on Beneš's own initiative. The essence of the conversation which lasted about one and a half hours consisted in the fact that in Beneš's view the European democracies were threatened less by the existence of the USSR than by that of the fascist dictatorships. Although he was sure that in the event of an encounter with the fascist dictatorships the democracies would come out on top, it was nevertheless necessary to avoid war with all its horrors. Therefore, all countries concerned for the preservation of peace—and among them he includes us—must establish good relations with one another in order to repulse the onslaught of fascist dictatorships—specifically Hitler's Germany. Accordingly, he has in mind the establishment of friendly relations between the USSR and the Little Entente. In Czechoslovakia, a country which has no dispute with the USSR, the matter has ripened to such an extent that the resumption of diplomatic relations presents no serious difficulties. One can say practically the same for Yugoslavia where the hostility of the king towards us has recently diminished. Only Rumania remains. Beneš announced that in the next session of the Council of the Little Entente he would raise the question of normalizing relations with the USSR. . . .

Rosenberg.

Dokumenty Vnesnei Politiki SSSR, vol. 16 (Moscow, 1970), no. 390.

IV

Challenge and Response, 1934 – 36

The years 1934 – 36 brought a succession of challenges to the international order: an abortive Austrian Nazi *putsch* in July 1934, Hitler's announcement of conscription and rearmament in March 1935, Mussolini's invasion of Abyssinia in October, Japan's repudiation of all naval treaty limitations in January 1936, Hitler's reoccupation of the Rhineland in March and the outbreak of the Spanish Civil War in July.

Early in 1934 the British Cabinet formally recognized Germany as the ultimate potential enemy but there was no thought of stopping her. Sir Robert Vansittart, permanent under secretary of state for foreign affairs, admitted in April 1934 that a long-range British policy must take account of Germany's legitimate grievances. The search for agreement with Germany was propelled by an awareness that without rearmament and strong allies Britain had little room for manoeuvre. After the Stavisky riots of 6 February, 1934 France was widely regarded as the 'sick woman' of Europe. In any event France could offer little help outside Europe and the Mediterranean. Hence a revived Anglo-Japanese alliance was an attractive proposition but Roosevelt opposed it (**48, 49**). Personal contact with Hitler strengthened the case for conciliation. After the stories of Nazi horrors Hitler's visitors were relieved to find him no demagogue but sane, sober and sincere (**51**).

France's quest for allies was limited to Europe. Given Britain's refusal to conclude a military alliance France looked for a powerful continental ally. In talks with the Soviet Union France seemed to be dragging her feet and an alliance was delayed until May 1935 (**47**). The main reason for France's hesitation was that she had several options open: alliance with Moscow; an eastern Locarno linking Germany, the Soviet Union and eastern allies; a Franco-German *rapprochement*; alliance with Italy. The choice was complicated by ideological passions. After the Stavisky riots politics were increasingly polarized between left and right.

Mussolini's decision of December 1934 to attack Abyssinia was the culmination of long-standing colonial ambitions (50). Italy's hopes of colonial spoils had been disappointed in 1919. Plans for an attack on Abyssinia were not discussed until 1932 because it was only then that Italian forces completed the subjugation of the Senussi in Libya. The diplomatic disappointments of 1933 – 34, beginning with the miscarriage of the Four Power Pact of July 1933, confirmed Mussolini's resolve to act in Africa. What decided the issue was the conclusion of an alliance with France—the Rome Agreements of 7 January, 1935. Mussolini believed that in exchange for Italian help in defending Austria's independence, France would turn a blind eye to the conquest of Abyssinia.

By the spring of 1935 Italy's intentions were common knowledge but there was no common front against her. Italy was needed as a make-weight against Germany. When in 1934 Austrian Nazis attempted a *putsch* Mussolini alone of European leaders had shown his willingness to use force to maintain the status quo in central Europe. Meeting at Stresa on 11 – 14 April, 1935 Britain, France and Italy reaffirmed their Locarno obligations and agreed to consult together on the measures necessary for the maintenance of Austrian independence. But no mention was made of Africa. Britain and France were soon at odds over the Anglo-German naval agreement of 18 June, 1935 allowing German naval rearmament up to 35 per cent of British tonnage. French ministers who had been kept in the dark about the negotiations took umbrage.

Why did Britain and France allow Italy to overrun Abyssinia? The Italian attack on a League member seemed an open and shut case of aggression. There were three principal reasons: the desire to retain Italy as an ally, military unpreparedness, divided opinion in Britain and France. British and French attitudes are illustrated in the Paris conversations of 7 December, 1935 between Sir Samuel Hoare, foreign secretary, and Pierre Laval, French prime minister (52).

Anglo-French diplomacy in the Italo-Abyssinian war fell between two stools. The soft sanctions imposed by the League in November 1935 did not help Abyssinia but Italy was sufficiently isolated to put out feelers for better relations with Germany. Hitler welcomed the *Duce*'s overtures. In mid-February 1936 he was preparing for the remilitarization of the Rhineland (53). With the return of the Saar to Germany in January 1935 the Rhineland became Hitler's immediate target. The pretext for action was provided on 11 February, 1936 when the Franco-Soviet pact of 2 May, 1935 was submitted to the French parliament for ratification. Germany argued that the pact was incompatible with Locarno. Hitler hoped to persuade Mussolini to repudiate Locarno first, whereupon Germany would follow suit. Mussolini would not go so far but affirmed that in the event of a German move he would not cooperate with Britain in any action under Locarno. This was enough for Hitler and on 7 March German troops entered the Rhineland.

Hitler's decision to intervene in the Spanish Civil War was motivated by his opposition to Bolshevism. With Popular Front governments in Spain and France and the Soviet Union doubling its defence spending Hitler was apprehensive. The continuity of his thinking on the Soviet Union is confirmed in a memorandum of August 1936 on the Four Year Plan (57). He reasserted his belief in the need to secure living space in the east and insisted that the economy and army must be ready for war within four years.

In the Four Year Plan memorandum Japan was singled out as the only country, apart from Germany and Italy, standing firm against Bolshevism. Germany and Japan signed the Anti-Comintern Pact on 25 November 1936. It was not a defensive alliance but a declaration to consult together on measures to combat Comintern activities. Japan did not commit herself to a military alliance with Germany and Italy until the Tripartite pact in 1940. Japanese foreign policy was confused and uncertain. The chief agency in policy making was the army but it was not a monolithic force and several factions competed for influence. In 1936 members of the High Command, the foreign ministry, and the navy remained anxious to arrive at a *modus vivendi* with Britain. The 'Fundamentals of National Policy', approved by a five ministers conference on 7 August, 1936, registered the competing claims of the army and navy—the army wished to advance to the north, the navy looked to the south (56). Britain was included for the first time among Japan's potential enemies. The 7 August conference was followed by a large increase in defence spending, with the navy securing a third building programme for 66 new ships.

By November 1936 the increasing scale of foreign intervention in the Spanish Civil War had created a fear of imminent European war and pleas for American help. However American opinion was determined not to get embroiled in Europe. By defaulting on their war debts to the United States in 1933 Britain and France reinforced American isolationism. In August 1935, as Mussolini prepared to invade Abyssinia, Congress passed the Neutrality Act, forbidding the

shipment of arms to either aggressor or victim. The Neutrality legisla-
tion was extended in February 1936. Britain and France continued
their search for agreement with Germany, with the emphasis on
economic and colonial concessions.

47 The Soviet ambassador in Paris reports on France's delay in negotiating an alliance, 25 January 1934

Neither Paul-Boncour nor Léger [secretary general of the French
foreign ministry] have yet invited me to discuss the proposals about the
League of Nations and mutual defence. I am adopting a waiting
attitude, for I do not want it to appear that we are more interested
than the French in the question. Paul-Boncour's sluggishness is
without doubt to be attributed to the fact of his indecisiveness, this
being a reflection of the struggle now taking place in France and even
in the Cabinet itself between two doctrines: pro-Soviet and pro-
German. One should also take into account the direct pressure which
Britain is putting on France in favour of a Franco-German agreement
and Germany's return to the Disarmament Conference and to the
League of Nations. The indirect action of Italy is also tending in the
same sense. It is possible that in the near future Britain will offer
Germany and France her services as a mediator. So it looks as though
Paul-Boncour is delaying our negotiations pending clarification of the
Franco-German situation. The possibility cannot be excluded, how-
ever, that despite a firm promise to me not to make any announce-
ments to Poland or anybody else without prior agreement, Paul-
Boncour has put out feelers to Beneš and Beck. [Polish foreign
minister]. . . .

Dokumenty Vnesnei Politiki SSR,
vol. 17 (Moscow, 1973), no 26

48 Neville Chamberlain suggests an Anglo–Japanese alliance, 1934

Letter from Chamberlain, then acting prime minister, to Sir John Simon,
foreign secretary, 1 September, 1934

My dear John,
While I have been here I have been thinking a great deal about the

European situation, the coming Naval Conference and the position of the Government. It seems to me that some immensely important question, affecting the whole future of G[reat] B[ritain] and the Empire, may turn upon the actions we take this autumn, and the more I have turned it over the more convinced I have become that this is one of those crucial points in history which test the statesman's capacity and foresight.

The result of my cogitations has led me to certain conclusions which, as they would require Cabinet authority to carry out, I have embodied in a memorandum to the Cabinet. I propose to circulate this memorandum very soon, as time presses, but I am sending you with this letter an advance copy in the hope that you may have time to consider it before you go to Geneva.

I am sending it to you, not only because you are the Minister most directly concerned, but because I attach particular weight to your cool and analytical judgment. Moreover I can't help reflecting that if you could bring off an agreement with Japan such as I have suggested it would stamp your tenure of office with the special distinction that is attached to memorable historical events, and, incidentally would add greatly to the prestige of the National Government in the most difficult of all fields.

I have been immensely impressed and confirmed in my views by two things since I wrote this paper. One is the report from Sir R. Clive referred to in the PS which relates how he was actually offered a Pact of Non-aggression by Japan and how Hirota [Japanese foreign minister] impressed upon him the friendliness of the Emperor. The second is more recent, namely the semi-official statement of Japanese ideas about the Naval Conference in which suggestions were made very closely approximating to those I have sketched in my paper. (See *The Times*, 30 August)

Surely with these two confirmatory bits of evidence I must be on the right tack. But if we neglected even to enquire what were Japan's ideas about a Pact, what might not be said of us by future historians if we drifted unto unfriendly relations with Japan, lost our Far Eastern trade to them, had to look on helplessly while she marched from one aggression to another.

As for USA don't let us be browbeaten by her. She will never repay us for sacrificing our interests in order to conciliate her and if we maintain at once a bold and a frank attitude towards her I am not afraid of the result.

Although Van [sittart] has not seen my paper he knows it is on the stocks, and as a result of some remarks I made when he sent me Clive's report, he has written to me that he was having the whole question of the Pact very carefully examined.

He has therefore begun the good work; I hope you may think sufficiently well of the idea to pursue it and that you will some day be remembered (*inter alia!*) as the author of the 'Simon-Hirota Pact'.

DBFP, 2nd series, XIII, no. 14.

49 Roosevelt opposed to an Anglo-Japanese pact, 1934

Letter from Roosevelt to Norman H. Davis, chairman, American delegation, London naval conference, 9 November, 1934

[Washington] 9 November, 1934

Private and Confidential
Dear Norman:

I find yours of October thirty-first on my return from Hyde Park after election. Your golf game with Matsudaira [Japanese ambassador in London] must have been exceptionally interesting. The latest news by cable seems no more encouraging.

I hope you will keep two definite considerations always in mind. First, that Simon and a few other Tories must be constantly impressed with the simple fact that if Great Britain is even suspected of preferring to play with Japan to playing with us, I shall be compelled, in the interest of American security, to approach public sentiment in Canada, Australia, New Zealand and South Africa in a definite effort to make these Dominions understand clearly that their future security is linked with us in the United States. You will best know how to inject this thought into the minds of Simon, Chamberlain, Baldwin and MacDonald in the most diplomatic way.

The second point is that I get increasing information that Japan cannot stand the cost of a Naval race.

By the way, that continued reference to the Immigration Act is, in my judgment, nothing more or less than a smoke screen — whether it be laid by Japanese militarists or by Japanese Ambassadors.

If the worst comes to the worst and Japan in effect walks out on the three party conference, I am inclined to go along with your thought at the bottom of Page 5, that England and the United States should join in a statement. As a matter of practical fact, in such a case we could easily agree with the British by some form of dovetailing categories so that they would have more light cruisers and we more battleship strength or something along that line.

It is unthinkable that the British would go along with even a slight Japanese increase. It would mean a further increase five years from now. You will remember that 1930 did give Japan an increase over 1922.

I am glad you are patient. I would be much out of place in such a conference,

Always sincerely,

> Cited in: Edgar B. Nixon (ed.), *Franklin D. Roosevelt and Foreign Affairs*, vol. 1 (London, 1969), p. 263.

50   Mussolini on Abyssinia, 30 December 1934

Memorandum by Mussolini for Marshal Badoglio, chief of general staff. Directive and Plan of Action to solve the Abyssinian question.

1   The problem of Italian-Abyssinian relations has very recently shifted from a diplomatic plane to one which can be solved by force only: like all 'historical' problems of this kind it admits of one solution: a resort to arms.

2   The development of the Abyssinian situation poses these incontrovertible facts. The tendency of the Negus has aimed at centralizing the Imperial authority and reducing to a nominal level, through continuous violence, intrigue and bribery, the power of the *Rases* (Chieftains) living in the peripheral areas. A long period will be needed before Abyssinia can be described as a state in the European sense of the word; still, it is necessary to bear in mind that in modern history this process can be speeded up, in particular since the missions of some European countries have come to her assistance. This enables us to foresee that the trend towards centralization and unification can be crowned with success within a reasonably short time, provided it is not interrupted by external events.

3   This 'political' development constitutes a powerful factor to increase the military potentiality and efficiency of the Abyssinian Empire.

4   Moreover, all information indicates a similar progress towards the centralization of military power, as well as a general tendency to

transform — on a European pattern — both Abyssinia's internal organization for-war and, above all, her armaments. It might not be long before such a transformation is complete, especially because it is speeded up by European instructors, provided that it is not interrupted by external events. With regard to those arms carried by hand (machine guns, rifles, automatic weapons. . .) Abyssinia is equipped with really modern arms, the number of which is beginning to be considerable.

5 Taking into account what is said above, one logical conclusion can be drawn: *time is working against us*. The longer we delay the solution of this problem, the more difficult the task will be and the greater the sacrifices. . . .

6 I decide on this war, the object of which is nothing *more nor less than the complete destruction of the Abyssinian army and the total conquest of Abyssinia*. In no other way can we build the Empire. . . .

8 One essential condition, which is in no way prejudicial to our action, is having a peaceful Europe on our hands, certainly for the period of two years 1935 – 36 and for 1936 – 37, by the latter period the solution must be completed. An examination of the position, emerging at the beginning of 1935, leads to the conclusion that in the next two years war will be averted in Europe. . . . Elements making for stability are: the agreements between Italy and France. These agreements remove the danger of a renewed German attack on Austria. On the other hand, the inevitable result of the Italian-French agreements is an improvement of Italian-Yugoslav relations. . . . Moreover it can be said of Germany that her military machine has not even approximately reached that level of efficiency which would enable her to take the initiative in starting a war. . . . Poland, which had previously seemed to be a pawn in Germany's game, is now making a noticeable move in the direction of France. . . .

9 For our arms to achieve a rapid and decisive victory, we must deploy on a vast scale the mechanized forces, which are now at our disposal, and which the Abyssinians either do not possess at all or do so only in an insufficient degree, but which they will possess within a few years. . . .

10 The speedier our action the less likely will be the danger of diplomatic complications. In the Japanese fashion there will be no need whatever officially for a declaration of war and in any case we must always emphasize the purely defensive character of operations. *No one in Europe would raise any difficulties provided the prosecution of operations resulted rapidly in an accomplished fact. It would suffice*

to declare to England and France that their interests would be recognized. . . .

12 Since our preparations will be partly or fully completed only in the autumn of 1935 it must be a matter of policy to prevent all incidents which might anticipate the conflict. . . .

> G. Rochat, *Militari e politici nella pre-parazione della Campagna d'Etiopia: Studio e documenti*, 1932 – 1936 (Milan, 1971), no. 29

51 Clifford Allen's impressions of Hitler, January 1935

Private note by Lord Allen of Hurtwood, chairman of the Independent Labour Party.

On reaching the Chancellory to meet Herr Hitler I found it sur-rounded by a crowd of onlookers, who are always hoping for a glimpse of the Chancellor. My mind flitted back to the crowds that may some-times be seen around Buckingham Palace, though they are usually only to be found there on some special occasion. This new palace, I understand, was erected by Chancellor Brüning, a quiet, modest, and peace-loving statesman, who always preferred to do his work in some obscure domestic retreat of his own, rather than in the great palace which he had caused to be built. Once inside the gates, picked Storm Troopers dressed in the now familiar black uniforms, were encountered at almost every stage of my journey.

At last I was ushered into the room where the Chancellor works. Its beauty, grandeur and enormous size, which was equivalent to a ballroom, contrasted oddly in my mind with the pokey jumble of rooms which constitute Number 10 Downing Street. The Chancellor and I advanced to meet each other across this wide space. We then sat quietly together for our conversation.

I was anxious to form a personal judgement of this notorious man. My first instinct was to see to what extent I could compare him with Lenin, with whom I had talked in the famous Kremlin. The Russian, shrewd though he was, left upon me an impression of a profoundly astute but academic man. Herr Hitler immediately strikes one with his immense vitality. But what a contrast he is to the picture British people have formed of him. With me he was quiet, restrained, but nonetheless ruthless. Sincere to his fingertips, with a fanaticism somewhat resembling, I should imagine, that of Oliver Cromwell with his Ironsides. This man looks upon politics as a kind of religion, and, as history records over and over again, he too will persecute for his religion, kill for it and die for it. But nonetheless he believes in it with an honesty and determination which it is folly either to disguise or caricature.

Throughout the whole of our conversation there was nothing resembling what I had been led to expect. No speech making, little emotional gesticulation, no losing the point in excited endeavours to lay down the law or to overwhelm me with explosive explanations of his emotions or policy. Clearly he can be a man of violence, but then what revolutionary is not? This is a revolution which has occurred in Germany. . . .

Hitler sat there, not an explosive demagogue, but a man of volcanic energy, and perfectly clear about his case. We discussed the whole European situation in technical detail. We estimated alternative lines of foreign policy. We examined the motives and intentions of all the major countries in Europe. Whether it is the effect of two years of power, or whether it be that he has been subject to caricature I cannot say, but this was not a man to allow a moment of time to be lost or a word to be wasted. The argument was precise, the sequence quick and logical: nor was the conversation one-sided.

> Martin Gilbert (ed.), *Plough My Own Furrow: The Life of Clifford Allen* (London, 1965), pp. 357 – 8.

52 Hoare-Laval talks on Abyssinia, December 1935

Excerpt from record of a meeting at the Quai d'Orsay, 7 December 1935

M. Laval [French prime minister] expressed pleasure at welcoming the Secretary of State in Paris. The delay in the proceedings at Geneva had been shown to be fully justified by recent political developments in France. On the question of the petrol sanction M. Laval went on to explain that France had no direct interest in the matter since she was not a supplier of petrol. But the consequences of any step which might be taken were of just as direct an interest to her as to the United Kingdom. Both from M. de Chambrun at Rome and from Signor Cerruti in Paris the French Government had every reason to know that Italy regarded the petrol sanction as a military measure although she did not wish to say so outright. No country could exist without petrol and certainly no war could be carried on without it. It followed that Signor Mussolini might reply to a petrol sanction by some resolution taken in a spirit of despair. Indeed M. Laval himself was convinced that this would happen.

M. Laval recalled that before the war in Abyssinia had actually broken out he had expressed the wish that the embargo on Italian exports could be postponed until the processes of conciliation had failed. In the end, and since he had himself been forced to admit that the moment was not ripe for conciliation, he had given way to the British thesis as advanced by Mr Eden [minister for League of Nations affairs]. But now and with regard to petrol he wished to return to the idea of seeking conciliation first before reverting to the petrol embargo. From this point of view he would deplore even the fixing of a relatively remote date for the entry of petrol sanctions into force although the French, being uninterested in the supply of oil, could not oppose the embargo. It was not necessary to abandon the idea but negotiations should first be tried. Meanwhile the formula that the petrol embargo must be generally accepted would serve to secure delay. The United States could do nothing effective until Congress met, even if they could do it then, which M. Laval thought would not be before 6 January.

On the question of a common military front M. Laval stated that, after his interview with His Majesty's Ambassador, he had seen Signor Cerruti. He had warned him that Rome must not make a mistake in judging the French attitude: and he confirmed this through the French Ambassador in Rome. He regretted only the allusions to this delicate process which had appeared in certain organs of the British press: he hoped that all possible restraint might be placed upon the appearance of untimely and provocative newspaper articles.

Sir Samuel Hoare [Foreign Secretary] expressed gratitude for the opportunity of conversations in Paris. Mutual frankness if doubts on both sides were to be eliminated was essential. He was particularly grateful for the action taken *vis-à-vis* of Italy but he proposed to carry further the exploration of certain doubts which still lingered and which he should like to clear up. A 'mad dog' act by Italy seemed improbable and he had noted that both Signor Mussolini and the official press service in Rome had implied, contrary to the impression which M. Laval had received from M. de Chambrun and Signor Cerruti, that the petrol sanction would be regarded as an economic measure and not as a hostile act. But an outbreak by Italy was not out of the question and if it were to occur it would infallibly be directed against the British Fleet or against Egypt. While this was so there were many people, particularly Italians including Italian representatives in most of the capitals of Europe, who were saying that in spite of her assurances France would not be able, or would not be in a position to give military assistance in case of necessity. He wished M. Laval to speak quite frankly and to communicate any doubts which he might have as to the possibility of France being unable, if and when it came to the point, to give the assistance which she had undertaken to give. It was much better to know beforehand that for one reason or another France might not be in a position to fulfil her engagements. No criticism was implied by the question nor was it in any way intended that British policy towards Italy should be more provocative merely because Britain had reason to feel sure of French support.

M. Laval did not attach much importance to anything the Italians might say. But as regards possible doubts as to the ability of the French Government to fulfil their engagements he could say that it was quite clear that the policy of sanctions did not command universal approval in France. A section of French public opinion persisted in thinking that Great Britain's attitude towards Italy was largely determined by a dislike of Fascism. But when all was said and done France did not break her engagements, and it was precisely for this reason that she regarded herself as equally interested with us in the question of the petrol sanction. The French people habitually observed their obligations, but they must feel that everything possible was being done to find a way out of the present crisis: otherwise some would persist in thinking that the lack of consideration evinced in British policy towards Italy was in part responsible for the situation. France would do what she had promised, but to enable her to do so she must be on a footing of complete equality with the United Kingdom.

Monsieur Laval went on to explain that through the Veterans' Leagues of Italy and France he had new confirmation which he could not disregard that the petrol embargo meant war and that France must help forward a solution which would not humiliate Italy. From the same sources it had been emphasized to him that the return of the Italian troops to their country without glory or territorial acquisitions meant revolution and rather than that Italy would fight.

M. de Chambrun [French ambassador in Rome] had reported that Signor Suvich [under-secretary, Italian foreign ministry] did not wish to put forward new proposals for a settlement, but he had replied by urging the need for negotiations and he had invited Signor Cerruti [Italian ambassador in Paris] urgently to induce his government to furnish new proposals. No reply had however so far been forthcoming from Signor Mussolini, whose speech of today M. Laval was inclined to judge rather unfavourably. But it was precisely on account of France's engagements towards us and her determination to honour them that he wished to persuade the United Kingdom to do everything possible to ward off what would be a dangerous adventure.

Sir Samual Hoare said that the petrol sanction would undoubtedly increase the danger of a 'mad-dog' act. He agreed with M. Laval that negotiations must be pressed on. But if the petrol embargo were to be postponed there must be good hope of these negotiations proving successful and to this end and as a beginning it was necessary to convince Italy that France and Great Britain, as well as the other Powers involved, were more united than ever before. Without publicity or threats the talks between the Naval Staffs ought to be carried further and supplemented by similar conversations by the Air Staffs and the General Staffs.

Sir Robert Vansittart emphasized the need for carrying on all three processes simultaneously — the fixing of the date for the embargo, the peace negotiations and the Staff conversations. He urged that these last conversations ought to be begun at once, in fact at the beginning of next week.

Monsieur Laval agreed.

Sir Samual Hoare said that Geneva was unlikely to agree to the embargo date being postponed unless Signor Mussolini was known to be talking seriously. The embargo itself was, he thought, originally a French proposal: no single Power seemed to be against it and in England it was felt that it was no reason for postponing a sanction because it seemed likely to be effective.

He must once more urge the importance of beginning the conversations between the various Staffs.

Monsieur Laval agreed to the naval conversations being enlarged so as to include all the defence services. The suggestions of such an expansion had indeed originally been a French one. He agreed with Sir Samuel Hoare that advantage should be taken of the presence of the French Admirals in London for the Naval Conference. He also agreed that the British Service Attachés in Paris might require assistance for the development of the conversations. He would have no objection to their being reinforced from London for this purpose.

Sir Samuel Hoare explained that the British Naval Staff were anxious to see certain essential preparations made by France in the Mediterranean area.

Turning to the question of the peace conversations he enquired what M. Laval would consider the best procedure to be adopted at Geneva on the supposition that the conversations with Italy had begun satisfactorily. It was essential to avoid any impression that the League of Nations was weakening.

M. Laval agreed. But he emphasized that Geneva would accept whatever France and Great Britain approved. If there were to be an exception it would no doubt be Moscow.

As regards peace conditions the Italian pretensions were excessive, but the British reservations were too severe. Mussolini must have at least a part of the territory he had conquered. Nor could he be expected to surrender to the vengeance of the Negus that part of the population which had yielded to him. Tigré must be ceded in part. In addition Italy wanted regions in which to settle her colonists south of the 8th parallel and excluding Ogaden which was of no value for the purpose; on the other hand he was fully prepared to see the Negus afforded access to the sea. Great Britain's ideas had hitherto been unduly restricted: he appealed to her to be more generous. It was the substance that mattered and the question of procedure was really of small importance.

Sir Samual Hoare emphasized that it was essential not to offer the appearance of rewarding aggression. As he saw it the main principles to be kept in view were the following:

1 the proposals must be kept within the framework of the report of the Committee of Five. Abyssinia must have a definite outlet to the sea.

2 Any question of mandate must be excluded.

3 The arrangement must be a judicious mixture of an exchange of territory and the conferring of economic concessions. The cession of territory by Ethiopia in the north must depend for its extent upon what was done in the south and southwest. As to Tigré he was prepared to agree that Italy must retain Adowa and Adigrat. But to go too far would lead to the Emperor's overthrow and provoke the accusation that all the League had managed to do was to ruin Abyssinia.

In the south there must be an exchange of territory against the port which Abyssinia was to receive: in the southwest the best way to deal with the question seemed to him to be an economic monopoly for Italy.

Sir Robert Vansittart said that above everything there must be joint Franco-British proposals. There must be no question of mediation in the sense that France put up British proposals to Italy and Italian proposals to Great Britain. And it was essential to remember that there must be some limit set to what Abyssinia could be expected to cede even in return for a port: to extend this limit would be to expose the League itself to the gravest danger.

M. Laval accepted the application of the principles laid down by the Committee of Five. But an international mandate over Abyssinia, in the form of the Plan of Assistance, did not interest Mussolini.

After some further discussions it was agreed that the Secretary of State should remain in Paris for another day so that the conversations could be resumed at 10.30 on 8 December.

DBFP. 2nd series, XV, No. 338

53 Hitler considers the reoccupation of the Rhineland, 1936

Memorandum by von Hassell, German ambassador in Italy, 14 February 1936

The Führer said that he was at present considering an extremely far-reaching question, about which he had so far spoken only to Herr von Neurath, Herr von Blomberg, Herr von Fritsch, Herr von Ribbentrop and Herr Göring, [respectively foreign minister, war minister, commander in chief of the army, Hitler's special adviser, minister president of Prussia] The question was whether Germany should take the Paris ratification of the Russian Pact (or even a favourable resolution by the Chamber) as grounds for denouncing Locarno and of once more stationing troops in the demilitarized zone. The latter, seen from the military point of view, was an absolute necessity. Until now he had always envisaged the spring of 1937 as the right moment. Political developments, however, made one wonder whether the psychological moment had not arrived *now*. Admittedly, the fact that militarily Germany was not yet ready and that she would be considerably stronger in 1937, was an argument for postponement; moreover, it was conceivable that at that later date there might be a Russo-Japanese conflict which would ease matters for Germany. But meantime this was quite uncertain and, as regards relative military strengths, the strength of the others, and especially of Russia, was increasing. At the moment, however, Russia was only intent on having peace in the West. England was in a bad state militarily, and much hampered by other problems; France was distracted by internal politics. In both countries there was strong opposition to the Russian Pact, which was to our advantage. He did not think that such a step on Germany's part would be answered by military action—though perhaps by economic sanctions; but these had meanwhile become thoroughly unpopular amongst the followers, who served as whipping boys, of the Great Powers.

He was now asking himself whether he should not approach Mussolini with the suggestion that he, for his part, should make use of the violation of the Locarno obligations, which the inclusion of Russia represented, as a pretext for denouncing the Pact, whereupon Germany would follow suit. The political advantages for both parties were obvious and, after all, Italy too had misgivings about the Russian Pact.

As regards the method, he had said to himself that it would be better for the matter to be brought to Mussolini's attention through special non-official channels, in order to convince him that it represented a personal decision made by the Führer himself, and in order that he should not betray us to the other side by passing on this suggestion. Herr von Blomberg, in a conversation with him and General Göring, had wondered whether the latter could not go to Rome. But the Führer did not see how such a journey could be kept secret.

I replied that when I had been summoned from Rome I had immediately thought that this question might be raised. It was clearly in the air. This was also shown by Flandin's [French foreign minister] answer (they were not going to let themselves again be confronted with *faits accomplis* and had already agreed upon the measures to be taken). Likewise, it was significant that the day before yesterday the first thing Aloisi [chief de cabinet to Mussolini] had asked me was what we would do if the Russian Pact were ratified.

Until now I had had the definite impression that our policy of 'lying low' had been very successful; it was of interest that the Japanese Ambassador had already told me twice that the others were waiting impatiently for some kind of action on the part of Germany in order to be able to pounce on it. But the Führer himself had already made it clear how difficult was the decision that had to be taken, and I would confine myself to Italy in the following: The view that dominated the situation there was undoubtedly that they had got into a terrible mess, and must seize upon any possible way out of it. Hence one could observe strong opposition, fostered by Grandi [Italian ambassador in London] to all action which might result in the burning of any bridges that might still exist. Since it now seemed as if oil sanctions were not going to be resolved upon (but would remain in suspension like the sword of Damocles), hopes of a compromise had grown, as had the desire not to get completely into the Western Powers' bad books. The Führer interjected that Starhemberg [Austrian Vice-chancellor] had told Papen [German envoy in Vienna] that he had gained the impression that Britain wanted to crush Mussolini. I replied that everything that I had said applied in the first place to the Foreign Ministry. Mussolini himself, and with him Ciano, [Italian minister for press and propaganda] had somewhat different ideas. Admittedly, in our last conversation Mussolini had not confirmed as positively as before his belief that Britain's aim was destructive. Nevertheless, this was the view he was most inclined to take, and he was therefore less opposed to clear, far-reaching decisions. I therefore believed that it would be perfectly possible to discuss this subject with him quite privately. But to do so, one point must be made quite clear, namely whether, in the event of Mussolini's refusing, we should carry out our decision all the same, or whether we should do so only in conjunction with him. After a brief pause for reflection, the Führer said that in the circumstances he thought it would be better to tell M[ussolini] that we would take the step in any case, but were suggesting to him that he should denounce the Treaty himself beforehand in order to avoid being placed in an extremely difficult position, also with regard to Germany, in consequence of our denunciation. If he denounced the Treaty and we followed suit, he would have gained the great advantage for Italy that Anglo-French policy would then be directed primarily against Germany. I replied that in any case one must be quite clear about this point in advance, and I repeated that, in view of Italy's exceedingly difficult position, there was no definite guarantee that Mussolini would accept the idea.

As for the method, I said I thought it quite out of the question for a mission such as General Göring's to be kept secret. Precisely because of the unusual course chosen, such a mission would, in fact, give the *démarche* a ten-fold importance in the eyes of the world, and, in my view, would achieve the opposite result to that which it was hoped to obtain by adopting this method. If the Führer decided in favour of getting in touch with Mussolini, then I should think that I myself, acting on his [the Führer's] personal instructions, could so conduct the conversation with Mussolini that he would not make use of the matter to betray us to the other side.

The Führer finally asked me whether I must return to Rome at once or whether I could go to Berlin; he wanted to discuss the matter further there, from Tuesday onwards, and would like me to be present. I replied that I had said in Rome that I would return at once; moreover, as we were giving a big reception on Monday my prolonged absence would probably attract a certain amount of attention. Nevertheless, if desired, I could go to Berlin. The Führer then said that it would, after all, be best if I went back at once, but that I should hold myself in readiness to come to Berlin after Tuesday if necessary.

DGFP, series C, IV, No. 564.

54   France's Popular Front leaders divided on Spain, July 1936

Letter from Fernando de los Rios, special envoy in Paris, to José Giral, Spanish prime minister, 25 July, 1936

Dear Friend—I refrain from entering into details because the advanced hour at which I start to write this letter, after a last conversation with the Government, or rather, with some of its prominent members, would make it impossible that it should leave by the Douglas aeroplane which is to carry it to Madrid so that it may be delivered to you personally. The fight that the Paris Press, with the sole exception, perhaps, of three newspapers, had started against a possible delivery of armaments, from the moment in which, owing to infidelities, it had knowledge of the coded telegram you sent to the Government last Monday to Tuesday night, became more acute when the aviators arrived, was stirred up by news of my own presence here, and as soon as the papers learnt, with details so minute as to reveal the existence of widespread treachery, all and every one of the points embraced by our requests. Last night, on my return from London, I was urgently summoned by the Leader of the Government to his house, where I found the four Ministers, who, as far as we are concerned, possess more influence within the Cabinet, owing to the nature of the departments they direct. The conversation was essentially political, and at their request I made a few considerations upon the character of the Spanish struggle, which cannot be looked upon as being strictly national owing to a series of reasons which we analysed: military frontier in the Pyrenees, Balearic Isles, Straits of Gibraltar, Canaries and breakage of the political unity of Western Europe.

Duty, therefore, and direct interest on the part of France to help us. How? We examined our demands and, from the attitude of the Ministers, I gathered that there existed a divergence of opinions.

A new question arose: that Spanish aviators should come to Paris to fetch the machines: I pointed out the semi-impossibility of this owing to our scarcity of personnel and to our intention of retaining the French pilots. I was told by one in a position to say this, that the whole consignment of aeroplanes and bombs was ready and could leave in the morning of today (25 July, 1936). . . . I retired to sleep and one hour later I was urgently aroused: the Air Minister, P. Cot, wished to visit me: he had inquired for me at the Embassy, and not finding me there, I was advised by mutual friends that in order not to awaken more suspicion I should go to his house: I went there, and he told me it was impossible to convince the Minister for Foreign Affairs of the legality of French pilots in taking aeroplanes to Spain: the formula was to take them to Perpignan, etc.: this is what I communicated to you last night, the 24th.

When I went this morning to the Air Ministry everything was going well: when I arrived at the Potez firm the difficulties seemed insurmountable. The Press campaign and the publication of the documents in which the Counsellor (of the Spanish Embassy) resigns looms so big that when Blum [French prime minister] went this morning to see the President of the Republic, he found him perturbed and in such a state of mind that he said, 'What is being planned, this delivery of armaments to Spain may mean war or revolution in France, and he asked that an extraordinary Cabinet meeting should be summoned at four o'clock in the afternoon.

The position of the President of the Republic is shared by several Ministers: the Cabinet was divided in its views, and the President of the Chamber, Herriot, has seen Blum and begged him to reflect, for he considers that this has never been done before, and that it may justify a de facto recognition by Germany and Italy of any semblance of government set up in a Spanish city and provide it with arms and ammunition in greater quantities than those France can supply. From half-past two until a quarter to four I have been with the Prime Minister and another Minister at the house of a third party: 'My soul is torn,' said Blum, who is as convinced as we ourselves are of the European significance of the struggle that is being fought in Spain. Never have I seen him so profoundly moved: 'I shall maintain my position at all costs and in spite of all risks,' he said. 'We must help Spain that is friendly to us. How? We shall see.'

At 3.30 I again met some of them: the fight had been stern, and a great rôle has been played in the discussion by a secret clause which fate revealed to me: in the Commercial Treaty or Commercial

Agreement signed in December 1935 by Martinez de Velasco, there exists under the form of a confidential note an understanding on the part of Spain to purchase from France armaments and munitions to the value of twenty million francs. The Minister of War had inquired last night about this, and asked if I knew something with reference to this clause, to which I answered 'yes', replying thus because, speaking in Embassy circles to Senor Castillo (the Counsellor) he had said something to me in half words which made me not a little suspicious: I asked for the dossier of the Treaty and found the confidential note in question, a note of which none of the present French Ministers was aware, which our Constitution forbids, and which has not been submitted to our Foreign Affairs Committee.

The resolution of the Cabinet has been to avoid delivery from Government to Government, but to grant us the necessary permits so that private industry may deliver to us and circulate such material as we may purchase. The method of executing this and facilitating it will be decided by a Committee of Ministers, on which we have some of our most faithful friends: tomorrow they will hold their most important and decisive meeting, and they anticipate that it is almost absolutely certain that we shall be able to take the aeroplanes out of the country after the 25th: on Monday or Tuesday, and we shall organize or, rather, I shall organize, aided by Cruz Marin and some other Spanish, as well as some excellent French, friends, the safe passage of the bombs, a difficult matter, especially for one who, like myself, is not an astute fox; but we shall see what necessity makes one capable of. The Potez 54 machines will be constructed, and we shall endeavour to shorten the terms. As regards all the armaments I think we can only deal with Hotchkiss.

Our conversations are overheard and everything that you say is published with slight alterations: for the good of Spain and the efficiency of the negotiations, it is advisable to speak with the utmost reserve, and to resort to prearranged words and make only occasional references to the necessity of employing such or such means for the struggle.

When you use words such as indispensable, urgent, essential, etc., you pave the way, given the secret organization which exists, for the sabotage of things that matter.

I want to tell you that tonight, acting on a request made to me by the Prefect of Police, I have taken up residence at a room at the Embassy: I regret it, but I do not think you will consider this indiscreet: I think it indispensable that the Ambassador should arrive quickly and assume the direction of this with full personality and responsibility.

To all the Cabinet my greetings and my best words of encouragement and faith in our Spain: for you besides the sincere embrace of
your old friend,

Yours

(Signed) Fernando de Los Rios.

> William Foss and Cecil Gerahty, *The
> Spanish Arena*, (London, Robert Hale,
> 1938) pp. 372 – 5.

55 Britain stresses the urgency of a non-intervention agreement on Spain, 7 August 1936

French foreign ministry memorandum of British and Belgian views,
Paris, 8 August, 1936.

1   Yesterday Sir George Clerk [British ambassador] spoke frankly to
M. Yvon Delbos [French foreign minister] about his government's
anxieties in the Spanish affair. An agreement on non-intervention was
a matter of extreme urgency—and pending an agreement it was
essential above all that no arms deliveries should take place otherwise
everything would be compromised.

2   The British ambassador was particularly afraid that if the conflict
persists General Franco, who needed support at any price, might be
tempted to use the Balearics to buy Italian help, or the Canaries for
German help. He thought that as a consequence the situation of
Gibraltar would be weakened.

3   The Belgian ambassador is anxious to see an agreement between
the five Locarno powers. Sir George Clerk, as an Englishman, said
that he is of the same opinion but added that allowance must be made
for French anxieties.

Both ambassadors did not conceal that their sympathy in the
Spanish affair is for the rebels, whom they considered to be the only
force capable of defeating anarchy and Soviet influence.

DDF, 2nd series, III, No. 108

56 Japan's aims, 1936

'Fundamentals of National Policy' 7 August, 1936

I

The basis of national policy is the need to consolidate national development internally and increase our prestige internationally through fairness and justice. Japan as the force for stability in east Asia in name and in fact must ensure the peace of the area and contribute to the well-being of men throughout the world, thereby living up to the ideals of the founding of our nation. Considering Japan's situation at home and abroad, the basic policies which she must adopt are to secure her position on the east Asian continent both diplomatically and militarily. The fundamental principles are as follows:

1 Japan must endeavour to eliminate the aggressive policies of the Powers in east Asia and share with people there cordial relations which are founded on the principles of co-existence and co-prosperity. This will be a manifestation of the spirit of the Imperial Way and a guiding light which we must use in pursuing our foreign policy.

2 Japan must complete her defence and armament programmes in order to guarantee her security and progress. Only thus can her position as a force for stability in east Asia be accomplished in name and in fact.

3 The basis of our continental policy must be to cope with the threat from the Soviet Union in the north in order to assure healthy development in Manchukuo and Japan-Manchukuo defence and, meanwhile, to plan our economic expansion by creating a strong coalition between Japan, Manchukuo and China against Britain and the United States. In bringing this about, we must bear in mind the need for cordial relations with other Powers.

4 We plan social and economic developments in the South Seas (Nampō Kaiyō), especially in the Outer Nanyō area, and contemplate the extension of our power by modest and peaceful means, avoiding clashes with other Powers. Thereby, we may anticipate the coming to fruition of Japan as a nation and the full development of Manchukuo.

II

Adopting these fundamentals as our criteria, we must reconcile our internal and external policies and bring our administration into line with present-day needs in the following ways:

1 In tackling Japan's security and armaments, the army must aim at dealing with the forces which Soviet Russia can deploy in the far east and increasing its garrisons in Kwantung and Korea so as to strike the first blow in the event of war breaking out with Soviet far-eastern forces.

2 The navy must aim at building up forces adequate to maintain ascendancy in the west Pacific against the American fleet.

With a view to the harmonious application of these fundamental policies, our foreign policy must be coordinated and amended. In order to enable beneficial and smooth progress to be made over diplomatic activities, the military should try to help through private channels, without assuming any public role [Part III, covering in the main financial and commercial policies, is omitted].

Ian Nish, *Japanese Foreign Policy*,
1869 – 1942. (London, 1977), 301 – 3.

57 Hitler on the Four Year Plan, August 1936

Politics are the conduct and the course of the historical struggle of nations for life. The aim of these struggles is survival. Even ideological struggles have their ultimate cause and are most deeply motivated by nationally determined purposes and aims of life. But religions and ideologies are always able to impart particular bitterness to such struggles, and therefore also to give them great historical impressiveness. They leave their imprint on centuries of history. Nations and states living within the sphere of such ideological or religious conflicts cannot opt out of or dissociate themselves from these events. Christianity and the barbarian invasions determined the course of history for centuries. Mohammedanism convulsed the Orient as well as the western world for half a millennium. The consequences of the Reformation have affected the whole of central Europe. Nor were individual countries — either by skill or by deliberate non-participation — able to steer clear of events. Since the outbreak of the French Revolution the world has been moving with ever-increasing speed towards a new conflict, the most extreme solution of which is Bolshevism; and the essence and goal of Bolshevism is the elimination of those strata of mankind which have hitherto provided the leadership and their replacement by world-wide Jewry. . . .

No nation will be able to avoid or abstain from this historical conflict. *Since Marxism, through its victory in Russia, has established one of the greatest empires as a forward base for its future operations, this question has become a menacing one. Against a democratic world which is ideologically split stands a unified aggressive will, based on an authoritarian ideology.*

The military resources of this aggressive will are in the meantime rapidly increasing from year to year. One has only to compare the Red Army as it actually exists today with the assumptions of military men of ten or fifteen years ago to realize the menacing extent of this development. Only consider the results of a further development over ten, fifteen or twenty years and think what conditions will be like then.

Germany

Germany will as always have to be regarded as the focus of the Western world against the attacks of Bolshevism. I do not regard this as an agreeable mission but as a serious handicap and burden for our national life, regrettably resulting from our disadvantageous position in Europe. We cannot, however, escape this destiny. Our political position results from the following:

At the moment there are only two countries in Europe which can be regarded as standing firm against Bolshevism — Germany and Italy. The other nations are either corrupted by their democratic way of life, infected by Marxism and therefore likely to collapse in the foreseeable future, or ruled by authoritarian Governments, whose sole strength lies in their military resources; this means, however, that being obliged to protect their leadership against their own peoples by the armed hand of the Executive, they are unable to use this armed hand for the protection of their countries against external enemies. None of these countries would ever be capable of waging war against Soviet Russia with any prospects of success. In fact, apart from Germany and Italy, only Japan can be considered as a Power standing firm in the face of the world peril.

It is not the aim of this memorandum to prophesy the moment when the untenable situation in Europe will reach the stage of an open crisis. I only want, in these lines, to express my conviction that this crisis cannot and will not fail to occur, and that Germany has the duty of securing her existence by every means in the face of this catastrophe, and to protect herself against it, and that this obligation has a number of implications involving the most important tasks that our people have ever been set. *For a victory of Bolshevism over Germany would lead not to a Versailles Treaty but to the final destruction, indeed to the annihilation, of the German people.*

The extent of such a catastrophe cannot be estimated. How indeed, would the whole of densely populated Western Europe (including Germany), after a collapse into Bolshevism, live through probably the most gruesome catastrophe which has been visited on mankind since the downfall of the states of antiquity. *In face of the necessity of warding off this danger, all other considerations must recede into the background as completely irrelevant.*

The development of our military capacity is to be effected through the new Army. *The extent of the military development of our resources cannot be too large, nor its pace too swift.* It is a major error to believe that there can be any argument on these points or any comparison with other vital necessities. However well balanced the general pattern of a nation's life ought to be, there must at particular times be certain disturbances of the balance at the expense of other less vital tasks. *If we do not succeed in bringing the German Army as rapidly as possible to the rank of premier army in the world so far as its training, raising of units, armaments, and, above all, its spiritual education also is concerned, then Germany will be lost!* In this the basic principle applies that omissions during the months of peace cannot be made good in centuries.

Hence all other desires without exception must come second to this task. For this task involves life and the preservation of life, and all other desires — however understandable at other junctures — are unimportant or even mortally dangerous and are therefore to be rejected. Posterity will ask us one day, not what were the means, the reasons or the convictions by which we thought fit today to achieve the salvation of the nation, but *whether* in fact we achieved it. And on that day it will be no excuse for our downfall for us to describe the means which were infallible, but, alas, brought about our ruin. . . .

It is, however, impossible to use foreign exchange allocated for the purchase of raw materials to import foodstuffs without inflicting a heavy and perhaps even fatal blow on the rest. *But above all it is absolutely impossible to do this at the expense of national rearmament.* I must at this point sharply reject the view that by restricting national rearmament, that is to say, the manufacture of arms and ammunition, we could bring about an 'enrichment' in raw materials which might then benefit Germany in the event of war. Such a view is based on a complete misconception, to put it mildly, of the tasks and military requirements that lie before us. For even a successful saving of raw materials by reducing, for instance, the production of munitions would merely mean that we should stockpile these raw materials in time of peace so as to manufacture them only in the event of war, that is to say, we should be depriving ourselves during the most critical months of munitions in exchange for raw copper, lead, or possibly iron. . . .

Nearly four precious years have now gone by. There is no doubt that by now we could have been completely independent of foreign countries in the spheres of fuel supplies, rubber supplies, and partly also iron ore supplies. Just as we are now producing 700,000 or 800,000 tons of petroleum, we could be producing 3 million tons. Just as we are today manufacturing a few thousand tons of rubber, we could already be producing 70,000 or 80,000 tons per annum. Just as we have stepped up the production of iron ore from 2½ million tons to 7 million tons, we could process 20 or 25 million tons of German iron ore and even 30 millions if necessary. There has been time enough in four years to find out what we cannot do. Now we have to carry out what we can do.

I thus set the following tasks:

    I   The German armed forces must be operational within four years.

    II The German economy must be fit for war within four years. . . .

> *Documents on Nazism*, 1919 – 1945, intro. and ed. by Jeremy Noakes and Geoffrey Pridham (London, Jonathan Cape, 1974), pp. 401 – 10.

V

Undeclared War, 1937 – 39

In the approach to the Second World War 1937 was a decisive year: Germany and Japan became set on a course of territorial expansion, the Rome-Berlin Axis was confirmed and consolidated, Britain and France decided to continue the search for agreement with Germany.

Mussolini's visit to Berlin in September 1937 set the seal on the German-Italian *rapprochement* and in October Italy joined the Anti-Comintern Pact which Germany and Japan had signed the previous year. The *Duce* who in 1934 had been the guardian of Austria's independence now conceded that Austria was a German state (**58**). The way was clear for the *Anschluss*.

On 5 November, 1937 Hitler summoned his advisers to a secret conference at the Reich Chancellery. The only extant record of the conference is the much-disputed Hossbach Memorandum drawn up by Hitler's adjutant, Colonel Hossbach (**59**). The Führer declared that Germany's problems would have to be solved by force by 1943 – 45 at the latest. In the meantime his immediate aims were the seizure of Austria and Czechoslovakia. After the Hossbach Conference German military planning, hitherto defensive in character, was remodelled with the emphasis on an offensive against Czechoslovakia — Operation Green (**61**).

1937 was also a decisive year for the international order in the Far East. In July 1937 Japan, without a declaration of war, attacked China and thus unleashed a war which lasted until 1945. Roosevelt turned aside British overtures for joint mediation in the Sino-Japanese conflict for fear of antagonizing the Japanese and inflaming isolationists at home. His famous 'Quarantine' speech at Chicago on 5 October, 1937 condemning a 'reign of terror and international lawlessness' did not mark a change in American foreign policy. Roosevelt had no specific remedies in mind and excluded any action on Spain and Japan. The Brussels Conference of November 1937 which met to discuss the Sino-Japanese war was a meeting of the signatories of the Nine Power Treaty of 1922 affirming China's independence. Roosevelt refused to have the conference in Washington and had nothing new to offer delegates (60).

With danger signals flashing from the Mediterranean and Far East, the British Cabinet decided that every effort must be made to improve relations with Germany and Italy since no reliance could be placed on France and the United States. Britain could not defend herself against 'Germany, Italy and Japan simultaneously' (62). An Anglo-French conference at the end of November 1937 had agreed on the need for a general settlement with Germany.

Following the *Anschluss* on 12 March, 1938 Hitler began to harass Czechoslovakia. The principal aim of the two western democracies was to conciliate Germany and so avoid a European war. After taking military advice on the possibilities of helping Czechoslovakia and Republican Spain Léon Blum's second Popular Front government concluded on 15 March, 1938 that, short of all-out war, little could be done to help its allies.

The excerpt from the diary of the Italian foreign minister, Count Ciano, conveys the atmosphere of the war of nerves created by Hitler in the last week of September 1938 (65). There is no evidence that Roosevelt's appeal to Hitler on 27 September had any effect on the German leader's decision making (64). But the significance of the appeal, together with previous messages to Hitler and Mussolini, lay in its impact on world opinion. The moral authority and prestige of the United States was unequivocally deployed in favour of conciliation and compromise. Witness Roosevelt's cable to Neville Chamberlain after the prime minister had accepted Hitler's invitation to a conference in Munich—'Good man'. It was precisely this moral commitment to appeasement which British and French leaders had striven for since the beginning of the crisis.

After Czechoslovakia, German diplomacy focused on the creation of a tripartite alliance of Germany, Italy and Japan. Hitler's foreign minister, von Ribbentrop, handed a draft to Ciano at the Munich conference (65). A German-Italian alliance—the Pact of Steel—was finally signed on 22 May, 1939. But no pact was signed with Japan. Tortuous negotiations dragged on until 23 August, 1939 when the Japanese, mortified by the news of the German-Soviet non-aggression pact, broke off talks.

The German-Japanese negotiations were difficult because the two countries had conflicting aims. Germany sought a general all-purpose alliance for use against one or more of her potential enemies—the

Soviet Union, Britain, France, the United States. Accordingly, German drafts did not designate any particular countries as targets. Japan however wanted merely a strengthening of the Anti-Comintern pact directed against the Soviet Union. In the document 'the army's hopes regarding current foreign policies' of 3 July, 1938 the army's main concern was an early victory in the China war. To this end it recommended the strengthening of the Anti-Comintern Pact and improving relations with the United States (63). Japan was prepared to exert some political pressure on Britain and France to give up their support of Chiang Kai-shek's government in China but it did not want war.

Why, then, did the negotiations last so long? The reason lay in the confused, ambiguous and faction-ridden nature of Japanese policy making. When fresh instructions were sent to Japanese envoys in Berlin and Rome on 25 January, 1939 a compromise position was adopted whereby the draft text accepted the German formula of 'one or more non-signatory nations' but the secret items of understanding made it clear that for Japan the alliance was mainly directed against the Soviet Union and that military aid was limited to a Soviet attack on one of the signatories (66). But it was a case of too many cooks. The 25 January instructions were soon outflanked as the foreign ministry, army, navy and ambassadors, not to mention the Germans, all weighed in with drafts and counter-drafts.

The German-Soviet non-aggression pact of 23 August, 1939 more than compensated Hitler for the breakdown of negotiations with Tokyo. A German-Soviet *rapprochement* lay in the logic of Versailles since both states had reason to be dissatisfied with the peace treaties. The Treaty of Rapallo in 1922 initiated German-Soviet political and military cooperation. Hitler had broken off these links and affirmed his opposition to the Soviet Union (57). It was Munich that paved the way to better relations. Isolated and excluded from a major European settlement the Soviet Union reappraised its policy.

Anglo-French guarantees to Poland on 31 March, 1939 did little to allay Soviet distrust of Western intentions. By April 1939 Germany and the Soviet Union needed each other. After the collapse of German-Polish talks Hitler wanted the Soviet Union's benevolent neutrality. Stalin's main concern was security. Faced with the danger of war on two fronts—Soviet and Japanese forces clashed on the Mongolian-Manchurian frontier in 1938 – 39—the Soviet leader insured himself by talking to both sides. The protracted negotiations with Britain and France for a tripartite alliance in the summer of 1939 convinced Stalin that the British were hedging to gain time. During the months of haggling in Moscow the one question that really mattered, namely, whether Poland and Romania would allow Soviet forces to cross their frontiers, was never raised. It was left to Marshal Voroshilov, commissar for defence, to ask this key question at the third session of the military talks on 14 August (**69**).

The one consolation for the two western democracies on 3 September, 1939 was that public opinion which had been so divided in 1938 was now united on the issue of resisting Germany (**68**).

58   Italy will not save Austria, November 1937

Conversation between Mussolini and von Ribbentrop, German ambassador in London, 6 November, 1937.

Finally, Ribbentrop discusses the Austrian question.

After stating that he is speaking in a purely personal capacity, he points out to the Duce that in the grand policy of Rome and Berlin, Austria now represents an element of secondary importance, and that he considers that at a certain moment it will be necessary to settle finally a question on which the enemies of the common Italo-German policy still speculate. The Duce replies that Austria is a German country by race, language and culture. The Austrian question must not be considered as a problem affecting Italy and Germany, but, on the contrary, as a problem of an international order. For his part he has stated, and repeats it now, that he is tired of mounting guard over Austrian independence, especially if the Austrians no longer want their independence. The Duce sees the situation thus: Austria is German state No. 2. It will never be able to do anything without Germany, far less against Germany. Italian interest today is no longer as lively as it was some years ago, for one thing because of Italy's imperialist development, which was now concentrating her interest on the Mediterranean and the Colonies. It must be added that the fact that the Austrians have not modified in the slightest their cold and negative attitude towards us has contributed to the decrease of Italian interest in Austria. According to the Duce, the best method is to let events take their natural course. One must not aggravate the situation, so as to avoid crises of an international nature. On the other hand, France knows that if a crisis should arise in Austria, Italy would do nothing. This was said to Schuschnigg, [Austrian chancellor] too, on the occasion of the Venice conversation. We cannot impose independence upon Austria which, by the very fact that it was imposed, would cease to be independence. On the Austrian question, therefore, it is necessary to abide by the formula enunciated during the conversation with Göring [Commander in chief, German air force] in the Karinhall: nothing will be done without previous exchange of information. . . .

> C.J. Lowe and F. Marzari, *Italian Foreign Policy*, 1870 – 1940 (London, Routledge and Kegan Paul, 1975), pp. 408 – 9.

59   The Hossbach Memorandum, 10 November 1937

Minutes of the Conference in the Reich Chancellery, Berlin, 5 November, 1937, from 4.15 to 8.30 p.m.

Present: The Führer and Chancellor,
Field Marshal von Blomberg, War Minister,
Colonel General Baron von Fritsch, Commander in Chief, Army,
Admiral Dr h. c. Raeder, Commander in Chief, Navy,
Colonel General Göring, Commander in Chief, *Luftwaffe*,
Baron von Neurath, Foreign Minister,
Colonel Hossbach.

The Führer began by stating that the subject of the present conference was of such importance that its discussion would, in other countries, certainly be a matter for a full Cabinet Meeting, but he — the Führer — had rejected the idea of making it a subject of discussion before the wider circle of the Reich Cabinet just because of the importance of the matter. His exposition to follow was the fruit of thorough deliberation and the experiences of his 4½ years of power. He wished to explain to the gentlemen present his basic ideas concerning the opportunities for the development of our position in the field of foreign affairs and its requirements, and he asked, in the interests of a long-term German policy, that his exposition be regarded, in the event of his death, as his last will and testament.
The Führer then continued:

The aim of German policy was to make secure and to preserve the racial community [*Volksmasse*] and to enlarge it. It was therefore a question of space. . . .

German policy had to reckon with two hate-inspired antagonists, Britain and France, to whom a German colossus in the centre of Europe was a thorn in the flesh, and both countries were opposed to any further strengthening of Germany's position either in Europe or overseas; in support of this opposition they were able to count on the agreement of all their political parties. Both countries saw in the establishment of German military bases overseas a threat to their own communications, a safeguarding of German commerce, and, as a consequence, a strengthening of Germany's position in Europe. . . .

Germany's problem could only be solved by means of force and this was never without attendant risk. The campaigns of Frederick the Great for Silesia and Bismarck's wars against Austria and France had involved unheard-of risk, and the swiftness of the Prussian action in 1870 had kept Austria from entering the war. If one accepts as the basis of the following exposition the resort to force with its attendant risks, then there remain still to be answered the questions 'when' and 'how'. In this matter there were three cases [*Fälle*] to be dealt with:

Case 1: Period 1943 – 1945

After this date only a change for the worse, from our point of view, could be expected.

The equipment of the army, navy, and *Luftwaffe*, as well as the formation of the officer corps, was nearly completed. Equipment and armament were modern; in further delay there lay the danger of their obsolescence. In particular, the secrecy of 'special weapons' could not be preserved forever. The recruiting of reserves was limited to current age groups; further drafts from older untrained age groups were no longer available.

Our relative strength would decrease in relation to the rearmament which would by then have been carried out by the rest of the world. If we did not act by 1943 – 45, any year could, in consequence of a lack of reserves, produce the food crisis, to cope with which the necessary foreign exchange was not available, and this must be regarded as a 'waning point of the regime'. Besides, the world was expecting our attack and was increasing its countermeasures from year to year. It was while the rest of the world was still preparing its defences [*sich abriegele*] that we were obliged to take the offensive.

Nobody knew today what the situation would be in the years 1943 – 45. One thing only was certain, that we could not wait longer.

On the one hand there was the great *Wehrmacht*, and the necessity of maintaining it at its present level, the ageing of the movement and of its leaders; and on the other, the prospect of a lowering of the standard of living and of a limitation of the birth rate, which left no choice but to act. If the Führer was still living, it was his unalterable resolve to solve Germany's problem of space at the latest by 1943 – 45. The necessity for action before 1943 – 45 would arise in cases 2 and 3.

Case 2:

If internal strife in France should develop into such a domestic crisis as to absorb the French Army completely and render it incapable of use for war against Germany, then the time for action against the Czechs had come.

Case 3:

If France is so embroiled by a war with another state that she cannot 'proceed' against Germany.

For the improvement of our politico-military position our first objective, in the event of our being embroiled in war, must be to overthrow Czechoslovakia and Austria simultaneously in order to remove the threat to our flank in any possible operation against the west. In a conflict with France it was hardly to be regarded as likely that the Czechs would declare war on us on the very same day as France. The desire to join in the war would, however, increase among the Czechs in proportion to any weakening on our part and then her participation could clearly take the form of an attack toward Silesia, toward the north or toward the west.

If the Czechs were overthrown and a common German-Hungarian frontier achieved, a neutral attitude on the part of Poland could be the more certainly counted on in the event of a Franco-German conflict. Our agreements with Poland only retained their force as long as Germany's strength remained unshaken. In the event of German setbacks a Polish action against East Prussia, and possibly against Pomerania and Silesia as well, had to be reckoned with.

On the assumption of a development of the situation leading to action on our part as planned, in the years 1943 – 45, the attitude of France, Britain, Italy, Poland, and Russia could probably be estimated as follows:

Actually, the Führer believed that almost certainly Britain, and probably France as well, had already tacitly written off the Czechs and were reconciled to the fact that this question would be cleared up in due course by Germany. Difficulties connected with the Empire, and the prospect of being once more entangled in a protracted European war, were decisive considerations for Britain against participation in a war against Germany. Britain's attitude would certainly not be without influence on that of France. An attack by France without British support, and with the prospect of the offensive being brought to a standstill on our western fortifications, was hardly probable. Nor was a French march through Belgium and Holland without British support to be expected; this also was a course not to be contemplated by us in the event of a conflict with France, because it would certainly entail the hostility of Britain. It would of course be necessary to maintain a strong defence [*eine Abriegelung*] on our western frontier during the prosecution of our attack on the Czechs and Austria. And in this connection it had to be remembered that the defence measures of the Czechs were growing in strength from year to year, and that the actual worth of the Austrian Army also was increasing in the course of time. Even though the populations concerned, especially of Czechoslovakia, were not sparse, the annexation of Czechoslovakia and Austria would mean an acquisition of foodstuffs for 5 to 6 million people, on the assumption that the compulsory emigration of 2 million people from Czechoslovakia and 1 million people from Austria was practicable. The incorporation of these two States with Germany meant, from the politico-military point of view, a substantial advantage because it would mean shorter and better frontiers, the freeing of forces for other purposes, and the possibility of creating new units up to a level of about 12 divisions, that is, 1 new division per million inhabitants.

Italy was not expected to object to the elimination of the Czechs, but it was impossible at the moment to estimate what her attitude on the Austrian question would be; that depended essentially upon whether the Duce were still alive.

The degree of surprise and the swiftness of our action were decisive factors for Poland's attitude. Poland—with Russia at her rear—will have little inclination to engage in war against a victorious Germany.

Military intervention by Russia must be countered by the swiftness of our operations; however, whether such an intervention was a practical contingency at all was, in view of Japan's attitude, more than doubtful.

Should case 2 arise—the crippling of France by civil war—the situation thus created by the elimination of the most dangerous opponent must be seized upon whenever it occurs for the blow against the Czechs.

The Führer saw case 3 coming definitely nearer; it might emerge from the present tensions in the Mediterranean, and he was resolved to take advantage of it whenever it happened, even as early as 1938. . . .

If Germany made use of this war to settle the Czech and Austrian questions, it was to be assumed that Britain—herself at war with Italy—would decide not to act against Germany. Without British support, a warlike action by France against Germany was not to be expected. . . .

In appraising the situation Field Marshal von Blomberg and Colonel General von Fritsch repeatedly emphasized the necessity that Britain and France must not appear in the role of our enemies, and stated that the French Army would not be so committed by the war with Italy that France could not at the same time enter the field with forces superior to ours on our western frontier. General von Fritsch estimated the probable French forces available for use on the Alpine frontier at approximately twenty divisions, so that a strong French superiority would still remain on the western frontier, with the role, according to the German view, of invading the Rhineland. In this matter, moreover, the advanced state of French defence preparations (*Mobilmachung*) must be taken into particular account, and it must be remembered apart from the insignificant value of our present fortifications—on which Field Marshal von Blomberg laid special emphasis—that the four motorized divisions intended for the west were still more or less incapable of movement. In regard to our offensive toward the southeast, Field Marshal von Blomberg drew particular attention to the strength of the Czech fortifications, which had acquired by now a structure like a Maginot Line and which would gravely hamper our attack.

General von Fritsch mentioned that this was the very purpose of a study which he had ordered made this winter, namely, to examine the possibility of conducting operations against the Czechs with special reference to overcoming the Czech fortification system; the General further expressed his opinion that under existing circumstances he must give up his plan to go abroad on his leave, which was due to begin on 10 November. The Führer dismissed this idea on the ground that the possibility of a conflict need not yet be regarded as so imminent. To the Foreign Minister's objection that an Anglo-French-Italian conflict was not yet within such a measurable distance as the Führer seemed to assume, the Führer put the summer of 1938 as the date which seemed to him possible for this. In reply to considerations offered by Field Marshal von Blomberg and General von Fritsch regarding the attitude of Britain and France, the Führer repeated his previous statements that he was convinced of Britain's non-participation, and therefore he did not believe in the probability of belligerent action by France against Germany. Should the Mediterranean conflict under discussion lead to a general mobilization in Europe, then we must immediately begin action against the Czechs. On the other hand, should the powers not engaged in the war declare themselves disinterested, then Germany would have to adopt a similar attitude to this for the time being.

Colonel General Göring thought that, in view of the Führer's statement, we should consider liquidating our military undertakings in Spain. The Führer agrees to this with the limitation that he thinks he should reserve a decision for a proper moment.

The second part of the conference was concerned with concrete questions of armament.

Certified Correct:

Colonel, (General Staff)　　　　　　　　　　　　　　　Hossbach.

DGFP series D, I, no. 19.

60　The United States must take firm action against Japan, November, 1937.

Telegram from chairman of the American delegation at the Brussels Conference to the secretary of state, 14 November, 1937.

For the President and the Secretary. The effort of this Conference to bring about conciliation has been doubly difficult because it was preceded by condemnation of Japan at Geneva and Washington. The French attitude has improved appreciably of late and Delbos [French foreign minister] has been cooperative and helpful. However, he is convinced entirely that it is futile to expect that normal pressure will have any appreciable effect upon Japan; that Japan is relying upon force and is impervious to reason; and that since Japan has spurned every effort towards conciliation the Conference must soon decide what further pressure the principal powers can and will exert.

Eden [Foreign secretary] seems to believe that there is still some chance that some way may be found to bring Japan into some sort of a negotiation; feels that this may have to be done by a few powers outside of the Conference and its reporting to the Conference; feels that we cannot usefully and with dignity continue much longer to confine ourselves to an expression of principles and pleas to Japan to accept our good offices only to be rebuffed; and is convinced that our efforts to bring about a practical and just settlement would succeed if Japan really believed that at least our two Powers would take some positive action. He has repeated to me that the British Cabinet favors doing anything that the United States may be willing to do and he agrees that whatever is done or is not done should be so handled as not to put the responsibility or blame on either country only and that whatever courses we pursue should be along parallel lines.

He has spoken of the possibility of embargoes without enthusiasm but with the indication that the British would be willing to proceed on that line if we were willing. I have told him that I have no authority even to discuss that possibility seriously. He has stated that although Great Britain could not possibly challenge Japan single-handed with the situation in Europe what it is, they could send several battleships, et cetera, to the Far East and he is inclined to think that a concentration of naval forces might be an advisable and useful gesture.

Delbos has tried repeatedly to discuss positive joint action with Eden and me but I have avoided such discussion. He told us on Friday that the Japanese Ambassador in Paris had threatened that if France did not soon stop transit of arms through Indo-China Japan would occupy Hainan and take retaliatory measures. He gave me the impression that while they did not want to knuckle down to Japan they were afraid not to do so unless they could get some assurance of aid from Great Britain and ourselves. I told him that I could of course give no such assurance but that I thought they were unduly afraid of what Japan might do as she has her hands very full and would be foolish to bring on herself trouble with some other power. He then told me that Stern and Henry [respectively former French minister of colonies and French envoy] had recently had a very encouraging conversation with the President on this question.

He showed me Henry's telegram giving an account of the conversation in which you were reported as having said in substance that you thought France ought to keep open the transit through Indo-China, that they had expressed their fear of retaliation on the part of

Japan and that you had replied that they ought to bear in mind that because of the inter-relation of communication and interest between Indo-China, Hong Kong, and the Philippines it was possible that the United States would regard an attack on one as in the nature of an attack on all.

I am going into some detail because I feel that unless we are pre-pared to participate in some positive steps in case Japan does not within the near future enter into some discussion looking toward a peaceful settlement, most countries will lose their nerve and fold their hands. The minimum step that will in my opinion hold them in line would be the adoption of a resolution calling for non-recognition of changes brought about by armed force, prohibition of government loans and credits and discouragement of private loans and credits. There are indications that Japan is nervous over this Conference and is maneuvering in various ways to undermine it; and she is believed to have been making veiled threats to practically all of the powers except Great Britain and ourselves.

What concerns me somewhat is that while Japan is now nervous for fear we may agree upon something positive, if we go on much longer without any evidence of intention to do anything more than preach she will soon become firmly convinced that she can pursue her course without any danger of interference.

> *FRUS*, 1937, IV, (Washington, 1954), 183 – 5.

61 General Jodl's amendment to 'Operation Green', 7 December, 1937

Jodl was chief of the national defence section in the high command of the armed forces.

1 The further development of the diplomatic situation makes 'Operation Red' increasingly less likely than 'Operation Green'. . . .

2 The political preconditions for the activation of 'Operation Green' have changed, following the directives of the Führer and Reich Chancellor, and the objectives of such a war have been expanded.

The previous Section II of Part 2 of the directive of the High Command of the Armed Forces of 24 June, 1937 is therefore to be deleted and replaced by the enclosed new version. . . .

The main emphasis of all mobilization planning is now to be placed on 'Operation Green'. . . .

II War on two fronts with main effort in south-east ('Operation Green')

I Prerequisites

When Germany has achieved complete preparedness for war in all spheres, then the military conditions will have been created for carrying out an offensive war against Czechoslovakia, so that the solution of the German problem of living space can be carried to a victorious conclusion even if one or another of the Great Powers intervene against us.

Apart from many other considerations, there is in the first place the defensive capacity of our western fortifications, which will permit the western frontier of the German Reich to be held with weak forces for a long time against greatly superior strength.

But even so the Government [*Staatsführung*] will do what is politically feasible to avoid the risk for Germany of a war on two fronts and will try to avoid any situation with which, as far as can be judged, Germany could not cope militarily or economically.

Should the political situation not develop, or develop only slowly, in our favour, then the execution of 'Operation Green' from our side will have to be postponed for years. If, however, a situation arises which, owing to Britain's aversion to a general European War, through her lack of interest in the Central European problem and because of a conflict breaking out between Italy and France in the Mediterranean, creates the probability that Germany will face no other opponent than Russia on Czechoslovakia's side, then 'Operation Green' will start *before* the completion of Germany's full preparedness for war.

2   The military objective of 'Operation Green' is still the speedy occupation of Bohemia and Moravia with the simultaneous solution of the Austrian question in the sense of incorporating Austria into the German Reich. In order to achieve the latter aim, military force will be required only if other means do not lead or have not led to success.

In accordance with this military objective it is the task of the German Wehrmacht to make preparations so that:

(a) the bulk of all forces can invade Czechoslovakia with speed, surprise and the maximum impetus;

(b) reserves, mainly the armed units of the SS, are kept ready in order, if necessary, to march into Austria;

(c) in the west, security can be maintained with only a minimum of forces for rearguard protection of the eastern operations. . . .

> *DGFP*, series D, VII, app. III (K),
> pp. 635 – 7.

62 The British Cabinet reviews its foreign and defence policies, 8 December, 1937

The Cabinet had before them a Memorandum by the Minister for Coordination of Defence (C.P. – 295 (37)) covering a Most Secret Report by the Chiefs of Staff Sub-Committee (C.I.D. Paper No. 1366 – B) on the Comparison of the Strength of Great Britain with that of certain other Nations as at January, 1938. The *draft* Conclusions reached by the Committee of Imperial Defence (303rd Meeting, Minute 3) after consideration of the above Report were as follows:

F.R. 10(38)10

(i) To take note of:
(a) The warnings contained in the Report of the Chiefs of Staff Sub-Committee (C.I.D. Paper No. 1366 – B):

F.R.I. (38) 1.

(b) The statement on foreign policy made at this meeting by the Secretary of State for Foreign Affairs, which, it was agreed, takes proper account of the facts of the situation, including those mentioned in the Report by the Chiefs of Staff:
(c) The Prime Minister's observations as summarized in the above Minutes.
(ii) That the Report by the Chiefs of Staff Sub-Committee (C.I.D. Paper No. 1366 – B) together with the above conclusions (but not the full Minutes) should be circulated to the Cabinet; it being left to the Prime Minister to explain the gist of the discussion to the Cabinet.

In compliance with the second of the conclusions quoted above, the Prime Minister made a statement to the Cabinet.

He pointed out that in paragraph 41 of their memorandum, the Chiefs of Staff Sub-Committee had summarized their conclusions. In paragraph 42 they had expressed the warning referred to in conclusion (i)(a) above. From this paragraph, he quoted the following extracts:

'From the above Report it will be seen that our Naval, Military and Air Forces, in their present stage of development are still far from sufficient to meet our defensive commitments, which now extend from western Europe through the Mediterranean to the Far East. . . . Without overlooking the assistance which we should hope to obtain from France, and possibly other allies, we cannot foresee the time when our defence forces will be strong enough to safeguard our territory, trade and vital interests against Germany, Italy and Japan simultaneously. We cannot, therefore, exaggerate the importance, from the point of view of Imperial defence, of any political or international action that can be taken to reduce the numbers of our potential enemies and to gain the support of potential allies.'

The Foreign Secretary, the Prime Minister continued, had circulated a short paper to the Committee of Imperial Defence dealing with certain aspects of the Chiefs of Staff paper but not pretending to give any general account of our foreign policy. At the meeting of the Committee, however, the Foreign Secretary had made a verbal statement, the general effect of which had been summarized in conclusion (i)(b). He then summarized the main considerations that had been brought to the notice of the Committee. It was true, as the Chiefs of Staff had pointed out, that we could not hope to confront satisfactorily Germany, Italy and Japan simultaneously and, when we looked round as to what help we could get from other nations, the results were not very encouraging. France was our most important friend. Though she was strong defensively and possessed a powerful army, the French Air Force was far from satisfactory. During the Anglo-French visit, M. Chautemps had admitted to an output of aircraft that was only about one-fifth (60 − 300) of our own. A long time must elapse before France would be able to give us much help in the air. The Power that had the greatest strength was the United States of America, but he would be a rash man who based his calculations on help from that quarter. Our position in relation to the smaller Powers was much better than formerly, but he did not think that they would add much to our offensive or defensive strength. In time of peace their support was useful, but in war less so. The Chiefs of Staff, as he had mentioned, said they could not foresee the time when our defence forces would be strong enough to safeguard our territory, trade and vital interests against Germany, Italy and Japan simultaneously. They had urged that our foreign policy must be governed by this consideration, and they had made rather a strong appeal to this effect. Of course, it would be possible to make an effort to detach one of the three Powers from the other two and it might even succeed. This, however, could only be done at the cost of concessions which would involve humiliations and disadvantages to this country by destroying the confidence of other nations. No one would suppose, therefore, that we should try and bribe one of the three nations to leave the other two. What the Foreign Secretary was doing was to try and prevent a situation arising in which the three Powers mentioned would ever be at war with us. He recalled that before the trouble had arisen in the Far East, we had been making great efforts to improve our relations with Japan and that considerable progress had been made. Owing to recent events, we had been compelled to break off these negotiations, but we had tried to keep open the position of resuming them later on. We had avoided threats ourselves and had restrained others from making them. The improvement in relations with Italy was not easy, but we had made some efforts to get better terms, in spite of the difficult attitude of Mussolini and we were about to make a further effort at that end of the Berlin-Rome Axis. As he himself had pointed out before, however, Germany was the real key to the question. In view of the recent consideration given by the Cabinet to the question of improving relations with Germany, it was unnecessary to develop that theme any further. He thought, however, that he had said enough to show that the strategic considerations urged by the Chiefs of Staff were fully taken into account in our foreign policy and that was what underlay the taking note by the Committee of Imperial Defence of conclusion (i)(b) quoted above, namely—

'(b) The statement on foreign policy made at this meeting by the Secretary of State for Foreign Affairs, which, it was agreed, takes proper account of the facts of the situation, including those mentioned in the Report by the Chiefs of Staff.'

In the course of a short discussion, attention was drawn to the late Prime Minister's undertaking as to the maintenance of parity between the Air Force of the United Kingdom and that of Germany.

The Minister for Coordination of Defence pointed out that Lord Baldwin's statement required interpretation. He had never taken it to mean that we must have exactly the same number of fighters and bombers as Germany in order to carry out the contemplated equality.

The Prime Minister said he did not intend to repeat Lord Baldwin's words and if the question were raised, he would make it clear that the Government did not consider it necessary to have precise equality in every class of aircraft. It might be necessary to make a statement on this subject before very long.

After some further discussion, the Cabinet agreed:

To take note of the Report contained in C.P. 296(37), together with the Prime Minister's remarks thereon and summarized above.

> *Cabinet Papers*, (Public Record Office, London), CAB 23/90A.

63   The aims of the Japanese army, July 1938

Document 'The Army's hopes regarding current foreign policies, 3 July 1938'.

I   General Foreign Policy

Policy

1   By strengthening the anti-Comintern axis and disposing of the China Incident decisively, to win de facto recognition by the Powers of our China Policy and persuade them to cooperate in the construction of a new China in accord with our wishes; to win their support for our posture; and by so doing to bring about a resolution of the Incident quickly and smoothly and also contribute to the success of the empire's foreign policy after the Incident has been settled.

2   To coordinate all diplomatic and economic activities on the principle of 'national policies first'.

Details

1   Diplomatic efforts should concentrate on the following:
   (a)   Strengthening of the anti-Comintern axis.
   (b)   Adopting positive measures to persuade the Soviet Union not to participate in the China Incident (there is no change in the fundamental policy of discouraging the Soviet Union's aggressive intentions towards East Asia).
   (c)   Inducing Britain to abandon its policy of supporting Chiang Kai-shek.
   (d)   Persuading the United States at the very least to retain a neutral attitude, if possible to adopt a pro-Japanese attitude, and especially to strengthen friendly economic relations.

2   The importation of arms into China should be stopped by diplomatic means as well as by military force.

3   The rights of the Powers in China should be respected so long as
     they do not interfere with the principles below. At the same time
     we welcome the participation of third countries friendly to Japan
     in the economic development of the new China.

     (a) The Empire of Japan will assist the new China in the deter-
         mination of all financial and economic policies, including
         matters relating to currency, customs, and customs rates;
         these are to be observed by third powers.

     (b) In north China and eastern Mongolia [Mokyo] the empire will
         assume actual control over the development of national
         defence resources.

     (c) In central China, usually in cooperation with the Powers, the
         empire will engage in industrial development projects.

     (d) In areas other than those specified in the two preceding items,
         the empire generally will acknowledge existing industrial
         development projects.

     (e) Trade with China, in principle, will be based on free
         competition.

     (f) No concessions granted by the Chiang regime since the
         beginning of the Incident will be approved.

4   Amicable mediation efforts by third powers should not be rejected
     so long as they do not contradict established policies concerned
     with solution of the Incident.

5   Intervention by third nations should be decisively blocked.

6   The empire should establish an effective propaganda organ to
     enable third powers to understand the true intention of the
     empire, to reverse quickly their pro-Chiang Kai-shek attitudes,
     and to create a worldwide anticommunist sentiment. For this
     purpose, the government should consider the employment of
     suitable persons from outside the government.

II   Operations to Strengthen the Anti-Comintern Axis

Policy

1   To strengthen political relations between Japan, Germany and
     Italy.

2   To strengthen economic cooperation of Japan and Manchukuo
     with Germany and Italy.

3   To endeavour to persuade needed countries to join the Anti-
     Comintern Pact. In particular, the adherence of Manchukuo
     should be brought about as quickly as possible.

Details

1   The Policy for the strengthening of political relations between
     Japan, Germany, and Italy should be as follows: Separate, secret
     agreements should be concluded with Germany, expanding the
     spirit of the Anti-Comintern Pact so as to convert it into an anti-
     Soviet military alliance; and with Italy, so that it can serve mainly
     for the purpose of blocking Britain.
2   In general, the following should be considered for strengthening
     economic cooperation between Japan and Manchukuo on the one
     hand and Germany and Italy on the other:
     (a) Promotion of a trade agreement and general economic
         cooperation between Japan and Manchukuo, and Germany
         and Italy.
     (b) Devising suitable measures to meet the demand for an
         expansion of industrial facilities, particularly machine-tool
         production.
     (c) Cooperation in the economic development of Manchukuo
         and China and, if necessary, granting economic privileges to
         Germany and Italy in China.
     (d) Taking up the question of returning to Germany its former
         colonies in the Pacific in order to strengthen Japan's relations
         with Germany, particularly in the realm of economic
         cooperation.
3   Efforts should be made to persuade countries such as Poland and
     Rumania to join the Anti-Comintern Pact as soon as possible.
4   Efforts should be devoted to creating a worldwide anticommunist
     sentiment.

III   Operations vis-a-vis the Soviet Union

Policy

To conduct various operations so as effectively to discourage the USSR
from participating in the China Incident.

Details

1   Our national strength should be increased, the economic

development of China and Manchukuo should be hastened, and our forces in Manchukuo should be enlarged so as to maintain and increase our strength *vis-à-vis* the Soviet Union.

2   Propaganda should be disseminated in Britain, the United States, and France, telling the truth about the Soviet Union and its untrustworthy behaviour, so as to discredit and isolate it internationally.

3   Direct relations with the USSR should be conducted fairly and firmly, with particular attention to insuring that the Soviet Union adheres to the letter of existing treaties.

4   Soviet schemes in China and its illegal activities *vis-à-vis* Japan and Manchukuo should be publicized in order to arouse domestic public opinion.

5   A nonaggression treaty between Japan and the USSR should not be concluded.

IV   Operations vis-a-vis Britain

Policy

To bring about British understanding of Japan's firm and fair attitude and adjust Anglo-Japanese economic relations in China, thereby causing Britain promptly to abandon its policy of support of Chiang Kai-shek.

Details

1   Britain should be convinced that prolongation of the China Incident is disadvantageous to its Far Eastern policy; and to the extent that Britain accepts Japan's policy for solving the Incident, friendly consideration should be given to British rights in south-central China.

2   Special care should be taken regarding measures that concern British rights in China, and unnecessary friction should be avoided.

3   Our diplomatic, economic, and propaganda agencies in the British bloc should be coordinated and improved. Japanese behaviour, both public and private, toward Britain should be restrained, so as to convince Britain of Japan's good faith and ability to accomplish its policies in China.

V   Operations vis-a-vis the United States

Policy

To persuade the United States at the very least to retain its neutral attitude during the period of the Incident and if possible adopt a pro-Japanese attitude, and especially to strengthen friendly economic relations.

Details

1   Efforts should be made to correct Japan's image by disseminating appropriate propaganda, especially by presenting the facts about the actual situation.

2   Every possible effort should be made to insure the security of American rights in China.

3   In addition, all other available action should be taken to strengthen friendly economic ties, especially to promote trade and to secure the introduction of American capital, for example:

(a) Strengthening trade with the United States in order to secure the resources needed for total mobilization.

(b) Establishing credit in the United States to meet the demand for an expansion of production, particularly of the machine industry.

(c) Cooperating in the economic development of Manchukuo and China and, if necessary, granting economic privileges to the United States in China.

(d) Adjusting Japanese-American relations by diplomatic negotiation whenever necessary for the attainment of the present policy.

VI   Operations vis-a-vis France

Policy

To persuade France to abandon its policy of support for Chiang Kai-shek particularly to discontinue supplying arms to China.

James William Morley, (ed), *Deterrent Diplomacy, Japan, Germany and the USSR* 1935–1940 (New York, Columbia University Press, 1976), app. 3 pp. 268–72.

64 Roosevelt suggests a conference on Czechoslovakia, September 1938

Telegram from President Roosevelt to Adolf Hitler, 27 September, 1938.

I desire to acknowledge Your Excellency's reply to my telegram of 26 September. I was confident that you would coincide in the opinion I expressed regarding the unforeseeable consequences and the incalculable disaster which would result to the entire world from the outbreak of a European war.

The question before the world today, Mr Chancellor, is not the question of errors of judgment or of injustices committed in the past. It is the question of the fate of the world today and tomorrow. The world asks of us who at this moment are heads of nations the supreme capacity to achieve the destinies of nations without forcing upon them as a price, the mutilation and death of millions of citizens.

Resort to force in the Great War failed to bring tranquillity. Victory and defeat were alike sterile. That lesson the world should have learned. For that reason above all others I addressed on 26 September my appeal to Your Excellency and to the President of Czechoslovakia and to the Prime Ministers of Great Britain and of France.

The two points I sought to emphasize were, first, that all matters of difference between the German Government and the Czechoslovak Government could and should be settled by pacific methods; and, second, that the threatened alternative of the use of force on a scale likely to result in a general war is as unnecessary as it is unjustifiable. It is, therefore, supremely important that negotiations should continue without interruption until a fair and constructive solution is reached.

My conviction on these two points is deepened because responsible statesmen have officially stated that an agreement in principle has already been reached between the Government of the German Reich and the Government of Czechoslovakia, although the precise time, method and detail of carrying out that agreement remain at issue.

Whatever existing differences may be, and whatever their merits may be — and upon them I do not and need not undertake to pass — my appeal was solely that negotiations be continued until a peaceful settlement is found, and that thereby a resort to force be avoided.

Present negotiations still stand open. They can be continued if you will give the word. Should the need for supplementing them become evident, nothing stands in the way of widening their scope into a conference of all the nations directly interested in the present controversy.

Such a meeting to be held immediately—in some neutral spot in Europe—would offer the opportunity for this and correlated questions to be solved in a spirit of justice, of fair dealing, and, in all human probability, with a greater permanence.

In my considered judgment, and in the light of the experience of this century, continued negotiations remain the only way by which the immediate problem can be disposed of upon any lasting basis.

Should you agree to a solution in this peaceful manner I am convinced that hundreds of millions throughout the world would recognize your action as an outstanding historic service to all humanity.

Allow me to state my unqualified conviction that history, and the souls of every man, woman, and child whose lives will be lost in the threatened war will hold us and all of us accountable should we omit any appeal for its prevention.

The Government of the United States has no political involvements in Europe, and will assume no obligations in the conduct of the present negotiations. Yet in our own right we recognize our responsibilities as a part of a world of neighbors.

The conscience and the impelling desire of the people of my country demand that the voice of their government be raised again and yet again to avert and to avoid war.

> Cited in: Richard D. Challener, *From Isolation to Containment*, 1931 – 1952 (London, Edward Arnold, 1970), pp 84 – 5.

65   Italy and the Munich crisis

Excerpts from the diary kept by Count Galeazzo Ciano, Italian foreign minister, 27 – 30 September, 1938

27 September. The Duce received Valle, Pariani, and Cavagnari [respectively chiefs of air, army and naval staffs] and gave orders for an initial mobilization sufficient to ensure armed neutrality in the first phase. Then he had a long conference with me.

He is still perplexed about the attitude which the French and the English will adopt and, in the event of their declaring war, about their military tactics. An attack on the Siegfried line? Out of the question. And as Germany, once Czechoslovakia has been liquidated, will not attack in the west, one cannot rule out the possibility that the conflict may be resolved without a clash between the giants. In any case, the Duce wants to settle forthwith the basis of the political understanding with Berlin and to create organs of military cooperation. With this end in view he proposes a meeting between me and Ribbentrop [German foreign minister]. The Germans accept and suggest bringing the soldiers too. Keitel [Chief of German general staff] on their side, Pariani and Valle on our side. We are to meet in Munich at 12 noon on Thursday.

No new moves on the diplomatic chess-board, except a confirmation from Berlin that 'the day is tomorrow'. In the afternoon I received Villani, to whom I repeated the usual recommendations of calm; the Japanese Ambassador, who, unofficially, declared himself convinced that Tokyo will intervene on our side; and Cristich, who came to repudiate the conduct I have mentioned of their Minister in Tirana. He told me that, according to the Czech Minister, Russian intervention will take the concrete form of an air attack on Poland.

Chamberlain [British prime minister] spoke on the wireless at 8 tonight — his tone was depressed. It is that of a man who has abandoned all hope of peace. In fact, short of a miracle. . . .

28 September. 10 a.m. Four hours to go before the outbreak of hostilities, when Perth [British ambassador in Rome] telephones to ask for an interview. I receive him at once. He says, with much emotion, that Chamberlain appeals to the Duce for his friendly intervention in these hours, which he considers the last in which something can be done to save peace and civilization. He repeats the guarantee already offered by England and France for the return of the Sudetenland. I ask Perth whether I am to regard his *démarche* as an official invitation to the Duce to assume the role of mediator. Yes. In that case there is no time to lose — the offer deserves to be given consideration. I tell Perth to wait for me at the Palazzo Chigi. I go to the Duce. He agrees at once on the impossibility of meeting Chamberlain's request with a flat refusal. He telephones Attolico [Italian ambassador in Berlin]: 'Go to the Führer and tell him, having first said that in any eventuality I shall be at his side, that I recommend that the commencement of hostilities should be delayed for 24 hours. Meanwhile I undertake to study what can be done to solve the problem.' I go back to the Palazzo Chigi. I inform Perth that hostilities are to begin today and confirm that our place is beside Germany. His face quivers and his eyes are red. When I add that nevertheless the Duce has accepted Chamberlain's request and has proposed a delay of 24 hours, he bursts into a sobbing laugh

and rushes off to his Embassy. A little later he asks for another interview. He brings with him a message from Chamberlain to the Duce
and a copy of another sent to Hitler: a concrete proposal for a
Conference of Four with the task of reaching a radical solution of
the Sudeten problem within seven days. It cannot be rejected—by
rejecting it Hitler would draw the hatred of the world upon himself
and have the sole responsibility for the conflict. Palazzo Venezia—the
Duce decides to support the English request, particularly as the Führer
has now, at Mussolini's desire, had a phonogram of instructions made.
I telephone to Perth, to inform him, and to Attolico, to give him
directions. Naturally I cancel the meeting with Ribbentrop and Keitel
arranged yesterday.

Blondel [French Chargé d'Affairs in Rome] too, it transpires from a
telephone call, is preparing to make a *démarche*. Not a hope—it is not
our intention that France shall interfere. The whole face of the
question would be changed and the German would, rightly, smell a
rat. I telephone to Perth: 'It transpires that France is preparing to put
her oar in. I advise you that any *démarche* by Blondel would simply
defeat its own ends. Find a way of preventing it. Our work would be
imperilled.' He agrees and undertakes to comply with my request.

3 p.m. Attolico telephones that Hitler agrees in principle, making
certain reservations of secondary importance. He lays down one
condition, however: the presence of Mussolini, which he regards as the
sole guarantee. The Duce accepts. We leave at 6 tonight, in order
to be in Munich, where the Conference is to take place, at 10.30 in
the morning.

I return to the Duce with the American Ambassador, bearing a very
tardy message from Roosevelt. I remain alone with the Duce. 'As you
see', he says, 'I am only moderately happy, because, though perhaps at
a heavy price, we could have liquidated France and Great Britain for
ever. We now have overwhelming proof of this.'

We leave at 6. The unanimous prayers of Italy are with us.

29 – 30 September. In the train the Duce is in a very good humour.
We dine together and he speaks with great vivacity on every subject.
He criticizes Britain and British policy severely. 'In a country where
animals are adored to the point of making cemeteries and hospitals
and houses for them, and legacies are bequeathed to parrots, you can
be sure that decadence has set in. Besides, other reasons apart, it is also
a consequence of the composition of the English people. Four million
surplus women. Four million sexually unsatisfied women, artificially
creating a host of problems in order to excite or appease their senses.

Not being able to embrace one man, they embrace humanity.'

At Kufstein we meet the Führer. We get into his carriage, where spread out on a table are all the maps of the Sudetenland and the western fortifications. He explains the situation: he intends to liquidate Czechoslovakia as she now is, because she immobilizes forty of his divisions and ties his hands *vis-à-vis* France. When Czechoslovakia has been, as she must be, deflated, ten divisions will be enough to immobilize her. The Duce listens with concentration. The programme is now fixed: either the Conference is successful in a short time or the solution will take place by force of arms. 'Besides', adds the Führer, 'the time will come when we shall have to fight side by side against France and England. All the better that it should happen while the Duce and I are at the head of our countries, and still young and full of vigour.'

But all that seems superseded by the atmosphere which in fact has been created — an atmosphere of agreement. Even the people waving as the train passes make one realize their joy at the event which is in the air.

After a brief stop at the palace where the Duce and I are staying, we go to the Führerhaus, where the conference is to take place. The others have already arrived and are gathered round a table on which snacks and drinks are set out. The Führer comes half-way down the stairs to meet us and, with the rest of his suite, singles out us, the Italians, by a marked distinction of treatment. Brief, cold handshakes with Daladier [French prime minister] and Chamberlain — then the Duce, alone, goes over to a corner of the room where the Nazi leaders surround him. There is a vague sense of embarrassment, particularly on the part of the French. I talk to Daladier, and then to François-Poncet [French ambassador in Berlin] about trivial things. Then to Chamberlain, who says he wants to talk to the Duce. He thanks him for all that he has already done. But the Duce, coldly, does not take advantage of the opening, and the conversation peters out.

We enter the conference room. The four chiefs; Ribbentrop, Léger [Secretary general of the French foreign ministry], Wilson [adviser to Chamberlain] and I; and Schmidt, the interpreter. The Führer speaks — a few words of thanks and an exposition of the situation. He speaks calmly, but from time to time he gets excited and then he raises his voice and beats his fist against the palm of his other hand. Then Chamberlain. Then Daladier. Lastly the Duce, who affirms the necessity for a rapid and concrete decision, and with this end in view proposed to use as a basis for discussion a document which has in fact been telephoned to us by our Embassy the previous evening, as expressing the desires of the German Government.

The discussion develops formally and without very much anima-tion. Chamberlain is inclined to linger over legal points; Daladier defends the cause of the Czechs without much conviction; the Duce prefers to remain silent and sum up and draw conclusions when the others have finished their dissertations.

We adjourn for lunch, which takes place in the Führer's private house — a modest apartment in a large building full of other residents. It has, however, many very valuable pictures.

The conference is continued in the afternoon and virtually breaks up into little groups which try to work out the various formulas. This permits us to talk with greater confidence, and the ice is broken.

Daladier, particularly, is loquacious in personal conversation. He says that what is happening today is due solely to the pig-headedness of Beneš [Czechoslovak president]. In the last few months he has repeatedly suggested to Beneš that the Sudetens should be given autonomy. That would at least have deferred the present crisis. He grumbles about the French warmongers, who would have liked to push the country into an absurd and indeed impossible war — for France and England would never have been able to do anything really useful for Czechoslovakia, once she was attacked by the forces of the Reich.

The Duce, slightly annoyed by the vaguely parliamentary atmo-sphere which conferences always produce, moves round the room with his hands in his pockets and a rather distracted air. Every now and then he joins in the search for a formula. His great spirit, always ahead of events and men, has already absorbed the idea of agreement and, while the others are still wasting their breath over more or less formal problems, he has almost ceased to take any interest. He has already passed on and is meditating other things.

However, he joins in the discussion again, when it turns to the question of including in the agenda the problem of the Polish and Hungarian minorities. The others, without exception, would gladly have said nothing about it. In fact they try to evade its discussion. But when there is a strong will, the strong will always predominates and others coalesce around it. The problem is discussed and solved by means of a formula which I do not hesitate to describe as very brilliant.

Meanwhile conversations *à deux* are taking place. There is a hint at the possibility of the Duce delaying his departure in order to permit a meeting between him and Chamberlain. But the idea is ruled out by the Duce, as he thinks that this might offend German susceptibilities. First I and then the Duce talk to Chamberlain. We tell him more or less the same things: we disinterest ourselves in Spain; withdrawal of 10,000 volunteers in the near future; goodwill for a speedy implementation of our Pact of 16 April. Chamberlain hints at the possibility of a Conference of Four to solve the Spanish problem.

At last, at one in the morning, the document is completed. Everybody is satisfied, even the French — even the Czechs, according to what Daladier tells me. François-Poncet has a moment of shame while he is collating the document. '*Voilà comme la France traite less seuls alliés qui lui étaient restés fidèles*', he exclaims.

We sign, shake hands, and depart.

In Italy, from the Brenner to Rome, from the King down to the peasants, the Duce receives welcomes such as I have never seen. He says himself that this enthusiasm was only equalled on the evening when the Empire was proclaimed.

Ribbentrop has handed me a project for a tripartite alliance between Italy, Germany, and Japan. He says it is 'the biggest thing in the world'. He always exaggerates, Ribbentrop. No doubt we will study it quite calmly and, perhaps, put it aside for some time.

> Malcolm Muggeridge (ed.), *Ciano's Diary*, 1937 – 38 (London, Methuen 1952) pp. 163 – 8.

66 Japan instructs its ambassadors in Germany and Italy on the conclusion of a tripartite pact, 25 January, 1939

From: Foreign Minister Arita Hachiro
To: Special Plenipotentiary to Italy, Ambassador Shiratori Toshio, and Special Plenipotentiary to Germany, Ambassador Oshima Hiroshi, instructions concerning the conclusion by Japan, Germany and Italy of a Treaty of Consultation and Mutual Assistance.

1 At the Five Ministers Conference held on 26 August of last year [1938], it was decided that the strengthening of the Anti-Comintern Pact should be based on the principle that the new treaty would be merely an extension of the pact, that it therefore should not depart from the principles of the Anti-Comintern Pact, and that the new treaty was not to be directed against countries such as Britain and France unless the Soviet Union were involved. In order for the Empire

of Japan to establish its position as a stable power in East Asia and in order to carry out smoothly Japan's conception of its New Order in East Asia, it is extremely important that Japan avoid involvement in European problems not directly relevant to Japan, and that Japan avoid such situations as would result in making enemies of nations such as Britain and the United States. Therefore, it has been decided that the strengthening of cooperation between Japan, Germany, and Italy should remain limited for a time to anticommunism and that conclusion of a full treaty of alliance would be inadvisable for the empire.

2 Since we were unable to convey the decision of the Five Ministers Conference clearly to our representatives abroad, Germany and Italy have not proposed a three-power treaty. While there was some difficulty for our government in altering the decision of the Five Ministers Conference, it has been decided that it would not be appropriate to insist on our previous decision, because we were responsible for Germany's and Italy's misunderstanding of Japan's policy. The ministers concerned met on the 19th of this month to consider the question and agreed upon the government's policy as described in Attachment A. On the basis of that policy statement, the Japanese government draft of the proposed treaty is included in Attachment B.

3 The Japanese draft is a compromise designed to be as advantageous to Japan as possible, while incorporating the import of the German and Italian drafts by including as targets third countries not related to the subversive activities of the Comintern. At the same time, in order to minimize its adverse impact on third countries, Japan will explain to the outside world that the new treaty will be no more than a strengthening of the Anti-Comintern Pact. Please understand that for many reasons the decision in Attachment A is not to be amended. Therefore, I hope you understand this latter point and will negotiate with Germany and Italy according to the attached documents.

4 The present Japanese-German Anti-Comintern Pact was concluded on the basis of pursuing an anti-Comintern policy on the one hand and maintaining joint pressure on the USSR on the other. In practice it has been used to solve various problems arising between the two countries regardless of the literal text of the treaty; and the participation of Italy will greatly strengthen this feature.

It goes without saying that the importance of this kind of treaty is not in what is written in the documents but rather in the closer political relations between the allied states that will be promoted by the conclusion of the treaty. Already the Anti-Comintern Pact has enabled all three countries—Japan, Germany, and Italy—to influence third countries politically and to check them considerably. Therefore, it is my firm belief that although outwardly the present treaty is to be strengthened only concerning anticommunism, in actual practice it can exert considerable political pressure on Britain and France.

It is not difficult to imagine that Germany and Italy will hesitate to consent to a draft that camouflages the new agreement as an anti-Comintern pact, for by giving the treaty the appearance of an alliance, they seem to be thinking of using it for their diplomatic manoeuvring in Europe. Since we can all fully anticipate future political moves in the practical application of the treaty, I believe it will be possible to convince them if the proper method of explanation is selected and the right efforts are made.

5 Details of the agreement in Attachment B are described separately, as follows:

(a) The secret items of understanding are absolutely essential to our government; although they are in the form of an understanding, we attach to them a weight equal to that of the protocol.

(b) We plan to publish the present treaty after consultation with Germany and Italy and after carefully considering the domestic as well as the international situation from our own standpoint. As you know, Japan is presently negotiating with the USSR for the conclusion of a fisheries treaty; in view of our experience when concluding the existing Anti-Comintern Pact, I think it is best that this pact with Germany and Italy be published only after the formal or tentative conclusion of the fisheries treaty, or after such negotiations prove to be fruitless. Further instructions on this point will follow. . . .

Secret Items of Understanding

On this day,_____, in signing this treaty, the undersigned plenipotentiaries have agreed to the following:

1 Concerning Article 3 of the treaty and Item 1 of the secret supplementary protocol, military assistance will be offered if the Soviet Union should attack one of the contracting parties, whether alone or in concert with other non-signatory nations.

The above provision does not affect the obligation for the contracting parties to consult and reach agreement concerning military assistance depending upon the situation, even if the Soviet Union is not involved in the attack.

2 In view of the fact that the treaty and the signed protocol are to be made public, the contracting parties, when required to explain the treaty, will assert in concert that it is an extension of the treaty concluded against the Communist International on 25 November, 1936, and that the main purpose of this treaty is defence against nations that pursue subversive activities based upon policies of the Communist International. On the_____day of_____, _____.

> James William Morley, (ed.), *Deterrent Diplomacy: Japan, Germany and the USSR*, 1935 – 1940 (New York, Columbia University Press, 1976), app. 4, pp. 273 – 82.

67 Beck defines Poland's position, 24 March, 1939

Memorandum on a conference of senior officials with the Polish foreign minister, Josef Beck.

Secret

Minister: The tension of the situation requires an investigation of the whole complex of problems. The situation is serious and it cannot be ignored. And it is serious because one of the elements hitherto timely for the definition of the state's situation, that is, Germany, has lost its calculability, with which it was endowed even amidst difficult problems.

Therefore a number of new elements have appeared in our politics and a number of new problems in the state.

As far as the basic line of action is concerned, a straight and clear line has been established with the top factors in the state. We defined with precision the limits of our direct interests, and beyond this line we conduct a normal policy and undertake action dealing with it as with normal current work. Below this line comes our Polish *non possumus*. This is clear: we will fight. Once the matter is put this way, chaos is overcome by a considerable share of calm, and thinking becomes orderly.

Where is the line? It is our territory, but not only that. The line also involves the non-acceptance by our state, regarding the drastic spot that Danzig has always been, of any unilateral suggestion to be imposed on us. And, regardless of what Danzig is worth as an object (in my opinion it may perhaps be worth quite a lot, but this is of no concern at the moment), under the present circumstances it has become a symbol. This means that, if we join that category of eastern states that allow rules to be dictated to them, then I do not know where the matter will end. That is why it is wiser to go forward to meet the enemy than to wait for him at home.

This enemy is a troublesome element, since it seems that he is losing the measure of thinking and acting. He might recover that measure once he encounters determined opposition, which hitherto he has not met with. The mighty have been humble to him, and the weak have capitulated in advance, even at the cost of honour. The Germans are marching all across Europe with nine divisions; with such strength Poland would not be overcome. Hitler and his associates know this, so that the question of a political contest with us will not be like the others.

I started with the extreme problem, in order to establish immediately an outlet for our thinking on this matter. On this basis we shall start international action. We have arrived at this difficult moment in our politics with all the trump cards in our hand. This does not speak badly for us.

I would like you, Gentlemen, to use your influence on your junior colleagues in order to bestow on our Ministry the bearing commensurate with these serious premises.

> Waclaw Jedrzejewicz (ed.), *Diplomat in Berlin*, 1933 – 1939: *Papers and Memoirs of Jozef Lipski* (New York, Columbia University Press, 1968), pp. 503 – 4.

68   British and French public opinion polls, 1938 – 39

(a)   Britain, 1938 – 39

Should Great Britain promise assistance to Czechoslovakia if Germany also acts towards her as she did towards Austria? (Mar. '38)	Yes	33%
	No	43
	No op.	24

| Are you in favour of giving back any former German colonies? (Oct. '38) | Yes | 15% |
| | No | 85 |

If 'No', would you rather fight than hand them back? (Oct. '38)	Yes	78%
	No	22
	No op.	9

| Hitler says he has 'No more territorial ambitions in Europe'. Do you believe him? (Oct. '38) | Yes | 7% |
| | No | 93 |

In the present situation do you favour increased expenditure on armaments? (Oct. '38)	Yes	72%
	No	18
	No op.	10

If there were a war between Germany and Russia, which side would you rather see win? (Dec. '38)	Germany	15%
	Russia	85
	No op.	31

If you HAD to choose between Fascism and Communism which would you choose? (Jan. '39)	Fascism	26%
	Communism	74
	No ans.	16

Which of these statements comes nearest to representing your view of Mr Chamberlain's policy of appeasement? (Feb. '39)

1 It is a policy which will ultimately lead to enduring peace in Europe.   28%

2 It will keep us out of war until we have time to rearm.   46%

3 It is bringing war nearer by whetting the appetites of the dictators.   24%
       (No opinion 2%)

Are you in favour of giving back any former German Colonies (Mar. '39)	Yes	14%
	No	78
	No op.	8

If 'No' would you rather fight than hand them back? (Mar. '39)	Yes	69%
	No	19
	No op.	12

Would you like to see Great Britain and Soviet Russia being more friendly to each other? (Mar. '39)	Yes	84%
	No	7
	No op.	9

Is the British Government right in following a policy of giving military guarantees to preserve the independence of small European nations? (Apr. '39)	Yes	83%
	No	17
	No op.	14

Are you in favour of Mr Winston Churchill being invited to join the Cabinet? (May '39)	Yes	56%
	No	26
	No op.	18

Do you think the risk of war has increased or decreased since last autumn? (May '39)	Incr.	30%
	Decr.	57%
	No op.	13

Do you approve of the Government's decision to apply conscription, or are you in favour of leaving it to individuals to enrol voluntarily?	Conscrip.	58%
	Vol.	38
	No op.	4

Do you think the time has come for the 'Peace Front' countries to draw up a detailed plan for world peace as the basis of a conference to which all countries would be invited? (June '39)	Yes	61%
	Later	19
	Never	11
	No op.	9

Are you in favour of a military alliance between Great Britain, France and Russia? (June '39)	Yes	84%
	No	9
	No op.	7

(b) France, 1938 – 39

October 1938

Do you approve of the Munich agreement?	Yes	57%
	No	37%
	No op.	6%

| Do you think that England and France should resist any further demands by Hitler? | Yes | 70% |
| | No | 17% |

Do you think that Germany should be given colonies?	Yes	59%
	No	33%
	No op.	8%

June 1939

The European Crisis

Germany has just taken Czechoslovakia; Italy is occupying Albania. Do you think these annexations are dangerous to France?	Yes No No op.	77% 18 5
Do you think we will be drawn into a war this year or next?	Yes No No op.	37% 47 16
Do you think Spain will remain irrevocably attached to the Axis powers?	Yes No No op.	46% 46 8
Do you think that, if the Germans try to seize Danzig, we should stop them by force?	Yes No No op.	76% 17 7
Do you think that conscription in England will help the cause of European peace?	Yes No No op.	91% 6 3
Will we have war in 1939?	Yes No No op.	45% 34 21
Asked of those who responded in the affirmative: Is there a possibility of war starting this October?	Yes No No op.	67% 25% 8
Do you think it is a good idea to prolong the terms of the present Parliament for another two years?	Yes No No op.	36% 57 7
Asked of Parisians: In the event of another Franco-German war, do you think Italy will become an ally of Germany?	Yes No No op.	50% 32 18

The Far Eastern Crisis

July

Do you think that France and England should resist further Japanese penetration into China?	Yes No No op.	80% 13 7

Spain

Now that General Franco has won the Spanish War, do you think that France has an enemy on her borders?	Yes	74%
	No	21
	No op.	5

August

French Colonies

	Fight	40%
Should France fight rather than surrender the smallest part of its colonial possessions?	Surrender	44
	No op.	16

> *Public Opinion Quarterly*, March 1940, pp. 77 – 82; *Gallup International Public Opinion Polls*, vol. 2, *France*, 1944 – 1975 (London, Greenwood Press, 1977) pp. 1 – 3.

69 A meeting of the military missions of Britain, France and the Soviet Union, Moscow, 14 August 1939

Marshal Voroshilov [Soviet commissar for defence]: I want a clear answer to my very clear question concerning the joint action of the Armed Forces of Britain, France and the Soviet Union against the common enemy—the bloc of aggressors, or the main aggressor—should he attack. . . .

Do the French and British General Staffs think that the Soviet land forces will be admitted to Polish territory in order to make direct contact with the enemy in case Poland is attacked? And further:

Do you think that our Armed Forces will be allowed passage across Polish territory, across Galicia, to make contact with the enemy and to fight him in the south of Poland? Yet one more thing:

Is it proposed to allow Soviet troops across Rumanian territory if the aggressor attacks Rumania?

These are the three questions which interest us most. (Admiral Drax confers at length with General Doumenc.)

General Doumenc [head of French mission]: I agree with the Marshal that the concentration of Soviet troops must take place principally in the areas indicated by the Marshal, and the distribution of these troops will be made at your discretion. I think that the weak points of the Polish-Rumanian front are their flanks and point of junction. We shall speak of the left flank when we deal with the question of communications.

Marshal Voroshilov: I want you to reply to my direct question. I said nothing about Soviet troop concentrations. I asked whether the British and French General Staffs envisage passage of our troops towards East Prussia or other points to fight the common enemy.

General Doumenc: I think that Poland and Rumania will implore you, Marshal, to come to their assistance.

Marshal Voroshilov: And perhaps they will not. It is not evident so far. We have a Non-Aggression Pact with the Poles, while France and Poland have a Treaty of Mutual Assistance. This is the reason why the question I raised is not an idle one as far as we are concerned, since we are discussing the plan of joint action against the aggressor. To my mind, France and Britain should have a clear idea about the way we can extend real help or about our participation in the war. (There is a lengthy exchange of opinion between Admiral Drax and General Heywood.)

Admiral Drax [head of British mission]: If Poland and Rumania do not ask for Soviet help they will soon become German provinces, and then the USSR will decide how to act. If, on the other hand, the USSR, France and Britain are in alliance, then the question of whether or not Rumania and Poland ask for help becomes quite clear.

Marshal Voroshilov: I repeat, gentlemen, that this question is a cardinal question for the Soviet Union.

Admiral Drax: I repeat my reply once again. If the USSR, France and Britain are allies, then in my personal opinion there can be little doubt that Poland and Rumania will ask for help. But that is my personal opinion, and to obtain a precise and satisfactory answer, it is necessary to approach Pol..nd.

Marshal Voroshilov: I regret that the Military Missions of Great Britain and France have not considered this question and have not brought an exact answer.

> Ministry for Foreign affairs of the USSR, *Soviet Peace Efforts on the Eve of World War II* (September 1938 – August 1939): *Documents and Records*, ed. V.M. Falin *et al.*, part 2 (Moscow, 1973), no. 415.

Chronology

1918	8 January	Wilson's Fourteen Points
	3 March	Russo-German Treaty of Brest-Litovsk
	4 October	Germany requests an armistice
	30 October	Turkish unconditional surrender
	3 November	Austro-Hungarian Armistice
	11 November	German Armistice
1919	18 January	Paris Peace Conference opens
	14 February	League of Nations Covenant approved
	4 March	Comintern founded at Moscow
	24 March	Council of Four begins
	28 June	Versailles Treaty signed
	10 September	Treaty of St Germain-en-Laye with Austria
	12 October	British evacuate Murmansk
	27 November	Treaty of Neuilly with Bulgaria
1920	10 January	Versailles Treaty enters into force
	21 January	Formal closure of the Paris Peace Conference
	16 March	Allies occupy Constantinople
	19 March	Final United States Senate defeat of Versailles Treaty
	4 April	France occupies Frankfurt
	18 – 26 April	San Remo Conference
	25 April	Polish offensive against Russia
	4 June	Treaty of Trianon with Hungary
	16 July	Spa Protocol on reparations
	10 August	Treaty of Sèvres with Turkey
	14 – 16 August	Poles defeat Russians at Warsaw
1921	8 March	Entente occupation of Düsseldorf
	16 March	Anglo-Soviet Trade agreement
	18 March	Russo-Polish peace treaty of Riga
	20 March	Upper Silesian plebiscite

	5 May	London Schedule of Payments
	25 August	United States-Germany peace treaty of Berlin
	12 November	Washington Conference opens
1922	6 – 13 January	Cannes Conference
	6 February	Five Power Treaty of Naval Limitations
		Nine Power Treaty on China
		Four Power Treaty on Pacific Islands
	15 February	Permanent Court of International Arbitration established at the Hague
	15 March	German-Soviet military agreement
	10 April- 19 May	Genoa Conference
	1 August	Balfour note on war debts
	11 October	Mundanya armistice ends Chanak crisis
1923	11 January	Ruhr occupation begins
	28 February	Anglo-American war debt agreement
	14 July	Treaty of Lausanne with Turkey
	31 August	Italy occupies Corfu
	17 September	Italy seizes Fiume
	26 September	German passive resistance ends
	29 November	German currency stabilized
1924	1 February	Britain recognizes Soviet government
	9 April	Dawes Plan issued
	18 April	League reorganizes Hungarian finances
	5 July	Britain rejects Draft Treaty of Mutual Assistance
	16 July- 16 August	London Reparations Conference
	2 October	Geneva Protocol for Pacific Settlement of International Disputes
	25 October	Zinoviev letter published
1925	10 March	Britain rejects Geneva Protocol
	28 April	Britain returns to gold standard
	27 August	Last French troops leave the Ruhr
	16 October	Locarno treaties initialled
	22 October	Greece invades Bulgaria
1926	30 January	British forces evacuate Cologne
	24 April	German-Soviet treaty of Berlin
	12 July	Anglo-French war debt agreement
	10 September	Germany enters the League

	17 September	Thoiry talks
	26 September	International Steel Agreement
	3 – 6 October	First Pan-European Congress, Vienna
1927	2 – 23 May	World Economic Conference, Geneva
	27 May	Britain breaks off relations with Soviet Union
	20 June	Geneva Naval Conference
1928	27 August	Kellogg-Briand Pact
1929	7 June	Young Report issued
	31 August	Hague Conference Protocol on Young Plan
	3 October	Anglo-Soviet relations restored
	29 October	New York Stock Exchange collapse
	13 November	Bank for International Settlements established
1930	3 – 20 January	Second Hague Conference
	22 April	London Naval Treaty
	17 May	Young Plan replaces Dawes Plan Briand Memorandum on United States of Europe
	30 June	Last Rhineland zone evacuated
	14 September	German Reichstag elections (107 Nazis)
1931	21 March	Austro-German customs union announced
	11 May	Austrian Credit-Anstalt fails
	20 June	Hoover Moratorium proposed
	3 September	Germany abandons Austro-German customs union plan
	18 September	Mukden incident
	21 September	Britain abandons gold standard
1932	28 January	Sino-Japanese clash at Shanghai
	2 February	Geneva Disarmament Conference opens
	9 March	Manchukuo proclaimed
	11 March	League adopts non-recognition
	16 June- 9 July	Lausanne reparations conference
	21 July- 20 August	Imperial Economic Conference, Ottawa
1933	30 January	Hitler becomes German Chancellor
	24 February	League adopts Lytton report
	4 March	Roosevelt's inauguration
	27 March	Japan leaves the League
	31 May	Sino-Japanese truce

	12 June- 27 July	World Economic Conference, London
	15 July	Four Power Pact signed at Rome but not ratified
	14 October	Germany leaves League and Disarmament Conference
1934	26 January	German-Polish non-aggression pact
	July	Abortive Nazi *putsch* in Austria
	18 September	Soviet Union joins the League
1935	7 January	Rome Agreements between France and Italy
	January	Saar plebiscite
	9 & 16 March	Hitler announces conscription and a military air force
	14 April	Stresa agreements between Britain, France, Italy
	2 May	Franco-Soviet pact
	16 May	Czech-Soviet pact
	18 June	Anglo-German naval agreement
	27 June	Franco-Italian military convention
	3 October	Mussolini invades Abyssinia
	8 December	Hoare-Laval plan
1936	7 March	Hitler remilitarizes Rhineland and denounces Locarno pacts
	5 May	Addis Ababa falls and Italy proclaims annexation of Abyssinia
	11 July	Austro-German agreement
	17 July	Spanish Civil War begins
	2 August	France proposes non-intervention agreement
	1 November	Rome-Berlin Axis announced
	25 November	Germany and Japan sign Anti-Comintern Pact
1937	2 January	Anglo-Italian 'Gentleman's Agreement' signed
	24 April	Anglo-French declaration recognizing Belgium's return to neutrality
	31 May	Neville Chamberlain becomes prime minister
	7 July	Sino-Japanese war begins
	14 September	Nyon agreement

	24 – 29 September	Mussolini visits Germany
	5 November	Hossbach Conference
	6 November	Italy joins Germany and Japan in Anti-Comintern Pact.
	29 – 30 November	Anglo-French conference, London
	11 December	Italy leaves the League
1938	4 February	Ribbentrop replaces Neurath as foreign minister
	13 March	Germany annexes Austria
	16 April	Anglo-Italian agreement signed (implemented, 16 November 1938)
	28 – 9 April	Anglo-French coversations, London
	15 September	Chamberlain/Hitler meeting at Berchtesgaden
	18 September	Anglo-French conference, London
	19 September	Anglo-French plan for cession of Sudetenland to Germany
	22 – 3 September	Chamberlain/Hitler meeting at Godesberg
	25 – 6 September	Anglo-French conference, London
	29 – 30 September	Munich Conference and Agreement. Chamberlain and Hitler sign Anglo-German Declaration
	6 December	Franco-German declaration
	22 December	Italy denounces Rome agreements of 1935
1939	5 January	Beck visits Hitler at Berchtesgaden
	15 March	Germany occupies Bohemia and Moravia Hungary occupies Carpatho-Ukraine
	23 March	Lithuania cedes Memel to Germany
	28 March	Madrid surrenders to General Franco
	29 March	Anglo-French staff talks begin
	31 March	Provisional Anglo-French guarantee of Poland
	7 April	Italy invades Albania
	13 April	Anglo-French guarantees of Greece and Romania
	28 April	Hitler denounces Anglo-German Naval Agreement and German-Polish Non-Aggression Pact
	12 May	Anglo-Turkish declaration
	22 May	German-Italian Pact of Steel signed
	14 June	Japanese blockade British concession at

	Tientsin
12 August	Anglo-Franco-Soviet military talks begin in Moscow
23 August	German-Soviet non-aggression pact signed in Moscow
1 September	Germany invades Poland
3 September	Britain and France declare war on Germany

Further Reading

General accounts

R.A.C. Parker, *Europe, 1919 – 1945* (London, 1969); A.J.P. Taylor, *The Origins of the Second World War* (2nd edn, London, 1963)

Armistice and Paris peace conference

Harry Rudin, *Armistice, 1918* (New Haven, Conn., 1944); Arno J. Mayer, *Politics and the Diplomacy of Peacemaking: Containment and Counter-revolution at Versailles, 1918 – 19* (London, 1968); Howard Elcock, *Portrait of a Decision* (London, 1972); Harold Nicolson, *Peacemaking, 1919* (London, 1967); David Robin Watson, *Clemenceau: A Political Biography* (London, 1974); Inga Floto, *Colonel House in Paris: A Study of American Policy at the Paris Peace Conference* (Aarhus, Denmark, 1973); Paul C. Helmreich, *From Paris to Sèvres: The Partition of the Ottoman Empire at the Peace Conference of 1919 – 20* (Columbus, Ohio, 1973).

International relations in the 1920s

Sally Marks, *The Illusion of Peace* (London, 1976); Keith L. Nelson, *Victors Divided: America and the Allies in Germany, 1918 – 1923* (London, 1975); Anne Orde, *Great Britain and International Security, 1920 – 1926* (London, 1978); Christopher M. Kimmich, *Germany and the League of Nations* (London, 1976); Jon Jacobsen, *Locarno Diplomacy: Germany and the West, 1925 – 1929* (Princeton, N.J., 1972); R.H. Ferrell, *Peace in Their Time, The Origins of the Briand-Kellogg Pact* (New Haven, Conn, 1952); Charles S Maier, *Recasting Bourgeois Europe* (Princeton, N.J., 1975).

International crises, 1931 – 9

Edward W. Bennett, *Germany and the Diplomacy of the Financial*

Crisis, 1931 (Cambridge, Mass., 1962); *German Rearmament and the West, 1932 – 1933* (Princeton, N.J., 1979); Christopher Thorne, *The Limits of Foreign Policy: The West, the League and the Far Eastern Crisis of 1931 – 1933* (London, 1972); Frank Hardie, *The Abyssinian Crisis* (London, 1974); James Thomas Emmerson, *The Rhineland Crisis, 7 March 1936* (London, 1977); Dante Puzzo, *Spain and the Great Powers, 1936 – 1941* (London, 1962); J.W. Bruegel, *Czechoslovakia before Munich* (London, 1973); Roy Douglas, *In the Year of Munich* (London, 1977); *The Advent of War* (London, 1978); Jill Edwards, *The British Government and the Spanish Civil War, 1936 – 1939* (London, 1979); Anthony Adamthwaite, *The Making of the Second World War* (London, 1979).

Foreign Policies of the Powers

Britain:

Paul Hayes, *Modern British Foreign Policy: The Twentieth Century, 1880 – 1939* (London, 1978); W.N. Medlicott, *British Foreign Policy Since Versailles* (London, 1968); Correlli Barnett, *The Collapse of British Power* (London, 1972).

France:

J. Néré, *The Foreign Policy of France from 1914 to 1945* (London, 1975); Stephen A. Schuker, *The End of French Predominance in Europe* (Chapel Hill, 1975); Walter A McDougall, *France's Rhineland Diplomacy*, 1914 – 1924 (Princeton, N.J., 1978); Anthony Adamthwaite, *France and the Coming of the Second World War, 1936 – 1939* (London, 1977).

Germany:

Gordon A. Craig, *Germany, 1866 – 1945* (Oxford, 1978); John Hiden, *Germany and Europe, 1919 – 1939* (London, 1977); W. Carr, *Arms, Autarky and Aggression: A Study in German Foreign Policy, 1933 – 1939* (London, 1972).

Italy:

C.J. Lowe and F. Marzari, *Italian Foreign Policy, 1870 – 1940* (London, 1975); Denis Mack Smith, *Mussolini's Roman Empire*

(London, 1976); Esmonde M. Robertson, *Mussolini as Empire-Builder: Europe and Africa, 1932 – 36* (London, 1977).

Japan:

Ian Nish, *Japanese Foreign Policy, 1869 – 1942* (London, 1977); Richard Storry, *Japan and the Decline of the West in Asia, 1894 – 1943* (London, 1979) William Morley (ed), *Deterrent Diplomacy: Japan, Germany and the USSR, 1935 – 1940* (New York, 1976).

Soviet Union:

B.N. Ponomaryov, A.A. Gromyko and V.M. Kovostov (eds), *History of the Foreign Policy of the USSR*, vol. I, 1917 – 1945 (Moscow, 1966); I.K. Koblyakov, *USSR: For Peace Against Aggression, 1933 – 1941* (Moscow, 1976) A. Ulam, *Expansion and Co-Existence: A History of Soviet Foreign Policy* (New York, 1968).

United States of America:

Arnold A. Offner, *The Origins of the Second World War: American Foreign Policy and World Politics, 1917 – 1941* (New York, 1975) Melvyn P. Leffler, *The Elusive Quest: America's Pursuit of European Stability and French Security, 1919 – 1933* (Chapel Hill, 1979); Robert Dallek, *Franklin D. Roosevelt and American Foreign Policy, 1932 – 1945* (London, 1979).

Belgium:

David Owen Kieft, *Belgium's Return to Neutrality* (Oxford, 1972).

Poland:

Roman Debicki, *Foreign Policy of Poland*, 1919 – 1939 (New York, 1962) Anna M. Cienciala, *Poland and the Western Powers, 1938 – 9* (London, 1968).

Special Aspects

Germany and the Soviet Union:

Walter Laqueur, *Russia and Germany: A Century of Conflict* (London, 1965).

Germany and Italy:

Mario Toscano, *The Origins of the Pact of Steel* (2nd edn, Baltimore, Md, 1967); Elizabeth Wiskemann, *The Rome-Berlin Axis* (London, 1966).

Anglo-Soviet relations:

Richard H. Ullmann, *Intervention and the War* (Oxford, 1962), vol. 2. *Britain and the Russian Civil War* (Oxford, 1969); vol. 3, The Anglo-Soviet Accord (Oxford, 1973); Gabriel Gorodetsky, *The Precarious Truce: Anglo-Soviet Relations*, 1924 – 1927 (Cambridge, 1977).

Britain and France:

Neville Waites (ed.), *Troubled Neighbours: Franco-British Relations in the Twentieth Century* (London, 1971); Arnold Wolfers, *Britain and France Between Two Wars* (New York, 1940); W.M. Jordan, *Britain, France and the German Problem* (London, 1943).

Appeasement:

Martin Gilbert, *The Roots of Appeasement* (London, 1966); William R. Rock, *British Appeasement in the 1930s* (London, 1977).

The Diplomats:

Gordon A. Craig and Felix Gilbert (eds), *The Diplomats, 1919 – 1939* (reprint, London, 1968); Norman Rose, *Vansittart, Study of a Diplomat* (London, 1978); Martin Gilbert, *Sir Horace Rumbold* (London, 1973); Gordon Waterfield, *Professional Diplomat: Sir Percy Lorraine* (London, 1973).

The League of Nations:

Francis P. Walters, *A History of the League of Nations* (London, 1960); Ruth B. Henig (ed), *The League of Nations* (Edinburgh, 1973); James Barros, *Betrayal from Within* (London, 1969); James Barros, *Office Without Power: Secretary General Sir Eric Drummond* (London, 1979); George W. Egerton, *Great Britain and the Creation of the League of Nations* (London 1979).

Armed Forces:

D.C. Watt, *Too Serious a Business: European Armed Forces and the Approach to the Second World War* (London, 1975); Adrian Preston (ed), *General Staffs and Diplomacy before the Second World War* (London, 1978); Michael Howard, *The Continental Commitment: The Dilemma of British defence Policy in the Era of Two World Wars* (London, 1972); J.R.M. Butler (ed.), *Grand Strategy*, History of the Second World War: United Kingdom Military Series, Vol. I, *Rearmament Policy* by N.H. Gibbs (London, 1976); F.L. Carsten, *The Reichswehr and Politics*, 1918 – 1933 (Oxford, 1966); John Erikson, *The Soviet High Command*, 1918 – 1941 (London, 1962).

Economic history:

J.S. Davis, *The World Between the Wars, 1919 – 1939, an Economist's View* (London, 1975); Derek H. Aldcroft, *From Versailles to Wall Street, 1919 – 1929* (London, 1977); Charles P. Kindleberger, *The World in Depression, 1929 – 1939* (London, 1973); Alan S. Milward, *War, Economy and Society, 1939 – 1945* (London, 1977).

Collected essays and articles

Hans W. Gatzke (ed), *European Diplomacy Between Two Wars* (Chicago, 1972); Esmonde M. Robertson (ed), *The Origins of the Second World War: Historical Interpretations* (London, 1971).

Reference

J.A.S. Grenville, *The Major International Treaties, 1914 – 1973: A History and Guide with Texts* (London, 1974); Martin Gilbert, *Recent History Atlas* (Third Edition, 1977).

Biographical Sketches

STANLEY BALDWIN (1867 – 1947). Conservative MP 1908 – 37; prime minister 1923 – 24, 1924 – 29 and 1935 – 37. Created Earl 1937.

ARTHUR JAMES BALFOUR (1848 – 1930). Unionist prime minister, 1902 – 05; first lord of the admiralty, 1915 – 16; foreign secretary, 1916 – 19; lord president of the council, 1919 – 22, 1925 – 29; created Earl 1922.

JOSEF BECK, Colonel (1894 – 1944). Polish foreign minister 1932 – 39.

EDUARD BENEŠ (1884 – 1948). Czechoslovak representative at Paris Peace Conference, 1919; foreign minister, 1918 – 35; President, 1935 – 38; in 1941 became President of exiled Czech government in London, returning to Prague in 1945.

LÉON BLUM (1872 – 1950). Leader of French Socialist Party; prime minister of Popular Front governments in 1936 – 37 and 1938; arrested by Vichy government in 1940; imprisoned by Germans; prime minister, 1946 – 47.

ARISTIDE BRIAND (1862 – 1932). French prime minister and foreign minister, 1915 – 17; prime minister, 1921 – 22; foreign minister, 1925 – 31.

LORD ROBERT CECIL (1864 – 1958). Son of the 3rd Marquess of Salisbury. Conservative MP 1906 – 10 and 1911 – 23. Created Viscount Cecil of Chelwood 1923. Chancellor of the Duchy of Lancaster, 1924 – 27. President, League of Nations Union, 1923 – 45.

AUSTEN CHAMBERLAIN (1863 – 1937). Conservative MP 1892 – 1937. Chancellor of the Exchequer 1903 – 06 and 1919 – 21. secretary of state for foreign affairs 1924 – 29.

NEVILLE CHAMBERLAIN (1869 – 1940). Lord Mayor of Birmingham 1915 – 16; Director General of National Service 1916 – 17. Conservative MP 1918 – 40. Chancellor of the Exchequer 1923 – 24 and 1931 – 37. Prime minister 1937 – 40.

COUNT GALEAZZO CIANO (1903 – 1944). Son-in-law of Mussolini; Italian foreign minister, 1936 – 43; ambassador to Vatican, 1943; executed, 1944.

GEORGES CLEMENCEAU (1841 – 1929). Elected deputy 1876; minister of interior 1906; prime minister, 1906 – 09; prime minister 1917 – 20; failed to secure election to presidency of the French Republic in 1920 and retired.

LORD CURZON (1859 – 1925). Conservative MP 1886 – 98. Viceroy of India 1899 – 1905; secretary of state for foreign affairs 1919 – 24. Created Marquess Curzon of Kedleston 1921.

EDOUARD DALADIER (1884 – 1970). Radical Socialist deputy for Vaucluse, 1919 – 40 and 1946 – 58; prime minister 1934; prime minister 1938 – 40; deported to Germany 1943 – 45.

YVON DELBOS (1885 – 1956). Radical Socialist deputy for Dordogne, 1924 – 44; French foreign minister 1936 – 38

ANTHONY EDEN (1897 – 1977). Conservative MP 1923 – 57; minister for League of Nations Affairs 1935; secretary of state for foreign affairs, 1935 – 38; secretary of state for foreign affairs, 1940 – 45, 1951 – 55; prime minister 1955 – 57. Created Earl of Avon 1962.

PIERRE ETIENNE FLANDIN (1889 – 1958). Elected deputy for the Yonne in 1914; president of right-wing *Alliance Démocratique* group; prime minister 1934 – 35; foreign minister 1936; foreign minister under Marshal Pétain 1940 – 41.

FERDINAND FOCH, Marshal (1851 – 1929). A professional soldier; principal French field commander in 1916, in charge of the battle of the Somme; Supreme Allied Commander in France March 1918.

HERMANN GÖRING, Field-Marshal (1893 – 1946). Participant in the putsch of 1923; President of the Reichstag 1932; air minister and C-in-C German Air Force, 1933 – 45; prime minister of Prussia and minister of the interior, 1933; commissioner for the 4 – Year Plan 1936.

EDOUARD HERRIOT (1872 – 1957). Radical Socialist deputy for the Rhone, 1919 – 1940; prime minister of 1924 *Cartel des Gauches*; prime minister 1932; president of Chamber of Deputies, 1936 – 40; deported to Germany, 1943 – 45; president of National Assembly, 1947.

ADOLF HITLER (1889 – 1945). Enlisted in Bavarian infantry 1914; saw active service on the Western Front; founder of Nazi party; Chancellor of the Reich from 1933; head of state from 1934; C-in-C German armed forces from 1938; committed suicide 1945.

SAMUEL HOARE (1880 – 1959). Conservative MP 1910 – 1944; secretary of state for air 1922 – 24, 1924 – 29 and 1940; secretary of state for foreign affairs 1935; home secretary 1937 – 39; ambassador to Spain, 1940 – 44. Created Viscount Templewood 1944.

JOHN MAYNARD KEYNES (1883 – 1946). Economist; Principal Treasury Representative at the Paris Peace Conference 1919; leading negotiator of the American loan to Britain 1945. Created Baron 1942.

PIERRE LAVAL (1883 – 1945). French prime minister, 1931 – 32; foreign minister 1934 – 35; prime minister and foreign minister, 1935 – 36; prime minister and foreign minister, 1942 – 44; executed 1945.

ANDREW BONAR LAW (1858 – 1923). Leader of Unionist party, 1911 – 21, 1922 – 23; chancellor of exchequer and member of war cabinet, 1916 – 19; lord privy seal 1919 – 21; Conservative prime minister, 1922 – 23.

ALEXIS LÉGER (1887 – 1975). Secretary General of French foreign ministry 1933 – 40; went to United States after fall of France and resumed literary career under pseudonym of Saint-John Perse, awarded Nobel Prize for Literature 1960.

MAXIM LITVINOV (1876 – 1952). His original name was Meier Moiseevich Wallakh. He was born in Bialystok, a largely Jewish town on the borders of Russia and Russian Poland. Principal Bolshevik agent in London 1916. Married Ivy Low 1916; People's Commissar for Foreign Affairs 1930 – May 1939; Soviet ambassador to the United States, 1941 – 43.

DAVID LLOYD GEORGE (1863 – 1945). Liberal MP 1890 – 1945; prime minister, 1916 – 22; Created Earl 1945.

J. RAMSAY MACDONALD (1866 – 1937). Secretary of Labour Party 1900 – 12; Labour MP 1906 – 18 and 1922 – 37; prime minister and secretary of state for foreign affairs 1924 (Labour Government); prime minister 1929 – 35 (National Government); lord president of the council, 1935 – 37.

BENITO MUSSOLINI (1883 – 1945). Socialist agitator and journalist, 1904 – 15; President, Council of Ministers, 1922 – 6; Head of Government and prime minister, 1926 – 43; minister for foreign affairs, 1924 – 29, 1932 – 36; deposed 1943; executed 1945.

VITTORIO EMANUELE ORLANDO (1860 – 1952). Jurist and politician; Italian Prime Minister and leader of Italian delegation to the Paris Peace Conference 1919.

JOSEPH PAUL-BONCOUR (1873 – 1972). Socialist deputy; member of French delegation to League of Nations; prime minister and foreign minister, 1932; foreign minister 1934 and 1938.

RAYMOND POINCARÉ (1860 – 1934). French Prime Minister and Foreign Minister, 1912 – 13; President of the Republic, 1913 – 20; Chairman of Reparations Commission 1920; prime minister and foreign minister, 1922 – 24; prime Minister 1926 – 29.

JOACHIM VON RIBBENTROP (1893 – 1946). Ambassador of the Reich, 1935; led German delegation to London naval talks, 1935; Ambassador in London, 1936 – 38; foreign minister, 1938 – 45; executed 1946.

FRANKLIN D ROOSEVELT (1882 – 1945). Democratic Senator 1911; assistant secretary of the navy, 1913 – 20; Governor of the State of New York, 1929 – 33; President of the United States of America, 1933 – 45.

SIR JOHN SIMON (1873 – 1954). Liberal MP 1906 – 18 and 1922 – 40; secretary of state for foreign affairs, 1931 – 35; chancellor of the exchequer, 1937 – 40; lord chancellor, 1940 – 45. Created Viscount 1940.

JAN CHRISTIAN SMUTS (1870 – 1950). Boer general, British field marshal; South African Minister of Defence, 1910 – 19; prime minister of South Africa 1919 – 29; 1939 – 48; member of British war cabinet, 1917 – 19; one of South Africa's two Commissions at the Paris Peace Conference 1919.

JOSEPH STALIN (1879 – 1953). Joined Tiflis Marxist Social Democratic Organization, 1898; founded *Pravda* 1911; in October Revolution, 1917; elected General Secretary of Central Committee of Communist Party of Soviet Union, 1922; Marshal of the Soviet Union, 1943; Generalissimo 1945.

GUSTAV STRESEMANN (1878 – 1929). Elected to German Reichstag as representative of National Liberal Party 1907; supported German war effort and annexationist war aims, 1914 – 18; chancellor of Germany August 1923; foreign minister in series of Weimar Republic coalition governments, 1923 – 29.

SIR ROBERT VANSITTART (1881 – 1957). Entered diplomatic service 1902; principal private secretary to prime minister, 1928 – 30; permanent under-secretary, Foreign Office, 1930 – 7; chief diplomatic adviser to H.M.G., 1938 – 41.

WOODROW WILSON (1856 – 1924). Professor of Jurisprudence and Political Economy at Princeton, 1890; elected Governor of New Jersey, 1910; nominated Democractic presidential candidate in 1912; President of the United States of America, 1912 – 20; attended Paris Peace Conference 1919; suffered thrombosis and unable to carry out official duties for nine months, October 1919.

MAXIME WEYGAND (1867 – 1965). Professional soldier; chief of staff to Marshal Foch in 1914; High Commissioner for Syria and C-in-C of French forces in the Levant 1924; Chief of the French General Staff, 1930 – 31; Inspector General of the Army 1931 – 35; C-in-C in Levant, 1939; Chief of Staff of National Defence and Commander in Chief, May 1940.